Political Writings

AUGUSTINE

Political Writings

Translated by
MICHAEL W. TKACZ AND DOUGLAS KRIES

Edited by
ERNEST L. FORTIN AND DOUGLAS KRIES

with the collaboration of
ROLAND GUNN

Introduction by
ERNEST L. FORTIN

Hackett Publishing Company, Inc.
Indianapolis/Cambridge

Augustine: 354–430

Copyright © 1994 by Hackett Publishing Company, Inc.

All rights reserved

Printed in the United States of America

19 18 17 16   5 6 7 8 9

For further information, please address

Hackett Publishing Company, Inc.
P.O. Box 44937
Indianapolis, Indiana 46244-0937

www.hackettpublishing.com

Cover design by Listenberger Design & Associates
Text design by Dan Kirklin

Library of Congress Cataloging-in-Publication Data

Augustine, Saint, Bishop of Hippo.
    [Selections. English. 1994]
    Political writings/Augustine; translated by Michael W. Tkacz and
Douglas Kries; edited by Ernest L. Fortin, Roland Gunn, and Douglas
Kries; introduction by Ernest L. Fortin.
        p.   cm.
    Includes bibliographical references and index.
    ISBN 0-87220-211-9.
    ISBN 0-87220-210-0 (pbk.).
    1. Christianity and politics—Early works to 1800.   I. Tkacz,
Michael W., 1950– .   II. Kries, Douglas, 1958– .   III. Fortin,
Ernest L.   IV. Gunn, Roland, 1952– .   V. Title.
BR65.A52E6 1994
261.7—dc20   94–27554
                                              CIP

ISBN-13: 978-0-87220-211-5 (cloth)
ISBN-13: 978-0-87220-210-8 (pbk.)

Contents

Introduction

Although his knowledge of political theory far surpasses that of any other Latin Church Father, St. Augustine does not come across as first and foremost a political thinker. Most of his works make no mention of politics and none of them, not even the *City of God,* his most political book, is devoted exclusively to it. Only twice in these works does the adjective "political" occur, and even then only in quotations from Varro.[1] It is significant that the notion of the best regime, the guiding theme of classical political philosophy, hardly plays any role in his thought. He is aware of the fact that there are different regimes, some better than others, and on one occasion at least he enumerates them, but without going into the question of their relative merits.[2]

The same lack of interest in politics is reflected in Augustine's remark that "as far as this mortal life is concerned, which is lived out and ended in a few days," it matters little "under whose rule a human being marked for death lives, so long as those who govern do not force him to impiety and sin."[3] God distributes earthly kingdoms to whom he sees fit, to the good and the bad alike, lest his worshippers should covet these gifts as "something great"—*magnum aliquid*. It makes no difference that in this life some human beings should be kings and others subjects since all of them are destined for an afterlife in which there are neither kings nor subjects.[4] As Shakespeare would later have Antony and Cleopatra say, "Kingdoms are clay" and "'Tis paltry to be Caesar."[5]

If Augustine can be said to have any concern for politics at all, it is not for its own sake but because of the moral problems that it poses for Christians who, as citizens, are willy-nilly caught up in it. These problems have their common root in the nature of Christianity itself, which is essentially a nonpolitical religion. Unlike Judaism and Islam, the two other great monotheistic religions of the West, it does not call for the formation of a separate community or provide a code of laws by which that community might be governed. It takes it for granted that its followers will continue to live as full-fledged citizens of the political society to which they belong and share its way of life as long as they are not forced to indulge in practices that

are directly at odds with their basic beliefs, as were, for example, idolatry
and emperor worship.

If the New Testament is famous for anything in this regard, it is for
promulgating a set of lofty moral principles such as the ones contained in
the Sermon on the Mount (Mt 5:1–7:28); but since it says little or nothing
about the modalities of their application to concrete situations, these principles hardly suffice for the guidance of one's daily life. They are what are
sometimes called "common" principles, that is to say, principles that leave
unspecified the material content of the actions they command or prohibit.
It is not enough to be told that in dealing with one's fellow human beings
one ought to be just, kind, merciful, forgiving, and the like. One needs to
know how and under what conditions the actions so described will serve
both the common good and the true good of the individuals to whom this
type of behavior is to be shown. This is precisely what any reasonable code
of laws, including the one that accompanies the Decalogue in the Hebrew
Scriptures, the so-called "Code of the Covenant" (Ex 20:22–23:33), nor-
mally strives to do. Nor can one leave it at the vague rule of thumb that one
should do to others what one would have them do to us (Mt 7:12; Lk 6:31),
for as it stands the maxim could be taken to mean that two husbands may
engage in, say, wifeswapping if they both have a mind to do so.[6]

To further complicate matters, the New Testament often issues seemingly contradictory injunctions. In one place, it tells its followers to obey
their rulers (Rom 13:1; 1 Pt 2:13) and elsewhere that they should obey God
rather than men (Acts 5:29). At one moment it urges them to renounce the
world for Christ (Mt 19:21) and at another to conquer it in his name (Mt
28:19). Christ himself solemnly declares that he has not come to abolish
the Law and the prophets but to fulfill them and that "not an iota, not a
dot, will pass from the Law until all is accomplished" (Mt 5:17–19),
whereas St. Paul reminds us that with the coming of Christ human beings
are no longer under the Law and that those who continue to rely on it are
under a curse (Gal 3:10).

Lacking any clear and coherent political program of their own, Christians had no choice but to look elsewhere for the practical guidance needed
to order their collective lives. We know from the oldest accounts of the
debates surrounding this issue, the Acts of the Apostles and the Letters of
St. Paul, that a number of early Christians were tempted to "rejudaize"
Christianity by maintaining or reinstating the juridical prescriptions of the
Old Law. The move proved unacceptable inasmuch as Christianity all but
defined itself in opposition to such laws. The only alternative was to turn
to practical, i.e., moral and political, philosophy, the human science that

deals thematically with the governance of the individual as well as of society as a whole. Augustine was acquainted with this science mainly (though not exclusively)[7] through Cicero, Rome's preeminent philosophical authority and the mediator of Greek philosophy to a Latin world which up to that time had been profoundly hostile to it. His own account of the political life is best understood as an adaptation of Cicero's thought to the new situation created by the emergence of Christianity and, during Augustine's own lifetime, its virtual establishment as the religion of the Empire under Theodosius in 380.[8]

Pagans Against Christians

The occasion that moved Augustine to undertake this mammoth task was the crisis precipitated by the sack of Rome at the hands of Alaric and his Goths in the year 410, a dramatic event that made the vulnerability of the Empire evident to anyone with eyes to see. Christianity was promptly blamed for the disaster and the old charge that it was inimical to the well-being of civil society gained new currency among the pagan elite. Rome, so the argument ran, owed her greatness to the protection of her gods. By forsaking these gods she had incurred their wrath and lost their favor. The present calamity was an act of revenge on their part, a "judgment of Jove." It was a disaster of Rome's own making and all the more cruel for that reason.

Thus crudely stated, the argument could be rebutted by showing that practically the whole of Roman history had been marked by war and civil strife and that, since these evils antedated by centuries the rise of Christianity, they could not reasonably be laid at its door. Yet it was not an argument to be taken lightly. One sometimes wonders why, throughout the first five books of the *City of God* in particular but not only there, Augustine spends so much time recounting the absurd and mostly scurrilous deeds imputed to a host of obscure deities in whose existence educated pagans had long ceased to believe. The reason, one surmises, is not the fear that these fables would once again be mistaken for historical truths, assuming they ever were, but that they encapsulated the spirit of a cherished way of life whose refinement Christianity, "a religion out of joint with the natural assumptions of a whole culture,"[9] was in no position to match. Besides, the power of these tales to affect the morals of society was not proportionate to their quotient of reality, for the immoral behavior attributed to the gods legitimized the same type of behavior among human beings. Such had been Augustine's own experience, or so one gathers from his vivid description of the transition from the theatrical representations of Jupiter's adulteries to real adultery in *Confessions,* 1,16.[10] On a deeper level, the same mythology supplied the various countries of the ancient world with a plethora of national deities forever at war with one another, thus providing a divine warrant for the political strife that Christianity, with its teaching regarding the unity of the human race, sought to overcome.

It is interesting to note in passing that Augustine's bookish account of these gods has a strangely anachronistic flavor, focusing as it does most of the time on a crowd of lesser gods and goddesses about whom most of his contemporaries had probably never heard. These are the gods of the poets or of Rome's "mythical" theology, as Augustine calls it after Varro.[11] They are not the authoritative gods of its "civil" theology, on whom he seems reluctant to launch a frontal attack lest by denigrating them he should deprive Rome of whatever political support might still be derived from the misplaced belief in them.

This is not the whole story, however, for behind all the empty talk about tutelary deities lay the serious allegation that Christianity had brought about a decline in civic virtue and could reasonably be held to account for the deteriorating fortunes of the empire. By enlisting human beings in the service of a "higher"and "better" country,"[12] it divided the city and weakened its unconditional claim on the allegiance of its members. The dual citizenship that it imposed on its followers entailed a devaluation of the political order and rendered more difficult, if not impossible, the full measure of dedication to the city and what it stood for. Its doctrine of the universal fellowship of human beings and of their equality before God, its precept enjoining the love of one's enemies, and its admonition to the effect that one should requite evil with good all tended to undermine the military strength of the city and rob it of its most powerful defense against external foes. In the minds of Augustine's fellow Romans, the danger was far from illusory. Faced with the apparent and almost tragic impossibility of reconciling Christian belief with loyalty to their country, some of Augustine's close friends had for many years refused baptism even after having been instructed in the Faith.[13]

No doubt, one could point to a similar depreciation of the political order in classical philosophy, which placed the human being's highest good in the theoretical life rather than in the life of dutiful citizenship. But philosophy was limited to an intellectual elite. By its very essence it was destined to remain the preserve of a small number of wellborn and well-bred natures. There was no danger of its having the same direct impact on the life of the city.

Augustine's answer to this objection blends in typical fashion arguments drawn from both scriptural and philosophic sources. It consists in saying, in substance, that Christianity does not destroy patriotism but reinforces it by making of it a religious duty. The Old Testament prophets and the New Testament writers alike command obedience to one's rulers and the laws of one's city. To flout these authorities is to defy God's ordinance inasmuch as they are used by him as an instrument of his mercy in the midst of a sinful world, as St. Paul teaches in Rom 13:1–8, to which Augustine constantly refers in this connection. This being the case, one cannot allege the service of God as an excuse for shirking one's civic responsibilities.

The chances of a head-on collision between one's religious and one's political duties are further lessened by the fact that Christianity is primarily a faith or a "sound doctrine" (1 Tm 1:10; Tt 1:9 and 2:1) and not a divinely revealed law governing all of one's actions and opinions. It is compatible with any reasonably just regime and, in temporal matters, does not impose a way of life of its own, different from that of the rest of the citizenry. Its universality is such that it can accommodate itself with little difficulty to the most diverse customs and practices. The only practices to which it is opposed are the ones that reason itself denounces as vicious or immoral. By censuring these practices and urging its adherents to shun them, it actually serves the best interests of the city. Its very judgment concerning the inherent limitations of civil society does not entail a repudiation of that society. For all its manifest imperfections, civil society is not only indispensable, it is the greatest good of its kind that human beings possess. Its aim is or should be earthly peace, which Christians also seek. In the pursuit of this common goal, Christians and non-Christians can be united and live together as citizens of the same political community.

Furthermore, any depreciation of the fatherland, if one can speak of a depreciation, is amply compensated for by the fact that Christianity demands and often obtains from its followers a higher degree of morality and virtue. It thus helps to counteract the forces of vice and corruption, which are the true causes of the weakness and decline of cities and nations. Hence,

> let those who say that the teaching of Christ is contrary to the republic give us an army of soldiers of the kind that the teaching of Christ commands. Let them give us such provincial subjects, such husbands, wives, parents, children, masters, servants, kings, judges, and finally such taxpayers and taxcollectors as are commanded by the Christian teaching; and then let them

dare tell us that this teaching is contrary to the republic. Indeed, let them
hesitate to confess that it is, if observed, a great benefit for the republic.[14]

Finally, it is unfair to assert without qualification that Christianity
breeds contempt for military valor. The new Testament does not order
soldiers to surrender their arms but rather commends them for their righteousness and virtue. The injunction to requite evil with good concerns not
so much external actions as the internal dispositions with which they are
performed. It seeks to insure that war, if it must be waged, will be carried
out with a benevolent design and without undue cruelty. One is compelled
at all times to do what is most likely to benefit one's fellow human beings.
In some instances, peace and the correction of wrongdoers are more readily
and more perfectly achieved by forgiveness than by castigation, whereas in
other instances one would only confirm the wicked in their evil ways by
giving free rein to injustice and allowing crimes to go unpunished.[15] What
Christianity reproves is not war itself but the evils of war, such as the love
of violence, revenge, fierce and implacable hatreds, wild resistance, and
the lust for power. By succumbing to these evils, human beings lose a good
far more precious than any of the earthly goods that an enemy could take
from them. Instead of increasing the number of the good, they merely add
themselves to the number of the wicked. Just wars are therefore permissible, but they must be undertaken only out of necessity and for the sake of
peace. The decision to wage such wars rests with the monarch or ruler, to
whom is entrusted the welfare of the community as a whole. As for the
simple soldier, his duty is to obey orders. He himself is not answerable for
the crimes that may be committed in cases where it is unclear whether the
orders are just or not.

Although Augustine agrees that there would be less strife among human beings if everyone shared the same faith, he never regarded universal
peace as a goal that could be attained in this life; nor for that matter did he
draw from his monotheistic faith the conclusion that all human beings
should be politically united in such a way as to form a single world society.
The only passage in which this question is explicitly addressed presents
the happiest condition of mankind and the one most conducive to virtue as
that wherein small cities or small kingdoms coexist side by side in neigh-
borly concord.[16] Even that condition, however, will never be fully or permanently realized. Like it or not, war is inevitable. The wicked wage war
on the just because they want to, and the just wage war on the wicked
because they have to. In either case, independent cities and small kingdoms eventually give way to large kingdoms established through the con-

quest of the weaker by the stronger. The best that can be hoped for in practice is that the just cause will triumph over the unjust one; for nothing is more injurious to everyone, including evildoers themselves, than that the latter should prosper and use their prosperity to oppress the good.

Christians Against Pagans

Augustine's attempt to show how one can be a devout Christian and at the same time a good citizen, timely as it may be, still represents only half of his political agenda, and perhaps not the more important one at that. Nothing has yet been said about the more subtle and still much debated question as to whether one can be a good citizen and remain a good Christian. There are of course painful situations in which compliance with the demands of a thoroughly corrupt regime would amount to a tacit repudiation of one's faith, and our own century offers more than one example of them; but these are not the only ones to pose a problem for thoughtful Christians. Experience teaches that no regime is ever perfectly just and that actual societies are inherently incapable of living up to the high moral standards laid down not only by the Bible but by the philosophers of classical antiquity. The evil in question is not reducible to sporadic acts of injustice engaged in by assorted crooks and gangsters, of whom there are always plenty around, for these can usually be dealt with by legal means. Al Capone may have got away with it for a while, but the Feds did catch up to him in the end. Besides, a few rotten apples do not spoil the harvest. Common criminals can only do so much harm. They have no interest in bringing down the whole of society, if only because that would leave them with nothing to exploit. No, the problem has much deeper roots. It lies not with lawbreakers but with the law itself, which is relative to the regime and shares in its imperfection.

As previously noted,[17] that regime is in the best instance either a monarchy, an aristocracy, a democracy, or some more or less felicitous combination of the three. But this means that the city is in fact ruled by a part, which only claims to rule for the benefit of the whole. Seldom if ever does a society distribute its honors to those who most deserve them or its wealth to those who best know how to use it. To opt for a new regime when that rare opportunity presents itself is not to replace injustice with justice but to exchange one set of injustices for another. Worse still, even the most decent of citizens cannot avoid all complicity with the systemic inequities or institutional preferences of his society. By the mere fact that he lives and works in it, pays his taxes, exercises his right to vote, and may hold public office, he contributes to the perpetuation of its unjust way of life. Civil society is constituted in such a way as to compel us to choose between playing the hammer or the anvil, between victimizing others or being victimized by them. In simple Aristotelian terms, it is only under the best regime that the good citizen and the good human being coincide; but the best regime is a practical impossibility, and so therefore is moral goodness, despite its being demanded of everyone. Evil, it seems, is built into the very structure of the universe.

Such at any rate is the radical way in which Augustine chose to formulate the problem of Christianity's relationship to the political order. Nowhere is this radicalism more apparent than in his notorious (and frequently misunderstood) discussion of the *respublica* or civil society. In the *City of God*, II.21, Augustine, quoting Scipio, Cicero's mouthpiece in the *Republic*, defines civil society as "a group of people united by a consensus concerning right and a community of interests." Reverting to the same theme later on, in XIX.24, he is obliged to strike from that definition any reference to right or justice on the ground that it is not to be found in any of them. Civil society, he says, is a group of people united, not by an acknowledgment of right, but by a common agreement as to the objects of their love, regardless of the moral quality of these objects. Only in this truncated sense can Rome be said to have been a republic. When all is said and done, cities are mere compacts of wickedness entered into not for the sake of virtue or the good life but for the sole purpose of preserving a modicum of peace among people who would otherwise constantly be at one another's throats.

The same grim thought is expressed in slightly different terms in another well-known chapter of the *City of God* (IV,4), where kingdoms are said to be nothing but robber bands or gigantic larcenies *(magna latrocinia)* and robber bands nothing but small kingdoms *(parva regna)*—that, save for the impunity with which his crimes are committed, what Alexander does on a grand scale and with a huge fleet is no different from what a pirate does by himself and with a lone ship. The passage in Cicero's *Republic* from which Augustine borrows this story is the one in which for the sake of argument Philus, one of the interlocutors in the dialogue, defends the thesis that justice is a matter of convention rather than of nature. People abide by it not because it is intrinsically desirable but for reasons of necessity, such as fear of punishment or self-interest. Down deep, the brightest among them know that it is only a pretense. Although no one wants to admit it publicly, every political group is organized for the benefit of those who run it. Even the best of cities is governed by laws that cannot but favor the particular interests of its dominant class and thus profit some of its members at the expense of others. The choice of one regime over another always involves a trade-off of some sort in which the gains registered on one front are offset by the losses incurred on another. There is no such thing as a commonweal or a true city.

Odd as Augustine's method of procedure may seem, there is nothing farfetched about it. It merely conforms to the familiar principle that the unqualified noun designates the perfected object. A thing is good to the extent that it possesses everything that belongs to it by reason of its nature—*bonum ex integra causa,* as the the old Scholastics used to say. "Perfection," from the Latin *perficere,* "to bring to completion," is synonymous with wholeness. A chariot with a missing spoke, let alone a missing wheel, is not a chariot in the full sense of the word. The same is true *mutatis mutandis* of cities, laws, and human actions. Another way of formulating the same problem is to say that instead of taking moral phenomena as they appear to decent nonphilosophers, as does Aristotle, for example, Augustine habitually chooses to study them in the light of their highest metaphysical principles or, as one might say, in the light of the Platonic ideas. Viewed in that light, all human endeavors fall short of the mark and must be qualified as defective.

Part of the problem with this approach of course is that it disregards the important consideration that cities, like chariots, exhibit varying *degrees* of goodness or badness that any prudent ruler is obliged to take into account. Augustine himself is the first to admit that there are commonsensical or "more plausible" *(probabiliores)* definitions of the city according to which Rome was indeed a republic, albeit one that was better administered by the ancient Romans than by their descendants.[18] The question is why, preferring an all-or-nothing approach, he insisted on painting the bleakest possible picture of the political life.

The answer to that question is not one that we, as products of a liberal democratic tradition that is unaware of or unsympathetic to the classical notion of the regime as a *total* way of life, are in a good position to understand. We may recall that in the *City of God* and the writings related to it Augustine set two goals for himself. The first was to counter the charge that Christianity was to blame for the Empire's weakness in the face of the threat posed to its existence by the massing of barbarians on its borders. The second was to entice the pagan elite of his time to embrace the new faith, something that a number of them were reluctant to do on the ground that it taught people to be more concerned with the good of their souls than with that of the fatherland and was thus incompatible with the duties of citizenship. The problem was brought home to Augustine in a poignant way by one of his friends, the aged Nectarius of Calama, a pagan whose heart still burned with patriotic fire, who had imbibed from Cicero's *Republic* the loyal citizen's sentiment that there is no limit in either time or measure to the claim that their country has upon the care and service of right-hearted men, and who could not countenance a religion that was liable to dampen that sentiment.[19]

The difficulty is that the means by which these two goals might be achieved were in obvious tension with each other. One consisted in moderating the patriotic zeal of Augustine's pagan friends so as to secure their attachment to the Christian faith; the other, in reinforcing the patriotic zeal of his fellow Christians so as to attach them more firmly to the service of their earthly country. The critique of Roman political life and Roman religion that permeates so much of the *City of God* was specifically designed to make the pagan nobility aware of the problematic character of their devotion to Rome, admirable as it may have been in other respects. Hence its manifest onesidedness—Rome was never a republic, the pagan virtues are nothing but vices, all rulers are pirates in disguise—for only by downplaying the merits of Roman political life and exaggerating its shortcomings could Augustine hope to persuade the pagan "holdouts" of his day that the time had come to embrace the new faith.

It is worth noting that much of Augustine's argument is inspired by Cicero's account of Roman history in Book II of the *Republic*. The difference is that Cicero, who is faced with the problem of restoring his fellow countrymen's badly shaken faith in a Rome that was being torn apart by civil war, deftly conceals her defects (but not without letting the informed reader know that he is fully aware of them), whereas Augustine lets the cat out of the bag and lays these defects out for everyone to see.[20] His is an attempt not to glorify Rome but to demythologize Cicero's account of its history by stripping it of its "embellishments."[21]

Augustine could afford to be more outspoken than his pagan predecessor about such matters because he had the Christian faith to fall back on in order to rekindle a measure of public-spiritedness in the hearts of his fellow countrymen. The gist of his argument, as we have seen, is that by elevating patriotism to the level of a religious duty, Christianity serves the city more effectively than the moribund pagan religion that his adversaries were trying to revive had ever done. True, Christianity makes a stronger claim on the allegiance of its followers than does the temporal society of which they are also members, but, as a religion that transcends all temporal societies, it does not abrogate their citizenship in any particular temporal society. What characterizes the Christian life on this level is a dual citizenship of a kind that had never been seen before. In order to be at once a good Christian and a good citizen, one had only to render to Caesar what is Caesar's and to God what is God's (Mt 22:21; Mk 12:17; Lk 20:25). To anyone who was convinced that everything is Caesar's, however, the new arrangement was less than satisfactory, especially since what remained of one's attachment to one's fatherland was supported not so much by a powerful natural inclination as by the detour of the love of an unseen and mysterious God.

Christians Against Christians

Augustine was not the first Christian theologian to be called upon to deal with this problem. Others had had to come to grips with it during the first part of the fourth century, most notably Eusebius and the architects of the Constantinian settlement. Augustine was familiar with their solution to it through a young Spanish priest by the name of Orosius, who had joined him in North Africa and was commissioned by him to compile from all available sources a list of the disasters that had plagued Rome not only "in these Christian times," as the expression went, but throughout most of its notoriously turbulent history.

The results of this inquiry are contained in Orosius's *Seven Books of History against the Pagans,* which has the distinction of being not only the first but the most unusual history of the world ever written. Whereas Augustine's main concern was with the city of God, Orosius concentrated on what may fairly be called the city of the devil. His relatively short work, which enjoyed enormous popularity during the Middle Ages, is a catalogue of all the evils known to have been perpetrated or endured by human beings since the beginning of recorded time. Even a superficial reading of the book reveals, however, that in discharging his mandate Orosius went well beyond the call of duty. His simpleminded thesis is that, far from boding ill for the Empire, Christianity was responsible for the untold favors that had accrued to it in recent times. Its auspicious birth under Augustus had coincided with an era of unprecedented peace and held out the promise of even greater benefits in the future. Indeed, all of human history up to that moment could be seen as a lengthy preparation for the advent and eventual triumph of the Christian faith. With a little coaxing, the life spans of the great empires of the past could be fitted into a neat pattern that revealed the hand of God at work in their midst. To the east, the Babylonian empire (assimilated for present purposes to the Assyrian empire) had lasted fourteen hundred years; to the north and the south, the Macedonian and the Carthaginian empires seven hundred years each; to the west, Rome was already more than a thousand years old. In time, the persecutions to which the first generations of Christians were subjected had abated. The Empire had not only seen fit to sanction the new religion but had adopted it as its official religion and abolished its rivals. Furthermore, there was little likelihood that these accomplishments would be annulled by subsequent reversals or the regression to a less desirable stage of human development. Just as the plagues vested on the Egyptians had stopped at ten, so too had the persecutions inflicted on the early Christians. In the meantime, the Old Testament prophecies relating to the blessings of the messianic age were gradually being fulfilled: swords were being turned into plowshares, justice and peace were on the verge of forging a lasting alliance, and under the aegis of the new emperors the kingdom of God was about to be inaugurated not just in heaven, as some less worldly-minded apologists for the Christian faith had predicted, but here on earth.

Granted, innocent people were still being made to suffer unjustly and the wicked occasionally revelled in undeserved prosperity, but this meant only that the former would go to heaven a little sooner and the latter to hell a little later.[22] Orosius himself, who had managed to escape from his own troubled Spain to more peaceful shores, could remain undaunted. Had he not discovered a new home in North Africa, where he joyfully found himself "a Roman among Romans, a Christian among Christians, and a man among men"—something that would not have been possible at any earlier moment in history? What more was needed to prove that things were getting better and would continue to do so as time went on?

However appealing Orosius's little scheme may have been to some of his contemporaries and his innumerable readers in the centuries that followed, it did not meet with the approval of Augustine, who never once mentions his collaborator in the eleven books of the *City of God* that remained to be written when Orosius's book came out and even seems to go out of his way to reject his interpretation. Traces of his dissatisfaction with the work of his "disciple" may be detected in Book XVIII.52,1, where Augustine explicitly takes issue with those who would equate the victory of Christianity with the fulfillment of the famous messianic prophecies of Isaiah and of Psalm 72:

Some have thought or do think that the Church will not suffer any more

persecutions than it already has—that is, ten—until the time of the Antichrist, so that the eleventh and last persecution will be that of the Antichrist.
I do not think that this view should be rashly asserted or believed. . . . They
hold that the last persecution, that of the Antichrist, resembles the eleventh
plague, in which the Egyptians perished in the Red Sea while chasing the
Hebrews, whereas the people of God passed through on dry land. I, however, do not think that the events which took place in Egypt prophetically
signified these persecutions. However carefully and cleverly those who hold
this view may have compared the plagues and the persecutions, they have
done so not through the prophetic spirit but through the conjectures of the
human mind, which sometimes hits the truth and sometimes is led astray.

Not only from the time of Christ but from as far back as that of Abel the
Church has gone forth on pilgrimage amid both the persecutions of the
world and the consolations of God; and so it will be "until the end of time."
As far as the future is concerned, its prospects remain as uncertain as ever;
for "amid the great vicissitudes of human events, no people has ever been
granted such security as would free them from the dread of attacks hostile
to this life."[23] Neither is it true that the rise and decline of the great world
empires fall into anything like the symmetrical pattern into which Orosius
had unscrupulously tried to nudge them. The Assyrian empire, for example, endured, not 1,400 years, but 1,240. No juggling of the historical
data will allow us to uncover an intimation of rational design in the random
succession of worldly powers.

The same skepticism pervades Augustine's reinterpretation of the notion of a "Christian era" or *tempora christiana*, which had recently been
injected into the debate as a term of derogation by Christianity's pagan
adversaries. Orosius had seized upon it not only to vindicate the Christian
faith—others had done as much—but to bolster his own incremental conception of the development of Roman history: "Behold how under Christians and in these Christian times civil wars, even when they prove
unavoidable, are brought to a happy issue. The victory has been won, the
city stands intact, the tyrant has been laid low."[24]

Augustine's appraisal of the situation is a good deal more sober. However beneficial he may have considered the spread of Christianity to be, he
certainly did not think it carried with it any guarantee of earthly prosperity. It has been argued that Augustine, too, had once succumbed to the
same "triumphant" assessment of the emergence of Christianity and
viewed the present age as the long-awaited fulfillment of the Old Testament prophecies, only to retract himself and subject his initial understand-

ing of the *tempora christiana* to a "drastic devaluation" in the light of the reverses of the first decades of the fifth century.[25] Whether or not this is the case is debatable.[26] There is little reason to believe that Augustine ever sought to endow the Roman empire with quasi-messianic attributes and even less reason to believe that he regretted his having once ascribed a temporal meaning to the prophetic utterances of the Old Testament. I know of no text in which he denies that *any* of these prophecies refer to temporal events. What he does deny, in his early as well as in his later works, is that they contain only *glad* tidings. The truth of the matter is that both happy and unhappy events have been foretold by the prophets and the Gospel. Commenting again on the convulsions of his time, he writes:

> These things should make us weep but not wonder; and we ought to cry to God that, not for our merit but according to his mercy, he may deliver us from such great evils. For, what else was to be expected by the human race, seeing that these things were so long ago foretold by both the prophets and the Gospel? We ought not, therefore, be so inconsistent as to believe these Scriptures when they are read to us and to complain when they are fulfilled. Just as this great pressure of the Lord God's olive-press brings forth the dregs of unbelieving murmurs and blasphemies, so too it should produce a steady outpouring of pure oil in the confessions and prayers of believers. For to those who never tire of hurling their impious complaints at the Christian faith and claim that, prior to the time when this doctrine was proclaimed throughout the world, the human race was not subjected to such great evils, an answer can readily be given from the Gospel. Indeed, as the Lord says, "That servant who does not know his master's will and does what deserves a beating shall receive a light beating, whereas the servant who does know his master's will and does what deserves a beating shall receive a severe beating" (Lk 22:47–48). Is it surprising that in these Christian times *(christianis temporibus)* this world, like the servant who knows his master's will and yet does what deserves a beating should be punished severely? These people notice the rapidity with which the Gospel is propagated but not the perversity with which it is despised by the many.[27]

If the new times, then, are not necessarily better or more peaceful than the old, one cannot claim for Christianity the politically salvific role that Orosius and his mentor, Eusebius, had assigned to it.

The attractiveness of Eusebius's imperial theology and its Orosian analogue is that it offered what was far and away the most elegant solution yet devised to the problem of the Christian's involvement in the complexities of Roman public life. As long as this involvement entailed the risk of complicity in a manifestly iniquitous rule, the Christian conscience could feel justified in adopting an attitude of uncompromising resistance to it. The One is reminded in this connection of the invectives of an earlier generation of Christian extremists, represented pre-eminently by Hippolytus of Rome, who had been taught by the Book of Revelation to identify the Roman Empire with "the harlot seated upon the seven hills" and "drunk with the blood of the saints and martyrs of Jesus."[28] Under such adverse conditions, it might well be asked what indeed the Church had to do with Caesar. The accession of a Christian or someone partial to Christianity to the imperial throne had brought about a complete reversal of the situation.

Small wonder that this felicitous turn of events should have been hailed as the most important milestone in the history of Christianity since the birth of Christ. If henceforth public affairs were to be administered in accordance with the rules of strict justice, if wars were destined to disappear, if the only wars remaining to be waged were demonstrably just wars, and if the newly converted empire was but an earthly reflection of God's eternal kingdom, any qualms that one might have about lending one's wholehearted support to it could be laid to rest. The conflict between the moral ideal of the Sermon on the Mount and the harsh necessities of the political life had at long last come to an end.

One finds it somewhat easier to sympathize with Eusebius's enthusiastic if seemingly uncritical endorsement of Constantine and the Christian empire. After all, he had witnessed the atrocities of the reign of Diocletian (he was sixteen when the emperor acceded to the throne) and had been forced to spend some time in jail as a young man. Given his closeness to the new seat of power, however, he could hardly have been unaware of darker side of his hero's policies.[29] There is much to be said for the suggestion that Eusebius's naiveté was more apparent than real, since by his own admission he had "related whatever might redound to the glory of religion and . . . suppressed all that could tend to its discredit."[30] Orosius's only excuse was his ignorance or his monumental shallowness.

Unfortunately, what both of them propounded as the final answer to the perennially vexed question of Christianity's relationship to the political order could be seen, and was seen by Augustine, as a new and more insidious danger for at least two reasons. The first is that, by binding Christianity to the promise of temporal rewards, it inevitably cast doubts on the genuineness of one's sentiments in regard to it. A believer may be drawn to Christianity for a variety of human reasons, but ultimately the faith that is demanded of him cannot be accepted for any motive other than the faith itself. The ambiguity of the Eusebian and Orosian scheme is that it rendered Christianity equally appealing to believers and nonbelievers. Without giving its claim to divine truth as much as a second thought, one might look upon the Church as a convenient solution to the most urgent social problems of the day. Properly organized and supported, it could be pressed into service to counteract the forces that threatened the dissolution of an inordinately large and unwieldy political structure. Its spirit of moderation and law-abidingness was likely to improve the manners of society, particularly at a time when the traditional sources of morality were showing signs of unmistakable weakness. Laws are effective to the extent that they are accompanied by habits of decency and self-restraint on the part of most citizens; left to themselves, they seldom inspire virtue and are even less capable of containing vice. Yet it was painfully obvious that neither education nor pagan religion, the two principal agencies on which governments had formerly relied for this purpose, was adequate to the task. A universal and despotic empire is not the most suitable locus of moral education, and the old religion of the city, which had been on the wane for years, was not about to be rehabilitated.

Much more could be expected from the new religion, which addressed itself to everybody regardless of language, ethnic background, or local tradition. Christians had long rejected the notion that they constituted a *triton genos* or third race, alongside Judaism and the nations of the pagan world. Unlike some of the religious sectarians of late antiquity, they were not given to living in isolation or to withdrawing from society altogether. One found them everywhere, mingling freely with the rest of the population, sharing their customs, their dress, and within prescribed limits their general way of life. The moral teaching to which they subscribed enjoined the practice of public as well as of private virtue. Once generally accepted, it could be counted on to curb the selfish passions and propagate sentiments of truth, justice, and harmony among people who would look upon themselves as common children of the one true God. Thanks to its influence, the dissensions racking the Empire were less apt to erupt into bloody strife. In Gibbon's memorable words, "a prudent magistrate might observe with pleasure and eventually support the progress of a religion which diffused among the people a pure, benevolent, and universal system of ethics, adapted to every duty and every condition of life, recommended as the will and reason of the supreme deity, and enforced by the sanction of eternal rewards and punishments."[31]

The cost on the other side of the political ledger was, all things considered, minimal. Even the disparagement of military valor, which at other moments and under different circumstances could only be seen as a liability, had suddenly turned into an asset, favoring the ends to which in its own interest imperial policy was committed. By the same token, emperors had little to fear from a religion that derived the institution of civil government from the will of God, frowned upon sedition, and discouraged worldly ambition with as much vigor as it extolled the virtue of obedience to one's divinely ordained rulers. If even under a Nero St. Paul had preached the duty of unconditional submission to tyrants, how much more willing would Christians be to acquiesce in the rule of a prince who was at the same time a patron and a defender. The new alliance was clearly advantageous to both parties. By a miraculous convergence, it served the best interests of both heaven and earth.

Little more was required to lay bare the essential weakness of any purely political defense of Christianity. It is significant that the *City of God* devotes barely more than two short chapters (V, 25 and 26) to Constantine and Theodosius, the most renowned of the early Christian emperors, and that in reviewing their reigns Augustine stresses their private virtues to the virtual exclusion of their political virtues. The conversion of the Roman Empire, acclaimed by others as a crucial turning point in the history of the Church, is dismissed as a mere episode in an ongoing process no single moment of which is to be privileged over any other. Just as Augustine tacitly rejects the Byzantine theology of Eusebius, so he passes over in silence the so-called Augustus theology of Orosius, with its typical emphasis on the providential connection between the *pax romana* and the emergence of Christianity. The birth of Christ under Augustus is duly recorded, but in a single line and as a chronological coincidence on which no prognosis can be based regarding the course of human events.[32]

There is yet another, perhaps more cogent reason for which upon reflection Eusebius's imperial theology in any of its forms appeared fraught with peril. If political institutions are destined to improve with the passing of time and if, along with that improvement, the evils to which they so often gave rise in the past are to vanish from the scene, one wonders what is to become of virtue or human excellence once the process has reached its completion. Later generations would be spared the trouble of overcoming the obstacles that had previously stood in the path of right action. The success of their endeavors would be assured without their having to make any of the sacrifices required of their less fortunate predecessors. One could look forward to the day when everybody could reap the rewards of virtue without having to shoulder its burden.

Augustine's question is whether virtue can still be called virtue if success is always guaranteed. There is surely nothing wrong with following a charted course of action whose outcome is never in doubt, but there is nothing glorious in it either. What gives virtue its distinctively human character is precisely the uncertainty with which in all interesting cases one is compelled to act. People are at best responsible for the goodness or badness of their actions, not for their results. They may deserve to be successful, but whether they are or not depends in large measure on circumstances that lie beyond their control and may not even be known to them at the time of the deed. A just judge who has done everything in his power to ascertain the facts of a particular case cannot be held to account for unwittingly condemning an innocent person, however wrong his judgment may be.[33] The paradox is that were it not for the possibility of evil virtue itself would be in jeopardy. Prudence loses its raison d'être once we are relieved of the need to deliberate about the uncertain course of action to be pursued in a given set of circumstances, as does moderation once the impediments to the accomplishment of what is right in that domain have been removed. The function of virtue is not to do away with evil but to conquer it. Even as it does so, its victory is never secure; for as long as the vices against which it struggles resist, the battle remains precarious, and even when defeated they do not permit a triumph of carefree ease.[34]

Nowhere is this struggle more apparent than when the deliberations bear on the use of force as a means of opposing injustice. In order to safeguard the purity of one's soul, one would like to be able to renounce all punitive actions, but this will never be more than a pious wish. A weak justice is not an appropriate response to the injustices of the world. It only leads to greater injustice by allowing the wicked to prevail over the just. Complete peace is not part of man's mortal condition. It belongs to that "other life" which alone is free from the corruption of sin and death and in which nothing either in ourselves or in others will be at war with any of us.[35]

To repeat what was said earlier, the *City of God* was first conceived as an effort to refurbish and develop the arguments by means of which Christian apologetics had traditionally sought to reconcile Christianity with the legitimate demands of the political life. It soon became apparent, however, that the crucial question was not whether civil society could survive Christianity but whether Christianity itself could survive its integration into civil society. The problem was the more acute as the new faith was never envisaged as a purely private concern but was rather called upon to play within society a moral role similar to that which had once devolved upon pagan religion. Before the *City of God* was completed, the conventional defense with which it began had turned into a highly original attack on some of Augustine's own coreligionists and a far more probing analysis of the political implications of the Christian faith than any that had hitherto been undertaken.

The solution adopted by Eusebius and his followers was predicated on the conviction that a converted Roman Empire could fully live up to the ethical demands of the Gospel. Augustine destroyed the ground of the argument by showing that the level of justice of which societies are capable is always considerably lower than that to which individuals can aspire. The dilemma that confronts us on this score is well illustrated by Augustine's just war theory, which, upon closer examination, turns out to be much more subtle than we might have suspected. According to that theory, a war is just only under certain conditions—for example, when waged to repel an unjust aggressor, defend an ally, secure a legitimate right of passage, or rescue victims of oppression in a country other than one's own. The theory stipulates that all other means of redress shall first have been exhausted, that the war shall be undertaken only out of necessity and for the sake of peace, and that it shall be prosecuted without unnecessary violence. In all such cases the assumption is that a war can only be just on one side; for "when we wage a just war, our adversaries must be sinning."[36] If Rome's wars were just, those of the invading barbarians were unjust.

But were the barbarians behaving unjustly toward Rome? The picture is far from clear. There is plenty of evidence to show that in many if not most cases they were themselves acting out of necessity and under presssure from powerful hordes to the east before whom they had little choice but to flee. Besides, in the course of the negotiations Rome had had few scruples about breaking faith with them, to the point of indulging in unspeakable treacheries. Thousands of barbarians serving in the Roman army were mercilessly butchered once the reaction against them had set in, and others, after having been promised asylum, were reduced to the most abject slavery upon their arrival.[37] Rome, too, bore its share of the responsibility for the evils that were befalling it. Augustine all but says it was only getting what it deserved.

Beyond that was the nasty question of the justice of Rome's own borders, often hinted at but rarely broached openly in the literature of the period. It was no secret that these borders had been acquired through conquest or unjust aggression. But how can a war undertaken for the defense of unjust borders be considered just? The problem is not unlike the one that came up over a thousand years later in the wake of the Spanish conquest of the New World. Even if one grants the legitimacy of wars of civilization and agrees that according to natural justice the European invaders had some right to vast tracts of land that were not being put to good use,[38] one can hardly hold it against the native Americans for taking up arms in their own defense.

All in all, Augustine's just war theory left much unsaid, albeit not unnoticed. If anything can be thought to have motivated it, it is the conviction, not that wars can ever be completely just, but that under more or less favorable circumstances they might become a trifle less unjust. There are limits to how far one can go in establishing a nation's right to the territory over which it rules or in laying down rules for the defense of that territory. For Augustine, the choice was between civilization and barbarism, and it was in the light of this choice that the decision to support one side or the other had to be made. No one had fewer illusions than Augustine about the justice of the Roman Empire. If his heart was still with it, it is because he thought that the prospects for justice, slim as they always are, were greater within it than outside of it. Unlike so much of twentieth-century political science, Augustine never called for the extrusion of ethics from the realm of politics; but neither did he ever dream that the two realms could be simply identified.

It follows that for Augustine the notion of a Christian polity, whether it be upheld seriously or for reasons of expediency, is at best a comforting and at worst a fatal illusion, possibly leading to fanaticism, as it often has over the centuries.[39] Christian wisdom and political power are not only distinct but always more or less at odds with each other in accordance with the vicissitudes of history and the inclinations of our "restless hearts."[40] Some regimes are obviously superior to others but nothing suggests that any of them will ever be able to fulfill our deepest longings. Christianity as Augustine understands it does indeed provide a solution to the problem of human life, but it is not a solution that is attainable in and through political society. Like that of the classical philosophers, it remains nonpolitical or, better still, transpolitical. To have made this point clear for the first time is arguably Augustine's most precious contribution to the political theology of the West.

Ernest L. Fortin
Boston College

Notes

1. *City of God,* VI,12; VII.23,2.

2. It is not clear whether Augustine fully understood the meaning of the classical debate regarding the best regime. Whereas Cicero had endorsed the traditional view that a decent civil society may be ruled either by a king, a few nobles, or the many—*multitudo (De re publica,* I.26,42), Augustine speaks of a king, a few nobles, or the "whole people" *(universus populus),* thereby implying that all citizens can have an equal or just share in the governance of the city *(City of God,* II.21,2). The change may or may not have been deliberate, but either way it tended to obfuscate one of the basic problems of political philosophy. By "the many" or the people, Cicero meant the uneducated poor as distinguished from the nobles, whom they habitually outnumber and whose influence they often outweigh or effectively neutralize. Even the mixed regime, i.e., the regime in which all three classes are associated, cannot properly be described as the rule of "all" inasmuch as one class invariably predominates over the other two.

3. *Ibid.,* V.17.

4. *Ibid.,* IV.33.

5. *Antony and Cleopatra,* I.1,35; V.2,2.

6. *De Libero Arbitrio,* I.3,6.

7. Some of his information came from other sources, particularly Varro, Virgil, Seneca, and the Roman historians.

8. Through Cicero, as well as through other sources such as the ones just mentioned, Augustine was well acquainted with the classical notion of the naturalness of civil society. Since the publication of R. W. and A. J. Carlyle's monumental *A History of Mediaeval Political Thought in the West* (6 vols., Edinburgh, 1903–36), it has become fashionable to oppose two sharply different views of civil society, one religious and the other philosophical. According to the first, civil society would be rooted in sin and would have an exclusively remedial or punitive function; according to the second, it would be rooted in human nature and have a primarily educational function. Recent years have witnessed a healthy reaction against this somewhat simplistic view, for it is clear that the philosophers of classical antiquity saw the function of civil society as being both remedial and educational. See, for recent accounts of the problem, G. Post, *Studies in Medieval Legal Thought: Public Law and the State, 1100–1322* (Princeton Univ. Press, 1964), esp. 494–561. C. Nederman, "Nature, Sin and the Origins of Society: The Ciceronian Tradition in Medieval Thought," *Journal of the History of Ideas* 49 (1988). 13–26, and "Aristotelianism and the Origins of Political Science," *ibid.* 52 (1991), 179–94. P. J. Weithman, "Augustine and Aquinas on Original Sin and the Function of Political Authority," *Journal of the History of Philosophy* 30:3 (July, 1992), 353–76.

9. P. Brown, *Augustine of Hippo: A Biography* (Berkeley and Los Angeles, 1967), 301. In *Confessions,* III.5, Augustine notes that he first found the Sacred Scriptures "unworthy of being compared to the majesty of Cicero."

10. See also *City of God,* II.7.

11. Cf. *ibid.,* VI.6.

12. Augustine, *Letter* 91,1.

13. See, for example, *Letters* 151,14 and136,2 (not included in this volume).

14. *Letter* 138,2; see also 137.5,20 and 91,3.

15. *Against Faustus the Manichee,* XXII.74; cf. *Letter* 138.2,12.

16. *City of God,* IV.15.

17. *Supra,* n. 2.

18. Cf. *City of God,* XIX.21,4.

19. Augustine, *Letter* 91,1.

20. Further details on this specific point in E. L. Fortin, "The Patristic Sense of Community," *Augustinian Studies* 4 (1973), 194–96.

21. Cf. *City of God,* II.21,4, where the justice described by Cicero is called a colored painting rather than a living reality.

22. Orosius, *Historia,* VII.41.

23. *City of God,* XVII.13.

24. *Historia,* VII.33.

25. R. A. Markus, *Saeculum: History and Society in the Theology of St. Augustine* (Cambridge, 1970), 35.

26. For additional details and bibliographical references concerning the debate, cf. E. L. Fortin, "Augustine's *City of God* and the Modern Historical Consciousness," *Review of Politics* 41/3 (1979), 333–34. Also, for a summary presentation of Orosius's relationship to Augustine, R. A. Markus, "The Roman Empire in Early Christian Historiography," *Downside Review* 81 (1963), 340–54.

27. *Letter* 111,2.

28. Hippolytus, *In Danielem,* IV.8–9.

29. The year in which Constantine convoked the Council of Nicaea is also that in which he had his own son and his sister's son murdered. Orosius is candid enough to say that this was done for "unknown reasons" *(Historia,* VII.28).

30. Edw. Gibbon, *Decline and Fall of the Roman Empire,* chap. 16, with reference to Eusebius, *Historia Ecclesiastica,* 8,2.

31. Gibbon, *ibid.,* chap. 20.

32. *City of God,* XVIII.46; cf. III.30.

33. *Ibid.,* XIX.6.

34. Cf. *Ibid.,* XIX.27 (not included in our selections).

35. *Ibid.* See also *Enar. in Psalm* 148,1–2.

36. *City of God*, XIX.15. (The quotation has been omitted in our excerpt from this chapter.)

37. R. Bainton, *Christian Attitudes toward War and Peace* (New York and Nashville: Abingdon Press, 1960), 99–100.

38. In classical political theory, property belongs in the strictest sense to the one who knows best how to use it and is disposed to act in accordance with that knowledge. Everyone nevertheless recognized that this was not a principle that cities could adopt as a matter of course, for any attempt to do so would result in chaos.

39. Augustine's stance and posture in regard to religious freedom has provoked much controversy among scholars, some holding him to be the originator of modern liberalism and others the father of religious intolerance and persecution. What seems clear is that, while he advocated the *practice* of toleration whenever possible, he never made toleration into a universal principle. In this, his position resembles closely that of all of the leading thinkers of classical antiquity. On this touchy issue see, most recently and in my opinion most adequately, M. White, "Pluralism and Secularism in the Political Order: St. Augustine and Theoretical Liberalism," *The University of Dayton Review* 22/3 (Summer, 1994).

40. *Confessions*, I,1.

Brief Chronology

354   Birth of Augustine to Roman citizens of modest means in the small Numidian town of Thagaste (present-day Souk Ahras, in eastern Algeria).

371   Beginning of a four-year stay in Carthage to study rhetoric. Takes a concubine.

373   Reads Cicero's *Hortensius*, a protreptic or introduction to philosophy, and is inflamed with the desire for wisdom. First signs of his attraction to Manichaeism. Birth of his son, Adeodatus (?).

375   Beginning of his teaching career, first at Thagaste and a year later in Carthage.

383   Sails for Rome in the hope of finding better students and greater opportunities for worldly advancement.

384   Named professor of rhetoric in Milan, then the capital of the Empire, where he will meet Ambrose, the local bishop, who will be instrumental in his conversion to Christianity.

385   Monica, his mother, arrives in Milan from North Africa.

386   Reads the *libri platonicorum*, or "books of the Platonists," and through them learns of the existence of incorporeal substances. Converts to Christianity in October of that year.

387   Baptized by Ambrose during the Easter Vigil. Goes back to Rome in the fall. Death of Monica at Ostia, where she was waiting for the boat that would take her to Africa.

388   Returns to Thagaste and leads a life of leisurely contemplation with a group of close friends. Publishes his first dialogues *(Contra academicos, De beata vita, De ordine, Soliloquies)*.

389?   Death of Adeodatus at the age of seventeen.

391   Establishes a monastic community at Hippo Regius on the North African coast (present-day Annaba) and is ordained a priest.

392 Engages in a public debate with Fortunatus, a prominent Manichee.

394 Beginning of a prolonged polemic against the Donatists.

395 Appointed bishop of Hippo Regius, the second largest diocese in Africa, over which he will preside until his death.

397 Begins the *Confessions*, which are completed in 401.

410 Sack of Rome by Alaric and the Goths.

411 Beginning of a controversy with the Pelagians that will last to the end of his life.

413 Begins to write *The City of God*. Death of Marcellinus in September.

427 Completes *The City of God*.

430 Death of Augustine at Hippo on August 28, just as the Vandals are laying siege to the city.

Note on the Editing and Translating

Chief among St. Augustine's political writings is the monumental *City of God*. The majority of the material included in this volume consists of selections from that enormous work. In abridging *The City of God*, our goal was to give the reader a sense of the whole plan and argument of the work while at the same time emphasizing the sections particularly relevant to politics. As a result, some passages are included from virtually all of *The City of God's* twenty-two books, while considerably more material is included from certain key books, such as Book XIX. A brief introduction precedes each of the individual books. These are intended to provide a context within which the selections may more profitably be studied.

The abridgment of *The City of God* is followed by a topical arrangement of selections from Augustine's letters and other works. Brief introductions to these have also been provided. Footnotes have been included throughout in order to provide students with the most essential information for understanding Augustine's arguments and references.

The translations attempt to preserve both the literal meaning of the texts and the vigor of Augustine's style. As part of the attempt to be literal, we have consistently translated certain key Latin terms with the same English equivalents. As part of the attempt to preserve the vigor of Augustine's style, we have fought on all fronts against the temptation toward excessive wordiness.

Augustine's Latin is often marked by long and intricate sentence structures that are quite foreign to contemporary English. We have frequently broken these into two or more shorter sentences. Since the passages contained in this volume are excerpts from larger works, we have occasionally omitted some of the transitional words that Augustine uses to tie together two chapters, only one of which is included here. Paragraph indentations have been added freely.

Augustine's biblical quotations have been translated directly from his own Latin text. Because Augustine relied heavily on early Latin translations of the Scriptures, our translations sometimes differ from the ones found in present-day English Bibles.

Rendering Augustine into English is now an undertaking with a fairly long history. Even though all of our translations are new and based on the best critical editions currently available, we did not think it wise to ignore the labors of our predecessors and have therefore consulted them freely. Special mention should be made of the translations of *The City of God* prepared by McCracken, Green, Wiesen, Levine, and Sanford for the *Loeb Classical Library* (Harvard University Press, 1957–72, 7 vols.), by Dods for the *Nicene and Post-Nicene Fathers of the Christian Church* (Charles Scribner's Sons, 1887, 1st series, vol. 2), and by Bettenson (Penguin, 1972). We have also frequently taken into consideration the French translation by Combès in the *Bibliothèque Augustinienne* edition of Augustine's works (Desclée De Brouwer, 1959–60, 5 vols.).

We acknowledge, with gratitude, the contribution of Fr. Fredric Schlatter, s.j., who gave important assistance with a number of thorny passages, and of Catherine Brown Tkacz, who spent many long hours poring over our work and offering suggestions for its improvement. Thanks are due also to Edith Gunn, Bryan M. Benson, and Ronald C. Lee.

Political Writings

The Reconsiderations

Introduction

St. Augustine began working on The City of God *in 413; it would take him some thirteen years to complete it. Not long after finishing it, and only a few years before his death (in 430), he composed a book entitled* The Reconsiderations. *In this work he comments briefly on the contents of each of his earlier literary efforts and relates the events that prompted him to write them. In speaking of* The City of God, *Augustine first describes the circumstances that caused him to take up this enormous project and then sketches an outline of it.*

Reconsiderations II.43

Rome was invaded and sacked by the Goths under King Alaric. The attack caused great destruction. The worshippers of the many false gods, whom we call by the customary name of "pagans," blamed the Christian religion for the disaster and began to blaspheme the true God more sharply and bitterly than usual. Consumed with zeal for the house of God (Ps 69:10), I resolved to write the books on *The City of God* against their blasphemies and errors. The work occupied me for several years because I kept being interrupted by numerous other matters that could not be put off and to which I first had to attend.

At last, however, this enormous work, *The City of God*, comprising twenty-two books, was completed. The first five refute those who want their affairs to prosper and to this end deem it necessary to engage in the cult of a multitude of pagan gods. They contend that the evils in question spring up and proliferate because the worship of these gods is now prohibited. The next five books argue against those who, while admitting that such evils have never been and never will be lacking among mortal human beings, and that they vary according to place, time, and the individuals involved, great at one time and less so at another, nevertheless maintain

1

that the cult whereby sacrifices are offered to the many gods is useful for the sake of the life after death. In these ten books, therefore, those two false opinions held by the adversaries of the Christian religion are refuted.

However, lest someone should reproach us with only criticizing others without offering any solutions of our own, the second part of this work, which comprises twelve books, does just that, although whenever necessary we state our own views even in the first ten books and refute our adversaries even in the last twelve. Of these final twelve books, the first four treat of the origin of the two cities, one of which belongs to God and the other to this world; the second four treat of their development or progress; the third four treat of their final and deserved ends. Thus, all twenty-two books, although dealing with both cities, were named after the better one. Hence, the work is entitled *The City of God*.

Book I

Introduction

The first book of The City of God *focuses on the immediate problems posed for Christians by Alaric's sack of Rome on 24 August 410. Responding to the pagans who were blaming Christianity for that catastrophe, Augustine begins by noting that the Christian faith had in fact mitigated the harshness of the invaders, since they had respected Christian sanctuaries. In this context, he brings up the example of the fall of Troy, a most relevant point because Rome's national epic, the* Aeneid *of Virgil, suggested that Rome had been founded by Trojan refugees fleeing the destruction of their city. In addition to attacks from outside the church, there were also the concerns of those Christians who could not understand why God would permit such a disaster. Beginning in Chapter 8, Augustine turns to such concerns, discussing the problem of divine providence and human suffering and consoling the Christian virgins who had been raped by the barbarians rather than commit suicide. The issue of suicide leads Augustine into a discussion of acceptable forms of killing. In the selections included in this volume, he considers especially the killing of plants and animals and killing in response to a special command of God.*

Preface

I have undertaken to defend the most glorious city of God against those who prefer their own gods to the founder of that city. This defense, which I promised you, my dearest son Marcellinus,[1] considers the city of God both in the fleeting course of time when, living by faith, it travels among the impious and also in the stability of its eternal abode. It now awaits that

---

1. Marcellinus was a Christian Roman official who arrived in Carthage in 410. A pious Catholic political figure, he became Augustine's friend and also seems to have been an intermediary between Augustine and influential pagan circles. He

3

stability through patience, "until justice is turned into judgment" (Ps 93:15); but then it will obtain, through its excellence, final victory and perfect peace. The task which I undertake is great and arduous, but God is our help (Ps 61:9).

I am aware of the powers required to persuade the proud of how great the virtue of humility is. It brings about a loftiness that human arrogance cannot seize but which divine grace gives, a loftiness that transcends all earthly triumphs wavering in unstable mutability. The king and founder of this city of which we will be speaking has made clear the meaning of the divine law in the Scriptures of his people, in which it is said, "God resists the proud, but gives grace to the humble" (Prv 3:34; Jas 4:6; 1 Pt 5:5). However, this privilege, which belongs to God, the swollen spirit of the proud soul also grasps at, for it loves to be praised in these words: "to spare the defeated and to conquer the proud."[2] Thus, I must not pass over in silence the subject of the earthly city, which, even as it enslaves peoples in its quest to dominate, is itself dominated by the very lust to dominate. If the ability is given to me, I will speak of this earthly city insofar as the plan of this work requires.

Chapter 1

The reason for this is that the enemies against which the city of God must be defended come out of the earthly city. Many of them, once the error of impiety is corrected, become quite suitable citizens of the city of God. However, many of them are so ablaze with the fire of hatred and are so ungrateful for the obvious benefits of the redeemer of the city of God that they still speak against that city even though they could not today utter a single word against it if, while fleeing the hostile sword, they had not found the life of which they are so proud in its sacred places. Are not even those Romans whom the barbarians spared on account of Christ now hostile to the name of Christ? The shrines of the martyrs and the basilicas of the apostles testify to this, for they took in both their own and strangers who were fleeing the sack of the city.

All the way up to those places the bloodthirsty enemy raged. There the

---

was executed in 413, a victim of a general purge of Roman government officials in Africa.

2. Virgil, *Aeneid* VI. 853. Virgil (70–19 B.C.) was the most celebrated Roman poet; his *Aeneid* became the national epic and played a foundational role in Roman education.

raving of the butcher recognized its limit. There even the ones who were spared outside of those places were led by merciful foes, so that they would not be attacked by other foes who did not have such mercy. Moreover, even those who elsewhere were raging cruelly in wild fury held back all savage slaying and curbed all greed for getting captives after they came to those places where what the law of war allows was forbidden. In this way many escaped who now disparage these Christian times.[3]

The evil things which the earthly city endured they impute to Christ. The good things which occurred on account of Christ, resulting in their being alive due to the respect given to Christ, they do not impute to our Christ but to their own fate. If they were to discern correctly the rough and harsh suffering they endured at the hands of their foes, they ought to ascribe it to that divine providence which customarily uses wars to improve or obliterate the corrupt ways of men. That providence also makes the lives of the just and praiseworthy strong through such afflictions, and having found them acceptable, it either conveys them to a better place or detains them in this world for other purposes.

Contrary to the customs of war, the cruel barbarians spared them.[4] Some they spared wherever they found them on account of the name of Christ; others they spared in the largest places most consecrated to the name of Christ. These places were selected on account of their capacity to hold a great multitude, so that the mercy would be more abundant. This they ought to attribute to these Christian times; hence, they ought to give thanks to God; hence, in order to escape the punishment of eternal fire they ought to run truthfully to his name—the name which many of them mendaciously usurped in order to escape the punishment of temporal destruction. Among those whom you see insolently and shamelessly insulting the servants of Christ are many who would not have escaped destruction and annihilation unless they had pretended to be servants of Christ. And now

---

3. The phrase "Christian times" was used by non-Christians as a reproach against the newly Christianized empire; it was also used in a positive sense by Christians. See R. A. Markus, *Saeculum: History and Society in the Theology of St. Augustine* (Cambridge University Press, 1970), 22–44; but see G. Madec, "*Tempora Christiana*: Expression du triomphalisme chrétien ou récrimination païenne," in P. Mayer and W. Eckermann, eds., *Scientia Augustiniana* (Würzburg, 1975), 112–36; also Ernest L. Fortin, "Augustine's *City of God* and the Modern Historical Consciousness," *Review of Politics* 41 (1979), 333–35.

4. See Orosius, *Seven Books of History Against the Pagans* VII. 39. He mentions a decree by Alaric that made Christian holy places sanctuaries.

his name, to which they fled with deceitful mouths in order to enjoy temporal light, they resist through ungrateful pride, a most impious insanity, and a perverse heart, only to be punished in everlasting darkness.

Chapter 2

Many wars have been recorded which were waged either before the founding of Rome or since its birth and hegemony. Let the enemies of the city of God read these accounts, and let them show us a single city seized by foreigners where the troops who took it spared those they found taking refuge in the temples of their gods; or let them show us when a barbarian leader, upon storming a town, ordered that none of those found in this or that temple were to be harmed.

Did not Aeneas see Priam before the altars "defiling by his blood the fires he himself had consecrated"?[5] Did not Diomedes and Ulysses "cut down the guards of the supreme citadel, seize the sacred statue, and with bloody hands boldly grasp the sacred ribbons of the virgin goddess"?[6] The next passage in the *Aeneid*, "from that point the hopes of the Greeks ebbed and slipping backwards retreated,"[7] is not true, for indeed what happened next was that the Greeks conquered; next they destroyed Troy with sword and fire; next they hacked Priam to pieces as he fled to the altars.

Certainly Troy did not perish because it lost Minerva, for what had Minerva herself lost first so that she might perish? Perhaps her guards? This is quite true, for once they were killed, she could be carried away. It was not the men who were being protected by the image, but the image by the men. How then could she be worshipped in order that she might guard the fatherland and the citizens, when she was unable to guard her own guards?

Chapter 8

Someone may say, "Why, then, was the divine mercy extended even to the impious and the ungrateful?" Why would we hold this position, if not because the one who offered the mercy is the God who daily "makes his

---

5. *Aeneid* II. 501–2. Despite the piety of Priam, the king of Troy, the gods did not protect him, nor did the Greeks spare him when his city fell.

6. *Aeneid* II. 166–68. Diomedes and Ulysses were Greek warriors. Augustine refers to their capture of the Palladium or statue of the goddess Minerva, who was supposedly protecting Troy.

7. *Aeneid* II. 169–70.

sun rise upon the good and the evil and the rain fall upon the just and the unjust" (Mt 5:45)? Some of these impious ones, considering this, set themselves straight by repenting of their impiety. Others, as the apostle says, despising "the wealth of God's goodness and forbearance . . . according to their hardness of heart and unrepenting heart," store up a treasure "of wrath for themselves on the day of wrath, when the just judgment of God will be revealed and each one will be repaid according to his works" (Rom 2:4–6). Nevertheless, the patience of God invites the evil to repentence, as the whip of God instructs the good in patience. In like manner, the mercy of God embraces the good to nurture them, just as the severity of God corrects the evil to punish them.

Surely it pleased divine providence to prepare future goods for the just which the unjust will not enjoy, and future evils for the impious which will not torment the good. Nevertheless, he wills that temporary goods and evils be common to all, in order that such goods as evil people are seen to have may not be desired more eagerly, and in order that such evils as often adversely affect good people may not be avoided dishonorably.

However, what sort of use one makes of things which are called either "advantageous" or "adverse" is of the utmost importance. The good man is neither elated by temporary goods nor broken by temporary evils, but the evil man is punished by the misery of such evils because he is corrupted by the enjoyment of such goods. Still, God often plainly shows his working even in the distributing of goods and evils, for if every sin were punished by an obvious penalty now, nothing would be thought to be reserved for the last judgment; on the other hand, if no sin were punished clearly by the divine nature now, no one would believe in the existence of divine providence. It is similar with favorable things. If God did not grant them to some petitioners through a most evident generosity, we would say that such things do not belong to him. Likewise, if he granted them to all petitioners, we would think that, except for the sake of such rewards, we were not required to serve him. Nor would such service make us pious, but rather greedy and avaricious.

These things being so, whenever the good and the bad are afflicted equally, it is not the case that there is no distinction between them, for the distinction is not based on what they both endure. The dissimilarity of the sufferers remains despite the similarity of their sufferings, and although they are subjected to the same torment, the virtue and the vice are not the same. Subjected to the same fire, gold glows with a reddish gleam but chaff smolders. Subjected to the same threshing sled, the straw breaks into small pieces, but the grain is freed from the husk. The olive oil is not mixed with the lees just because both are forced out by the weight of the same olive press. So one and the same onrushing force tries, purifies, and refines the good, but condemns, devastates, and exterminates the evil. Thus, visited by the same affliction, the evil curse and blaspheme God, but the good beseech and praise him. It is not the kind of suffering but the kind of person who suffers that is so important. Stirred by equal motion, filth emits a horrible stench but perfume a sweet odor.

Chapter 11

Many Christians were killed, and many were destroyed in hideous ways. If this is difficult to bear, it is nevertheless common to all who have been born into this life. This I know: no one has died who would not have died eventually. . . . Hence, how they are to die ought not be a concern to those who necessarily will die, but rather to what place they will be compelled to go when they die. Accordingly, since Christians know the death of a pious, poor man licked by the tongues of dogs to be far better than that of an impious, rich man clothed in purple and fine linen, how did those horrible kinds of death hurt those who had lived well?[8]

Chapter 16

The enemies of the city of God truly think they accuse the Christians of a great crime when, exaggerating the account of their captivity, they add on stories of violations perpetrated not only against married women and virgins about to be married, but even against consecrated women. . . . Here we are not concerned so much to respond to the unfriendly as to console our own people. Hence, in the first place, let it be asserted and established that virtue, which consists in right living, commands the parts of the body from its throne in the mind, and that a body becomes holy through the exercise of a holy will. If such a will remains unshaken and stable, then, so long as he is not strong enough to avoid the attack without sinning, the sufferer is not to be blamed no matter what another does to or with the body. . . .

Chapter 18

. . . Holiness does not belong to the body because its parts are whole, or because they have not been handled. The parts of the body can suffer violence or injury through diverse accidents. Sometimes doctors, in aiding

---

8. The story of the religious pauper named Lazarus is related in Lk 16:19–31.

the body's health, do things to its parts which are horrible to behold. While examining by hand the integrity of a certain virgin, a midwife destroyed it, either through malevolence, inexperience, or accident. I do not believe that anyone is so stupid as to think that anything having to do with the holiness of her body itself was lost, although the integrity of that part was lost.

Accordingly, if the mind maintains the intention through which even the body deserved to be sanctified, then the violence of another's lust does not take away the body's sanctity, which is preserved by the persistence of one's own continence. Imagine, in contrast, some woman with a corrupted mind, violating the intention she had vowed to God, and on her way to be corrupted by her deceiver. Do we say that, while still on her way, she is holy in body, even though the holiness of her mind, through which the body was made holy, has been lost and destroyed? Avoid that error.

Let us rather be advised that just as the holiness of the body is not lost when the holiness of the mind remains while the body is overpowered, so the holiness of the body is lost when the holiness of the mind is violated even if the body is untouched. Accordingly, a woman violently overpowered and raped by the sin of another without any consent of her own does not have any cause to punish herself by voluntary death. How much less cause does she have prior to this happening to her! She ought not commit certain homicide when the shameful crime that is completely another's might still not be committed.

Chapter 20

. . . Certain people attempt to extend the commandment "You shall not kill" to wild beasts and domesticated animals, so that no one would be allowed to kill any of them. Therefore, why not also include green plants and whatever is nourished and attached to the ground by roots? Even these kinds of things, although they do not sense, are said to live. Hence, they are also able to die and consequently are also able, when violence is used, to be killed. Thus, the apostle, when he speaks of seeds of this sort, says, "What you sow is not brought to life, unless it dies" (1 Cor 15:36). Also, in a psalm it is written, "He killed their vines by hail" (Ps 78:47). Because of this, then, when we hear "You shall not kill," are we to consider it an abomination to pull up a bush? Are we, through extreme insanity, to rest satisfied with the error of the Manichaeans?[9]

9. Manichaeism was a religious sect founded in Persia in the third century. It

Therefore, rejecting this nonsense, when we read "You shall not kill," we do not understand this saying to be about shrubs, since they do not have sensation. Nor do we understand it be be about irrational animals that fly, swim, walk, or crawl, since they are not united to us through reason, and so it is not given to them to have a community with us. Because of this, through the most just ordering of the Creator, both their living and dying are subordinated to our own uses. Plants and animals having been eliminated, what remains is that we are to understand the saying "You shall not kill" to be about human beings: you shall not kill someone else nor yourself, for to kill oneself is to kill a human being.

Chapter 21

Divine authority itself, it is true, made certain exceptions to the prohibition of killing a human being. In these exceptions, by giving either a law or an express command addressed to a specific person as the occasion required, God ordered some human beings to be killed. But he who acts on someone else's orders, like a sword aiding its user, is not himself a killer. Therefore, not in the least did those who waged war on God's authority act contrary to the precept that says, "You shall not kill," and neither did those who exercised a position of public power according to God's laws—that is, according to the government of the most just reason—and punished criminals with death. Abraham, too, is not only not blamed for a crime of cruelty, but is even praised in the name of piety, because he willed to kill his son, not out of wickedness but out of obedience.

It is right to question whether one should hold that it was on account of a command of God that Jephthah killed his daughter who ran to meet him because he had vowed to sacrifice to God the first one who ran to meet him as he returned victorious from battle (Jgs 11:29–49). Nor would Samson be excused for crushing himself along with his enemies by the collapse of the house if the Spirit, who was working miracles through him, had not secretly commanded it. Thus, with the exceptions of those killed either through a just and general law or through a special command of God, the

---

spread rapidly through the Roman empire and Augustine himself was attracted to its teachings as a young man. Among other things, the Manichaeans were vegetarians who believed that plants suffer when harvested. On Manichaeism, see also the introduction to the section on "War." For a more complete account of Manichaeism, see Samuel N. C. Lieu, *Manichaeism in the Later Roman Empire and Medieval China: A Historical Survey* (Manchester University Press, 1985).

very fountain of justice, anyone who kills a human being, whether it be himself or anyone else, entangles himself in the crime of murder.[10]

Chapter 29

Therefore, the whole family of the highest and true God has its consolation, which is neither false nor based on a hope in wavering and unsteady things. It also has a temporal life that is not at all to be lamented, for through it this family is educated for eternal life. Like a traveller, it uses earthly goods without being ensnared by them, and it is both tested and corrected by evils. . . .

Chapter 34

. . . Romulus and Remus,[11] seeking to enlarge the population of the city they were creating, are said to have established an asylum where anyone might flee and escape all punishment. This is a precedent to marvel at, for it anticipates the honor lately given to Christ. The recent destroyers of the city established the very thing that its founders had previously established. Yet, what is so great about the deed of Romulus and Remus if they did this in order to build up the number of their own citizens, while the destroyers did it in order to preserve a large number of their enemies?

Chapter 35

May the redeemed family of Christ the Lord and the pilgrim city of Christ the King respond to its enemies with these replies or with fuller and more appropriate ones if they can find any. May it keep in mind that among

10. In this chapter Augustine considers three instances in which Old Testament figures might seem to have violated the commandment that prohibited killing. He defends Abraham's sacrifice of Isaac (Gn 22), since it was commanded by God. He is not so sure about Jephthah, however, who vowed to sacrifice the first to greet him when he returned home from battle and kept his vow even though the first to greet him turned out to be his only daughter (Jgs 11:29–40). Jephthah seems to have done this on account of his own vow, Augustine suggests, and not in obedience to a command of God. Augustine is likewise cautious about the case of Samson, who killed himself along with his enemies (Jgs 16:28–30). His action may be approved only if it was done by order of the Spirit.

11. Romulus was the legendary founder of the city of Rome. According to the Roman historian Livy (c. 59 B.C.– A.D. 17), Romulus murdered Remus before he

those same enemies hide its future citizens. Living among them, may that city not think it fruitless to bear their hostilities until such time as it obtains their confessions of faith. . . .

founded the asylum. See Livy's *History of Rome* I. 6–8. Augustine returns to this topic in V. 17.

Book II

Introduction

In Books II–IV, Augustine delivers a lengthy argument designed to show that disaster had befallen Rome since its foundation and hence long before the rise of Christianity. The particular focus of Book II is the moral decline of the Roman people, which Augustine considers to be the real disaster to have afflicted the city. He affixes the blame for this catastrophe squarely on the pagan gods and their lack of concern for moral character. Chapter 4 contrasts the Christian God's call for the moral regeneration of his followers with the obscene rites demanded by the pagan gods. Chapters 14 and 15 turn to the role of the poets in propagating unedifying tales about the gods. In Chapters 19 through 21, Augustine appeals to two famous non-Christian authors to drive home his point. Even the historian Sallust recognized that the once noble Roman republic had degenerated into "the worst and most disgraceful" republic of all, and if the views of Cicero's Republic *are accepted, the Roman republic had in fact ceased to exist long before the rise of Christianity.*

Chapter 4

Why were the gods of the Romans unwilling to take care that they did not have the worst sort of morals? To be sure, the true God justifiably neglected those who did not worship him. But why did those gods, whose worship ungrateful men complain is prohibited to them, establish no laws to guide their worshippers in living well? Certainly, it was right that, just as these worshippers were concerned with the worship of their gods, so the gods should have been concerned with their worshippers' conduct.

Our adversaries respond that anyone who is evil is so by his own will. Who would deny this? Even so, it was the obligation of the gods men consulted not to keep hidden the precepts of the good life from the peoples

13

who worshipped them, but to promulgate them clearly. Through sooth-sayers they should have called upon and convinced sinners, openly warned those doing evil of punishment, and promised reward to those living rightly. When, though, did such a message ever shake the temples of those gods with a prompt and clear voice?

As adolescents, we too used to attend their absurd and sacrilegious spec-tacles. We would watch the entranced dervishes and listen to the musi-cians. We would take pleasure in the shameful games that were put on for the gods and goddesses, especially for the virgin Caelestis and Berecynthia, the mother of all the gods.[1] On the solemn day of her purification, the vilest actors publicly chanted before her couch things so indecent that they were unfit, I do not need to say for the mother of the gods, but even for the mothers of senators or any decent men. Indeed, such shameful things were not even fit for the mothers of those disgusting actors. There is, in the human respect for parents, something that even depravity cannot destroy. Those actors themselves would have been ashamed to say or do at home in the presence of their mothers the filthy things in which they publicly en-gaged in the presence of the mother of the gods and a teeming crowd of watchers and listeners of both sexes. If this crowd was present because drawn by curiosity, it should have departed in confusion because of the offense to its modesty.

If these rites are sacred, what is sacrilege? If these rites are purifica-tion, what is pollution? These rites were called "trays," as if a banquet were being celebrated at which impure demons fed on delicacies. Who does not realize what sort of spirits delight in such obscenities except those who are either unaware of the existence of impure spirits who, un-der the name of "gods," deceive human beings, or those who live in such a way as to seek the favor and fear the anger of these gods rather than of the true God?

Chapter 14

Next we ask, Why are the poets who write such fables, who are prohibited by the law of the Twelve Tables from damaging the reputation of the citi-zens but cast shameful abuse on the gods— why are they not held to be

---

1. This aspect of Roman worship, unlike many of the others discussed by Augustine, was still practiced during his lifetime. For other instances of Augustine's treatment of contemporary non-Christian religious practices, see IV. 27 and VII. 26.

dishonorable like the actors?[2] Is it right that the actors of these poetic fictions and these god-dishonoring stories should be disgraced while their authors are honored? Or perhaps the palm of victory should be given to Plato the Greek, who, when fashioning in speech how the city ought to be, recommended that the poets be expelled as enemies of the truth?[3] He certainly resented the insults leveled at the gods and did not want the minds of the citizens tainted and corrupted by such fictions.

Now compare the humanity of Plato in expelling the poets from the city so as to keep them from misleading the citizens with the divinity of the gods in demanding theatrical plays in their own honor. Plato, while unable by means of arguments to persuade the frivolous and lascivious Greeks, nevertheless advised them not to write such things. In contrast, those gods by their commands extorted the actual performance of these things from the grave and modest Romans. And not content with having them staged, they had them dedicated, consecrated, and solemnly celebrated in their honor. To whom, then, would the city more honorably award divine honors—to Plato opposing these disgraceful and abominable things or to the demons rejoicing in this deception of men whom Plato could not persuade of the truth? . . .

Roman law approximates Plato's arguments condemning all poetic fictions. The law at least denies to poets the right to slander men. Plato banished the poets from his city; the Romans at least banish the actors of poetic fictions from the political community, and if the Romans had dared to defy the gods who demand the plays of the actors, perhaps they would have banished them altogether. Therefore, the Romans could neither receive nor expect from their gods laws establishing good morals or correcting bad ones, because by their own laws they overcome and condemn the gods. The gods demand theatrical games in their honor; the Romans remove theater people from all honors. The gods command that they be celebrated with poetic fictions that are insulting to the gods themselves; the Romans

---

2. Augustine may be referring to VIII.1B of the Twelve Tables, the most ancient laws of the Romans, which made it a capital offense to compose or sing an incantation that would dishonor or disgrace someone. See also Cicero's *Republic* IV. 10.

3. The allusion to a city fashioned in speech is a reference to the city discussed in Plato's *Republic* (see esp. IX, 592a). The allusion to the expulsion of the poets (see esp. III, 398a) refers to a lengthy section of the *Republic* (Books II, III, and X) in which Plato argues for the careful control of poetry in the city. Augustine's point is thus that Plato was more concerned with the moral well-being of the city than were the Roman gods.

prevent the impudence of poets from insulting human beings. . . .

How, then, could such gods prevent imminent evils of mind and morals by good precepts and laws, or root them out once they had been implanted, when they themselves were busy sowing and cultivating crimes, whether real or fictitious, with which they desired the people to become familiar through theatrical performances, so that in this way the basest lust might be enkindled in the human will as if by divine authority? . . .

Chapter 15

Is it not flattery rather than reason that led them to choose their false gods? They did not consider Plato, whom they regard as a demigod and who labored with so many arguments to keep human morals from being corrupted by the evils of the mind (the ones most to be avoided), worthy of even a small shrine. Rather, they preferred their own Romulus to many other gods, even though their more or less secret doctrine ranks him as a demigod rather than a god. Indeed, they even appointed a *flamen* for him.[4] This was a kind of priest so distinguished in Roman religion—the distinction was symbolized by their conical hats—that only three divinities had *flamens* appointed for them: Dialis for Jupiter, Martialis for Mars, and Quirinalis for Romulus. . . .

Chapter 19

Look at the Roman republic which, "having changed little by little from the most beautiful and best, has become the worst and most disgraceful."[5] I am not the first to say this. Their own authors, from whom we learned it for a fee, said it long before the coming of Christ. Look at how, before the coming of Christ and after the destruction of Carthage, "the morals of the ancestors were not changed little by little as previously, but swept away by a torrent to such an extent that the youth were corrupted by luxury and greed."[6]

Let them read to us the precepts against luxury and greed given to the

---

4. As Augustine says, a *flamen* was a special priest who had an important role to play in the official religious life of Rome. By the time of Augustine, the public worship of Romulus had ceased.

5. This is a quotation from Sallust's *War with Catiline* 5, 9. Sallust (86–34 B.C.) was a famous Roman historian and political figure. Augustine relies heavily on his work throughout Book IV.

6. Sallust, *History* I, 16 (fragment).

Roman people by their gods. If only these gods had kept silent about chastity and modesty and not demanded from the people shameful and disgraceful things, giving them a pernicious authority through their false divinity. Let them read our many precepts against luxury and greed given through the prophets, the Holy Gospel, the Acts of the Apostles, and the epistles. Such precepts are everywhere read to the people gathered to hear them. How excellent and divine they sound, not like the clatter of philosophical disputation, but like the oracle of God sounding from the clouds.

Nevertheless, they do not blame their own gods for the luxury, the greed, and the wild and dissolute morals which, prior to the coming of Christ, changed the republic into "the worst and most disgraceful." Instead they reproach the Christian religion for any sort of distress which their pride and voluptuousness has suffered in recent times.

If "the kings of the earth and all peoples, leaders and all judges of the earth, youths and maidens, the youthful and the elderly" (Ps 148:11–12), those of every age capable of understanding, both sexes, even those very tax collectors and soldiers that John the baptist addressed (Lk 3:12–14)— if they would hear and obey the precepts of the Christian religion concerning just and upright morals, then the republic would embellish the domain of the present life with its own happiness and would ascend to eternal life to reign in supreme happiness. However, because this person hears, that one scorns, and many are better friends with the evil allurements of the vices than with the advantageous austerity of the virtues, the servants of Christ—whether kings or leaders or judges, whether soldiers or inhabitants of the provinces, whether rich or poor, whether free or slave, whether male or female—are commanded to endure even "the worst and most disgraceful" republic, if it is necessary, and through that endurance to prepare an illustrious place for themselves in that most holy and majestic assembly of angels, in that heavenly republic where the will of God is law.

Chapter 20

. . . What sane man would not compare this republic, I do not say to the Roman empire, but to the palace of Sardanapalus, a king so given to sensual pleasures that he had it inscribed on his tomb that in death he possessed only those things which his passion had absorbed and consumed while he was alive?[7] With this sort of king, who, indulgent himself, would not oppose their indulgence with any severity, the people would more

---

7. Sardanapalus: a legendary Assyrian king famous for his excessive luxury. See Cicero, *Tusculan Disputations* V. 35. 101.

freely consecrate a temple and *flamen* to him than the ancient Romans did to Romulus.

Chapter 21

If our enemies scorn the author who said that the Roman republic was the "worst and the most disgraceful," and if they do not care about the great shame and degradation of the "worst and most disgraceful" morals that fill it, but care only that it stand firm and survive, then let them hear no more about how it became the worst and most disgraceful, as Sallust narrates. Instead, let them hear that, as Cicero argues,[8] the republic had already at that time utterly perished and no longer existed at all.

Cicero brings forth Scipio, the destroyer of Carthage himself,[9] discussing the republic at a time when there was already foreboding that it was about to perish through the corruption described by Sallust. . . . At the end of the second book, Scipio says,

> Among lyres and flutes or singing voices, a certain harmony must be maintained out of the different sounds. Trained ears cannot bear false or discordant notes. This harmony, full of concord and agreement, is produced from the regulation of the most dissimilar voices. In the same way, the city, having been regulated by reason, harmonizes through a consensus of dissimilar elements from the upper, lower, and middle classes, just like musical notes. What the musicians call "harmony" in music, is "concord" in a city, a bond of preservation that is the tightest and the best of all in a republic, and in no way can it exist without justice.[10]

8. Cicero (106–43 B.C.): a Roman rhetorician, politician, and philosopher, famous for his eloquence and mastery of the Latin language. His works occupied a major position in Roman education in general and in Augustine's life in particular. In his *Confessions*, Augustine describes how reading Cicero's *Hortensius* inflamed him with a desire for wisdom (III. 4. 7–8). In the present chapter Augustine relates the discussion of Cicero's dialogue entitled *The Republic*, only part of which is extant. See also Augustine's remarks on Cicero in III, 30.

9. Scipio Africanus the Younger (c. 185–129 B.C.): a famous Roman general who captured the city of Carthage in 146 B.C., thereby ending the third and final Punic War. Cicero casts Scipio as one of the interlocutors in his dialogue, and it would seem that he speaks for Cicero himself in that conversation. This Scipio is not to be confused with Scipio Africanus the Greater, who defeated the great Carthaginian general Hannibal in 202 to bring about an end to the Second Punic War.

10. *Republic* II. 42.

After Scipio discusses somewhat more broadly and fully how great an advantage justice is to a city and how great a disadvantage is its absence, Philus, one of those present at the discussion, wades in and demands that this question be treated more thoroughly and that more be said about justice on account of what was then commonly supposed, namely, that a republic cannot be ruled without injustice. Scipio accordingly agrees that this question must be discussed and explicated. He replies that he thinks there is nothing that has already been said about a republic that could serve as a basis for proceeding further, unless it can be firmly established not only that it is false that a republic cannot be ruled without injustice, but also that it is most true that a republic cannot be ruled without supreme justice.[11]

The explication of this question is put off until the following day, when it is argued out with great conflict in the third book. Philus himself takes up the cause of those who think that without injustice a republic cannot be governed. Above all else, he apologizes for doing so, in order that it would not be believed that he himself actually held this position. He zealously pleads the cause of injustice against justice. Using arguments and examples resembling the truth, he undertakes to show that injustice is useful for a republic and justice useless.[12] Then Laelius, at the request of all the others, sets forth to defend justice and protects, to the extent that he is able, the position that nothing is so inimical to a city as injustice and that a republic cannot be governed or stand firm at all without a great deal of justice.[13]

After this question is treated to an extent that is viewed as sufficient, Scipio returns to the point where the discussion was interrupted. He repeats and recommends his brief definition of a republic, stating that a republic is "the affair of a people."[14] However, he defines a "people" to be not

11. *Republic* II. 44.

12. *Republic* III. 5–20.

13. *Republic* III. 21–29.

14. *Republic* I. 25; III. 31. With this definition, Scipio puns on the word "republic," saying that the *res publica* (republic) is the *res populi* (the thing, affair, or property of the people). Perhaps the English word "commonwealth" more closely approximates Scipio's point: the commonwealth is the weal (or well-being) of the community. However, translating *res publica* as "commonwealth" would obscure the connection to the Roman republic of which Scipio (and Augustine) are speaking; moreover, the English word has lost much of its original force. Hence, *res publica* has been translated as "republic" throughout.

every fellowship of a multitude, but a "fellowship united through a consensus concerning right and a sharing of advantage." Next, he shows the great advantage of definition in argumentation, and from his own definitions he then concludes that a republic, i.e. the affair of a people, exists when a people is governed well and justly, whether it is by a single king, a few aristocrats, or the whole people. However, when a king is unjust, he calls him, according to the Greek usage, a tyrant; when the aristocrats are unjust, he says their fellowship is a faction; when the people itself is unjust, he finds no customary name for it, unless it would also be called tyranny. In these latter three cases, he does not show that such a republic is then corrupt, as he had argued on the previous day. Rather, reasoning from his definitions, he teaches that a republic does not exist at all, because there is no "affair of the people" when a tyrant or a faction seize it. Nor is the people then a people if it is unjust, because there is no multitude united through a consensus concerning right and a sharing of advantage, as "people" was defined.

Therefore, when the Roman republic was of the quality described by Sallust, it was not then "the worst and most disgraceful," as he had said, but it did not exist at all according to this line of reasoning, which this dialogue on the republic conducted among the great leaders of that age makes clear. Also, Cicero himself, speaking in his own name and not in the person of Scipio or anyone else, quotes a verse from the poet Ennius at the beginning of Book 5: "The Roman republic stands firm on the morals and men of yesteryear."[15] Cicero goes on to say,

> This verse, through both its brevity and truth, seems to me to be just like a statement from some oracle. If the city had not had such morals, the men could not have founded or preserved for so long a republic ruling so far and wide; nor could the morals have done so, if these men had not been leaders. Thus, before our time, the morality of the forefathers brought forth outstanding men, and superior men maintained the old morality and the ways of our ancestors. Our age, however, has received the republic like a remarkable painting which is fading with age, and not only has it neglected to restore its original colors, but it has not even bothered to preserve, so to speak, its shape and basic outlines. What remains from the ancient morals upon which Ennius said the Roman republic stands firm? We see that they have fallen into such oblivion that not only are they not practised, but they are not

15. Ennius (239–c. 269 B.C.) was an influential Latin poet, though little of his work is extant.

even known. What shall I say of the men of our time? The morals themselves perished because of a lack of men. Not only must we answer for such a crime, but we must, as it were, plead our case against a capital charge. We preserve the republic in word, but the thing itself we lost long ago, and this is due not to some accident, but to our own vices.

Indeed, Cicero was confessing these things long after the death of Africanus, whom he portrays in the argument in his books *On the Republic*;[16] nevertheless, this was still before the coming of Christ. If these views had been thought and stated while the Christian religion was growing strong, who among our enemies would not have been of the opinion that the Christians should be blamed for them? Why, then, did their gods not bother to prevent the ruin and loss of the republic that Cicero, long before Christ came in the flesh, so mournfully laments as lost? Those who praise that republic even for those "men and morals of yesteryear" must consider whether true justice flourished in it or whether perhaps even then it was something that did not live through morals but was depicted through colors. Cicero himself unwittingly expresses this when he commends the painting.

However, we will examine this elsewhere, if God is willing.[17] In the appropriate place, I will attempt to show that according to the definitions of Cicero concerning what a "republic" is and what a "people" is, which were succinctly set forth in the speeches of Scipio (and also confirmed by many statements either of Cicero's own or of other speakers who are portrayed in the same dialogue), the republic never existed because true justice was never present in it. According to more accepted definitions, however, a certain sort of republic did exist, and it was directed better by the earlier Romans than by the later ones. Nevertheless, true justice does not exist except in that republic whose founder and ruler is Christ—if it is admitted that it, too, may be called a "republic," since we cannot deny that it is "the affair of the people." Yet even if such a use of this name "republic," which is commonly used for other things and in other ways, is perhaps too far removed from normal usage, certainly there is true justice in that city of which the Sacred Scripture says, "Glorious things are said about you, O city of God" (Ps 87:3).

---

16. Scipio Africanus the Younger died in 129 B.C.; Cicero is thought to have begun the *Republic* in about 54 B.C.

17. See XIX. 21 and 24.

Chapter 29

Crave these things of God instead, O praiseworthy Roman character, O children of Regulus, Scaevola, Scipio, and Fabricius.[18] Crave these things instead, and distinguish them from that most shameful vanity and most deceitful malignity of the demons. If there naturally shines in you anything praiseworthy, it will not be purified and perfected except by true piety and can only be ruined and punished by impiety. Choose now what you will follow, so that, without any error, you might praise not what is in yourself, but what is in the true God. In the past, you gained popular glory, but by the secret judgment of divine providence, you did not have the choice of true religion. Wake up, it is daytime—just as you have awakened in those in whose perfect virtue and sufferings for the true faith we glory! . . .

18. Augustine concludes his analysis of the moral life of the Roman republic with an appeal to four heroes of republican virtue. During the First Punic War (264–242 B.C.) the Roman general Regulus was captured by the Carthaginians. He travelled to Rome with a party of Carthaginian ambassadors to help secure terms of peace, agreeing to return to Carthage to face death if he failed to gain acceptance of the Carthaginian terms. Once in Rome, however, Regulus urged the Senate to reject those terms; he returned to Carthage where he was tortured and executed. Scaevola or Mucius attempted to win the freedom of Rome by assassinating the Etruscan King Porsena (c. 500 B.C.) even as Porsena was blockading it. Venturing forth from the safety of the city, he sneaked into Porsena's camp but was apprehended before he could kill the king. He was ordered to be burned alive; in a display of courage he stretched his right hand forth into the flames. The king decided to pardon him for such bravery. On Scipio, see the note on II. 21. Due to his severe distaste for luxury, Fabricius (fl. c. 280 B.C.) was a frequently cited example of austere republican virtue.

Book III

Introduction

Book III continues the analysis of the problems that beset Rome prior to the rise of Christianity. Now, however, instead of considering moral evil, Augustine turns to external disasters, the evils that the wicked think are the only evils. The book is organized chronologically. Augustine returns to the relationship between the fall of Troy and the founding of Rome, comparing the crime that led to the destruction of the former with the crime that lies at the very foundation of the latter. Following this discussion, he turns to the next period in Roman history, the rule of the kings. Our selections from this section focus on Numa Pompilius, who began the process of civilizing the unruly people, especially by means of religion. The final section of Book III is Augustine's discussion of the Roman republic. In Chapters 21 and 30, he shows that even after the long struggle of the three Punic wars ended with the final and total victory over rival Carthage, the republic still faced military difficulties. In particular, he describes the long and bloody civil wars that engulfed the republic, brought about Cicero's demise and ushered in the rule of Caesar Augustus, Rome's first emperor.

Chapter 6

If the sins of men so displeased those pagan gods that they deserted Troy and gave it over to fire and the sword on account of Paris's deed, then they should have been even angrier at the Romans for the killing of Romulus's brother than they were at the Trojans for the outrage perpetrated on a Greek husband. The murder of a relative in a newly-founded city should have angered them much more than adultery in a flourishing one. It is irrelevant to the point we are now making whether Romulus ordered his brother killed or killed him himself, a fact that many impudently deny, doubt out of shame, or conceal out of sorrow. We need not pause here to investigate carefully the testimony of the many writers on this event. It is clear that the brother of Romulus was killed neither by enemies nor by foreigners.[1]

If Romulus was the one who committed or ordered the deed (and he was more truly the head of the Romans than Paris was of the Trojans), why did the robber of another's wife provoke the anger of the gods against the Trojans while the killer of his brother won for the Romans the protection of those same gods? If, on the other hand, the crime was done or ordered by someone other than Romulus, then, in effect, the whole city did it, because it should have punished the crime but did not do so. Thus, the city killed not a brother but—what is worse—a father. Both brothers were founders of that city where one, wickedly killed, was not allowed to rule.

In my judgment, no evil can be attributed to Troy that would justify its being abandoned by the gods, thus causing its destruction. Nor can any good be attributed to Rome that would justify its being inhabited by the gods, thus causing its prosperity. Perhaps it might be said that the gods, having been conquered, fled from Troy to the Romans whom they deceived as well. Better still: those gods remained at Troy so that they might, as usual, deceive the new inhabitants, while at Rome, through the more perfect exercise of the same fallacious arts, they reaped greater honors.

Chapter 8

Was it prudent, then, to commit Rome to the guardianship of the gods of Troy after the example of the fall of that city? Might someone say that they were already living in Rome when Fimbria attacked and took Troy?[2] Why, then, did the image of Minerva remain standing?[3] Further, if they were in Rome when Fimbria destroyed Troy, perhaps they were in Troy when Rome itself was captured and burned by the Gauls.[4] Because of their very sharp hearing and very swift movements, they returned quickly to the Capitoline hill at the call of a goose in order to guard it, for it had not yet

1. On Romulus, see the note on I. 34.

2. Fimbria (d. 84 B.C.) conquered Troy shortly before his death. This sacking of the city is not to be confused with the capture of Troy by the Greeks centuries earlier.

3. In Book LXXXIII of Livy, which is not extant, it was apparently related that the image of Minerva stood unharmed even though her temple was demolished during the attack. See *Periochae* LXXXIII and Julius Obsequens 56b.

4. Rome was sacked by the Gauls in 387/6 B.C.

fallen. The warning came too late for them to return to defend the other parts of the city![5]

Chapter 9

The gods are also believed to have enabled Romulus's successor, Numa Pompilius,[6] to enjoy a peaceful reign and close the gates of Janus, which were usually open in wartime. He was thought to have merited this because he established many sacred rites among the Romans. It would certainly be proper to congratulate him for such a long period of peace if only he had known how to use it to pursue useful matters and, casting aside a most pernicious curiosity, had sought the true God with true piety. The gods did not secure this peace for him, but perhaps they would have deceived him less if they found him less at peace; for the less they found him occupied, the more they occupied him. Varro[7] tells us what this man undertook and by what skills he was able to associate the gods with himself and the city—a subject which, if it pleases the Lord, will be more thoroughly discussed in its proper place.[8]

For the time being, the question concerns the benefits of these gods. Peace is a great benefit, though it is a benefit of the true God and, like many benefits, such as sun, rain, and other supports of life, it also falls on the ungrateful and the wicked. Yet, if the gods are the ones who conferred this great good on Rome or Pompilius, why was it never given at a later date to the Roman empire during its laudable periods? Were the sacred rites more efficacious when they were first instituted than when they were later celebrated as established practices? At the earlier time they did not yet exist, but were invented; at the later time, they were already in existence and were maintained so that they might be beneficial. Yet, in Numa's reign there was a long period of peace of forty-three—or, as others would have it,

---

5. According to Livy (V. 47), the Gauls were about to attack the Capitol when the sacred geese woke up a Roman sentry who alerted the other defenders. The rest of the city was taken.

6. Numa Pompilius (715–673 B.C.) is most famous for giving the Romans their religious rites. See Livy I. 19.

7. Varro (116–27 B.C.) was considered by many of his contemporaries to be the most learned man of his time. He is said to have written 490 books, very few of which survive. Augustine makes extensive use of his now lost works on religion and philosophy.

8. See VII. 34.

thirty-nine—years; afterwards, once the sacred rites and the gods who were invoked by them had been established as guardians and guides, it is difficult to recall, out of the many years from the foundation of the city to the time of Augustus, barely more than one year after the first Punic War in which, by a great miracle, the Romans were able to close the gates of war.[9] How can this be?

Chapter 10

Will they respond that the Roman empire would not have spread so widely and achieved such great glory save by continuous and successive wars? A truly suitable cause! Why must Rome be disrupted in order to be a great empire? In the human body, is it not better to have a moderate stature with health rather than to attain a gigantic size through perpetual disturbances and, when you have acquired it, not to be at rest but to be afflicted by evils as great as your members are gigantic? What evil would there have been, or rather what good would there not have been, if those times had continued which Sallust sums up when he says, "In the beginning the kings (for that was at first the name of imperial authority on earth) differed; some of them exercised the mind and others the body; up to that time, human life was carried on without greed, each being satisfied with what was his own."[10] Was it proper that, in order for imperial authority to grow so enormously, what Virgil curses should come to pass: "Little by little came on a worse and colorless age, and raging war and love of gain"?[11]

Clearly, however, the Romans have a legitimate excuse for undertaking and waging such wars: they were forced to resist the threatening incursions of their enemies, not out of a desire to win human praise, but out of the necessity to protect their safety and liberty. This is clear. As Sallust himself writes:

> Once their state, now endowed with laws, customs, and land, seemed prosperous and powerful enough, as most often happens in human affairs, their opulence provoked envy. Accordingly, the kings and peoples on their borders attacked them. A few of their friends gave help, but the others, struck by fear, kept clear of the dangers. The Romans, however, alert in both domestic and military matters, hastened to make preparations, encouraging

9. Augustus closed the gates of the Temple of Janus Quirinus for the first of three times during his reign in 25 B.C.

10. *Catiline* 2, 1.

11. *Aeneid* VIII. 325–27.

one anther to go out against their enemies, protecting by arms their liberty, country, and parents. Afterwards, when they had repelled the dangers by their valour, they carried assistance to their allies and friends and made friends more by giving than receiving benefits.[12]

It is proper that Rome rose by these skills. However, in Numa's reign, how did it come about that peace lasted so long? Were enemies encroaching and threatening war, or was none of that happening, so that peace could persist? If Rome was even then afflicted by wars but did not go out to meet arms with arms, then whatever means they used to restrain their enemies without conquering them in battle or terrifying them with a martial assault, they might have used at all times. Rome, tranquil, could always have reigned with the gates of Janus closed. If this was not in Rome's power, then Rome had peace for as long as not her gods but the peoples on her borders willed it and did not provoke her with war—unless perhaps such gods would dare sell to one man what depends on the will or refusal of another man. To be sure, it is important to note that these demons are, to a certain extent, permitted to excite or terrify evil minds by their own wickedness. If they were always able to do this, and if another more secret and higher power did not often act against their power, they would always have in their power peace and military victory, since these almost always come about through human activity. However, peace and victory generally happen contrary to the will of the gods, as is confirmed not only by the many lying stories which hardly indicate or signify anything of the truth, but also by Roman history itself.

Chapter 21

. . . In the last Punic War, during a single campaign led by the younger Scipio (who on account of it also won for himself the title of "Africanus"),[13] the rival of Roman dominion was utterly destroyed. From that time on, however, the Roman republic was oppressed by burdens of evils. Indeed, the very prosperity and security of Rome's affairs led, on account of the Romans' exceedingly corrupt morals, to those burdensome evils. Thus, Carthage harmed Rome more by being so swiftly overthrown than it had previously harmed her by being for so long her adversary.

Caesar Augustus seems in every way to have wrested from the Romans their liberty, which, even in their own eyes, was no longer glorious but full

12. *Catiline* 6, 3–5.
13. On Scipio Africanus the Younger, see the note on II. 21.

of contention and destruction as it lost vigor and languished. He subjected all affairs to monarchic rule and, as it were, restored and revived the republic that was crumbling from the morbidity of old age. . . .

Chapter 30

With what effrontery, with what boldness, with what impudence, with what foolishness—or rather insanity—do they not attribute those disasters of the past to their own gods while they attribute the disasters of today to our Christ? The cruel civil wars were more bitter than all of the foreign wars, as is admitted by their own historians. These civil wars not only afflicted the republic, but are judged to have completely destroyed it. They began long before the coming of Christ, and, by a long series of criminal causes, led from the wars of Marius and Sulla to the wars of Sertorius and Catiline (of whom one was proscribed and the other supported by Sulla); and from this war to the war of Lepidus and Catulus (of whom one wanted to repeal the acts of Sulla and the other to defend them); and from this war to the war of Pompey and Caesar (of whom Pompey was a follower of Sulla, whose power he equalled or even surpassed, while Caesar could not bear Pompey's power because he did not have it himself; yet he exceeded it when Pompey was defeated and killed).[14] This led to the other Caesar, afterwards called Augustus, during whose rule Christ was born.[15]

Augustus himself waged many civil wars and in these many illustrious men died. Among them was Cicero, that eloquent master of the art of ruling a republic. Consider the conqueror of Pompey, Gaius Caesar,[16] who acted with clemency in civil victory and granted his adversaries life and dignity: a conspiracy of noble senators, asserting that he desired to be king

14. Augustine here recounts the many civil wars that engulfed the republic during the first century B.C. They began with the bloody conflict between Marius and Sulla in 88–82 B.C., which was later followed by the revolts of Sertorius, Catiline, and Lepidus. Pompey the Great (106–48 B.C.) and Julius Caesar (c. 100–44 B.C.) were originally allies, but a falling out led to war between the two. Pompey was decisively defeated in the Battle of Pharsalia in 48 B.C.

15. Caesar Augustus (63 B.C.–A.D. 14): the first Roman emperor. After his great uncle Julius Caesar was killed in 44 B.C., he engaged in a long series of intermittent wars and political struggles that eventually culminated with the defeat of Antony in 31 B.C. Having conquered all his rivals, he became master of the Roman world.

16. This is Julius Caesar, who was famous for the mercy he showed to those who sided with Pompey in the civil war between the two. Among those whom he pardoned was Cicero.

and claiming to act for the sake of the liberty of the republic, assassinated him, cutting him down in the Curia itself.[17] Then Antony, a man of quite different morals, corrupted and polluted with every vice, seemed to covet his power, but was vehemently opposed by Cicero for the sake of that same liberty of the fatherland.[18] There then emerged that young man of remarkable character, the other Caesar, adopted by Gaius Caesar as his son, who, as I said, was afterwards called Augustus.[19] This young Caesar was favored by Cicero so that his power might be used against Antony. Cicero hoped that he would depose Antony, put an end to his despotism, and establish a free republic. However, Cicero was so blind and improvident that the same young man, whose prestige and power he supported, permitted Cicero himself to be killed as a token of his reconciliation with Antony.[20] As for the liberty of the republic, which Cicero had many times proclaimed, young Caesar brought it under his own control.

17. Augustine refers to the famous assassination of Julius Caesar by a senatorial party on 15 March 44 B.C.

18. Antony was famous for his profligacy. He seems to have coveted powers as great as those previously held by Julius Caesar and was castigated for this by Cicero.

19. Augustus was adopted by his great-uncle, Julius Caesar.

20. As Augustine says, Cicero had originally supported Augustus (young Caesar) in order to counter Antony's power, which he considered to be dangerous to the republican cause. Augustus and Antony were reconciled in 43 B.C., and Augustus apparently permitted Antony to have his vengeance against Cicero.

Book IV

Introduction

With Book IV, Augustine turns from republican to imperial Rome and disputes the suggestion that the pagan gods could have had anything to do with the expansion of the Roman empire. In the first section of the book, he questions the morality of conquest and the very desirability of imperial rule. Despite its brevity, Chapter 4 is one of the most striking chapters of the entire City of God *because of its sweeping condemnation of kingdoms and empires. This chapter should be read in light of what is said about justice in Book II, Chapter 21, and Book XIX, Chapters 21 and 24. Augustine then turns to an open attack on the gods of popular religion, ridiculing the innumerable absurdities attributed to them. A sample from this section is Chapter 20, in which he scorns the manner in which the Romans had made "Virtue" into a goddess. As part of this attack on pagan religion, Augustine brings forth Scaevola's famous distinction between the theology of the poets, of the statesmen, and of the philosophers. Since even the Roman statesmen and philosophers did not accept the religion of the poets, the gods they speak of warrant no credence.*

Chapter 4

Without justice, what are kingdoms but great robber bands? What are robber bands but small kingdoms? The band is itself made up of men, is ruled by the command of a leader, and is held together by a social pact. Plunder is divided in accordance with an agreed-upon law. If this evil increases by the inclusion of dissolute men to the extent that it takes over territory, establishes headquarters, occupies cities, and subdues peoples, it publically assumes the title of kingdom! This title is manifestly conferred on it, not because greed has been removed, but because impunity has been added. A fitting and true response was once given to Alexander the Great by an apprehended pirate. When asked by the king what he thought he was doing by infesting the sea, he replied with noble insolence, "What do you think you are doing by infesting the whole world? Because I do it with one puny boat, I am called a pirate; because you do it with a great fleet, you are called an emperor."[1]

Chapter 6

Justin, who wrote Greek, or rather foreign, history in Latin and briefly, as did Trogus Pompeius, whom he followed, begins his book as follows:[2]

> In the beginning of the affairs of peoples and nations, power was in the hands of kings, who were raised to this supreme majesty not by wooing the people but by their moderation, which was acknowledged by good men. The people were bound by no laws. It was the custom to maintain rather than extend the boundaries of their rule and kingdoms were confined within the limits of the fatherland. Ninus, the king of the Assyrians, was the first to change this old, ancestrial custom of the peoples out of a new desire for empire. He was the first to wage war against the peoples on his borders and to conquer the peoples untrained in resistance. He pushed his conquests up to the borders of Libya.

Justin goes on to say,

> Ninus consolidated by lasting possession the vast empire thus acquired. Having vanquished his neighbors, he went on to others, strengthened by conscriptions of more men. By making of each victory an instrument of the next, he subjugated all the peoples of the East.

However faithful either Justin or Trogus may have been to the facts (that they were sometimes liars is shown by more reliable witnesses), nevertheless it is agreed among other writers that the Assyrian kingdom was extended far and wide by King Ninus.[3] Moreover, it lasted for so long that the Roman empire has not yet reached the same age.[4] As the experts in

---

1. The source for this story appears to have been Cicero's *Republic* III. 14.

2. Justin, who is thought to have lived in the second century A.D., produced a forty-four-volume abridgment of a universal history written by Trogus Pompeius, who lived in the time of Augustus.

3. King Ninus is a legendary figure who supposedly founded Assyria and established the city of Nineveh.

4. The legendary date for the founding of Rome is 753 B.C. If Augustine wrote

chronology write, this kingdom continued for 1240 years from the first year of Ninus's reign to the time it was transferred to the Medes.

Now, to inflict war on one's neighbors and then to proceed to others and, out of the sole desire to rule, to conquer and subdue peoples by whom one has not been molested, what else should this be called but grand larceny?

Chapter 15

Let our opponents consider the possibility that rejoicing over the extent of their reign is not appropriate for good men. To be sure, the iniquity of those against whom just wars were waged helped the empire to grow, because it surely would have stayed small if its neighbors were peaceful and just and did not, through wrongdoing, provoke war. Human affairs would have been happier that way. All kingdoms would have been small, enjoying concord with their neighbors. There would thus have been many kingdoms of peoples in the world, just as there are many homes of citizens in a city.

Waging war and extending the empire by subduing peoples is therefore viewed as happiness by the wicked, but as a necessity by the good. But because it would be worse if wrongdoers dominated those who are more just, it is not inappropriate to call even this necessity "happiness." Nevertheless, without doubt it is a better happiness to have concord with a good neighbor than to subjugate a bad one through war. It is a wicked prayer to wish for someone to hate or to fear so that there might be someone to conquer. If, then, by waging just wars, not impious or iniquitous ones, the Romans were able to acquire such a large empire, should not "the iniquity of foreigners" be worshipped like some goddess? Indeed, we see how much assistance she has given to the extension of the empire, making others into wrongdoers so that there might be someone to wage just wars against in order that the empire might grow. . . .

Chapter 20

They have made virtue a goddess; if that were possible, "Virtue" would indeed have been preferable to many other deities. Now, since it is not a goddess but a gift of God, let it be requested of him who alone is able to

---

this passage in about A.D. 414, then to his mind the age of Rome would have been approximately 1167 years.

grant it, and the whole crowd of false gods will vanish. But why is "Faith" believed to be a goddess and why does she too receive a temple and an altar? Whoever prudently acknowledges her makes of himself a home for her. Now how do they know what faith is, the first and foremost function of which is to believe in the true God? Why was virtue not sufficient? Does it not also include faith? Insofar as some have thought it proper to divide virtue into four kinds—prudence, justice, courage, and temperance—and since each of these has its own subdivisions, faith is among the parts of justice and holds the highest place for those of us who know that "the just man lives by faith" (Hb 2:4; Rom 1:17; Gal 3:11; Heb 10:38).

If faith is a goddess, I wonder why these worshippers of many gods have injured so many other goddesses by neglecting them when they could have dedicated temples and altars to them as well? Why does temperance not merit the status of a goddess, when several Roman rulers have achieved no small glory through her name? Why is courage not a goddess, she who assisted Mucius when he put his right hand into the flames, who assisted Curtius when for the sake of his country he threw himself into the precipice, who assisted Decius the father and Decius the son when they devoted themselves to the army?[5] (That is, if indeed true courage was present in all of them—a topic that is not pertinent here.) Why have prudence and wisdom merited no shrines? Is it because they are all worshipped under the general name "Virtue"? It would thus be possible to worship a single God, of whom the rest of the gods could be considered parts. Yet in that one virtue there is both faith and purity, which have merited altars in temples of their own.

Chapter 27

It is related that the most learned pontiff Scaevola had discussed three types of gods as having been handed down to us:[6] one by the poets, a second

5. On Mucius, see the note on II. 29. According to legend, a great chasm once opened up in the forum and the soothsayers stated that it could be filled only if Rome's greatest treasure was thrown into it. Curtius declared that Rome had no greater treasure than a brave citizen and leaped into the chasm, which closed over him. In the thick of battle, Decius the father and his son each rushed into the heart of the enemy's forces, sacrificing themselves in order to secure victory for their armies.

6. Scaevola served as supreme pontiff and authored an extensive work on Roman law. He was also a teacher of Cicero, who praises his virtues (see *On the Orator* I. 39, 180). Scaevola became a victim of the civil wars in 82 B.C.

by the philosophers, and a third by the rulers of the city. The first type, he says, is frivolous because of the many unworthy things invented by the poets about the gods. The second is not appropriate for cities because it comprises superfluous things as well as certain other things the knowledge of which would be harmful to the people. Concerning the superfluous things there is no great worry because, as the jurists say, "The superfluous things do no harm."[7] What, however, are those things which do harm when brought before the multitude? Scaevola answers: "The claim that Hercules, Aesculapius, Castor and Pollux are not gods because, as learned men say, they were human and died according to the human condition." What else? "The claim that cities do not have true images of the gods because the true God has neither sex nor age nor bodily parts." The pontiff is unwilling that peoples should know these things, for he does not think they are false. He therefore considers it expedient that cities should be deceived in religious matters. Varro himself does not hesitate to say this in his books on divine things. A fine religion to which the weak who need to be liberated may flee! When they seek the truth by which they may be freed, it is believed to be expedient to deceive them!

In these same books Varro is not silent about why Scaevola rejected the gods of the poets. It is because the poets so deform the gods that they could not even be compared with good men. They make one god commit theft, another adultery, or say or do something or other immorally or stupidly, as when the three goddesses competed for the prize for the greatest beauty and the two who lost to Venus destroyed Troy, as when Jupiter turned himself into a bull or a swan so that he might have intercourse with some woman, as when a goddess married a man, and as when Saturn devoured his children. Nothing miraculous or vicious can be fabricated which is not found in these stories of the gods and which is further removed from the divine nature.

O high pontiff Scaevola, take away the plays, if you can! Teach the people not to offer to the immortal gods those honors in which they may admire with joy the crimes of the gods and imitate them, if they can![8] If, however, the people answer you, "You pontiffs have brought these plays to us," ask the gods themselves, at whose instigation you have ordered them, not to order such plays to be shown. If the plays are evil and in no way to be believed of the majesty of the gods, the injury to the gods about whom they are contrived with impunity is that much greater.

7. *Justinian Code* VI. 23. 17.
8. See II. 4.

Yet the gods do not hear you, Scaevola; they are demons; they teach evil and rejoice in base things. The gods do not consider it wrong for such things to be contrived about them; quite the contrary, they are not able to bear the injury if the plays are not enacted at their festivals. Now, if you were to call Jupiter against them, primarily because more of his crimes are acted out in the plays, is it not true that, even though you call him the god who rules and administers the whole world, it is he to whom you do the greatest wrong because you have thought he should be worshipped with those others and should be considered their king?[9]

Chapter 33

God, the author and giver of happiness, because he alone is the true God, is the one who gives earthly kingdoms to both the good and the evil. He does not do this blindly or, as it were, fortuitously—because he is God, not fortune—but according to the order of things and times that is hidden from us but well-known to him. God, however, is not subject to this order of times but rules it as Lord and orders it as governor. Happiness he gives only to the good. Servants can have or lack it and kings can have or lack it, but it shall be complete in that life where no one is a servant. Therefore, he gives earthly kingdoms to the good or the evil so that his worshippers, who are still children as regard moral progress, may not desire these gifts from him as something great. It is the sacrament of the Old Testament,[10] in which the New Testament is hidden, that there even earthly gifts are promised, for even then spiritual people understood, though they did not yet openly declare, the eternity symbolized by these temporal things and the gifts of God in which true happiness may be found.

9. On this chapter, see Ernest L. Fortin, "Augustine and Roman Civil Religion: Some Critical Reflections," *Revue des Études Augustiniennes* 25 (1980), 238–56.

10. The phrase "sacrament of the Old Testament" is a literal translation of *sacramentum veteris testamenti*. In Augustine's time *sacramentum* had not yet become the technical term for the sacraments of the church. Augustine's point is that God's earthly gifts to Israel are signs that point beyond themselves to the spiritual realities set forth in the New Testament. See also X. 14.

Book V

Introduction

Book V concludes the first major section of The City of God, *which is devoted to a refutation of the view that the pagan gods are to be worshipped for the sake of prosperity in this life. Having shown in Book IV that the pagan gods had nothing to do with the expansion of the empire, Augustine now discusses how this expansion was in accord with the providence of the one, true God. This is the task of the important arguments of Chapters 9 and 11, in which Augustine explains his disagreement with the Stoic notion of fate on the one hand and Cicero's rejection of divine providence on the other. Our author then turns to the more specific question of the purpose of the Roman empire within God's providential plan. This crucial aspect of Augustine's political thought is considered in the selections from Chapters 15 through 19, in which it is argued that God used the Roman desire for glory and honor to curb human vice. In Chapters 24 through 26, with which the book ends, Augustine turns to the Christianized Roman empire. These pages include a description of the ideal Christian ruler (Ch. 24) and an outline of Roman political history since Constantine's legalization of the Christian faith.*

Chapter 9

The way in which Cicero takes on the task of refuting the Stoics indicates that he thought that his argument would have no effect unless he had first destroyed fortune-telling.[1] He does this by denying that there is any knowl-

---

1. Stoicism: a school of philosophy originally founded in Athens by Zeno of Citium (335–263 B.C.) Among its foremost Roman representatives were Seneca, Epictetus, and Marcus Aurelius. Among other things, the Stoics taught that all things are determined by fate, which they understood to be a chain of necessary causes having its origin in God.

edge of the future. He contends with all his powers that neither God nor man has such knowledge and that future events cannot be predicted. He therefore denies the foreknowledge of God and attempts to refute all prophecies, even those clearer than the light, by using empty arguments and by opposing certain oracles that are easily refuted—though even these oracles are not really refuted by him.[2]

In refuting the conjectures of the astrologers, however, his argument succeeds because their views are of the sort which self-destruct and refute themselves. Even so, those who assert that the stars determine fate are far more tolerable than those who deny the foreknowledge of the future, for to assert that God exists and at the same time to deny that he has foreknowledge of future events is clearly madness. . . .

No matter how vexed and tortuous the philosophers' debates and disputes may be, just as we confess the supreme and true God, so we also confess his will and his supreme power and foreknowledge. We are not afraid that what we do voluntarily might actually be done involuntarily because he, whose foreknowledge is infallible, foreknew that we would do it. It was this fear which concerned Cicero and caused him to oppose foreknowledge. It also caused the Stoics to hold that things do not always happen from necessity, even though they maintained that everything happens according to fate.

What was it, then, that concerned Cicero about the foreknowledge of the future, so that he tried to undermine it through detestable argumentation? It was undoubtedly this: if the future is foreknown, then things will happen in the order in which they are foreknown to happen, and if they happen in this order, then the order of things is, with respect to God who foreknows it, certain; and if the order of things is certain, then the order of causes is certain, because nothing happens without some efficient cause; but if there is such a certain order of causes according to which everything that happens does in fact happen, then, according to Cicero, everything which happens happens by fate. If, however, this is so, then nothing is in our own power and there is no free choice of the will. If we concede this, he says, then all of human life is subverted. The giving of laws is frustrated, as are blame, praise, criticism, and exhortation. There is no justice at all in establishing rewards for the good and punishments for the wicked.[3]

2. In this chapter, Augustine has in mind the arguments found in Cicero's *On Divination*, especially Book II, and in his *On Fate*, only part of which survives. On Cicero, see the note II. 21.

3. See *On Fate* 17. 40.

In order that such consequences, which are so disgraceful and absurd and harmful to human affairs, might not follow, Cicero rejects foreknowledge of the future and binds the religious mind in a dilemma, so that it must choose one of these two: either there is something subject to our will or there is foreknowledge of the future. He thinks that both cannot be true: if one is affirmed, the other is destroyed. If we would choose foreknowledge of the future, free choice of the will is destroyed; if we would choose free choice of the will, foreknowledge of the future is destroyed. . . .

We, against such bold sacrilege and impiety, say both that God knows everything before it happens and that we do by our will whatever we know and feel does not happen unless it is willed by us. We do not claim that everything happens by fate; in fact, we say that nothing happens by fate. We point out that the term "fate" is meaningless in its customary usage of referring to the position of the stars when someone was conceived or born, for it asserts something that is not real. We do not deny the order of causes in which the will of God has the greatest power, nor do we designate it by means of the word "fate," unless we take "fate" to mean "what is spoken," deriving it from *fari*, which means "to speak." After all, we cannot deny that it is written in the Sacred Scriptures that "God spoke once; I have heard these two things: that power belongs to God, and to you, Lord, belongs mercy, and you give back to each according to his works" (Ps 62:12). . . .

Even if the order of all causes is certain to God, it does not follow that nothing depends on the free choice of our own wills. Our wills are themselves included in that order of causes which is known with certainty by God and which is contained in his foreknowledge, for human wills are the causes of human actions. He who foreknew all the causes of things could not be ignorant of our wills, which he foreknew as causes of our actions.

Even the concession which Cicero grants, that nothing happens unless preceded by an efficient cause, is sufficient to refute him on this question.[4] How does it help him to say that nothing happens without a cause, but that not all causes are causes of fate, since there are also fortuitous, natural, and voluntary causes? That he admits that everything which happens would not happen unless it were preceded by a cause is enough to refute him. We say that those causes termed "fortuitous"—from which the word "fortune" is taken—are not non-existent, but that they are hidden. We attribute them either to the will of God or to the will of spirits of some kind. Concerning natural causes, we in no way separate them from the will of

4. See *On Fate* 10. 20–12. 28.

him who is the author and founder of all nature. Voluntary causes belong to God or angels or men or animals of various sorts—if the movements by which animals devoid of reason seek or avoid various things according to their own natures should really be called "voluntary." When I speak of the wills of the angels, I mean both the wills of the good angels, called the angels of God, and of the wicked angels, called the angels of the devil, or demons. So, too, by the wills of men I mean both the wills of the good and of the wicked.

From all this we conclude that the only efficient causes of all the things which occur are voluntary causes; that is, they are causes which come from that nature which is the spirit of life. To be sure, the air itself and the wind are also called "spirit,"[5] but because they are material, they are not the spirit of life. The spirit of life, however, which gives life to all things and is the creator of every body and every created spirit, is God himself, who is indeed uncreated spirit. In his will is the supreme power which assists the good wills of created spirits and judges the evil ones. He orders all of them, granting powers to some and not granting them to others. Just as he is the creator of all natures, so he is the giver of all powers, but not of all wills. Evil wills do not come from him, as they are contrary to the nature which does come from him. Bodies are mostly subject to wills—some to ours (that is, to the wills of all living mortal creatures, and more to the wills of human beings than to the wills of animals) and others to the wills of angels. Yet all bodies are subordinate to the will of God, to whom all wills are also subject, for wills have no power except that which he has given them.

The cause of things, therefore, which makes but is not made, is God. All other causes both make and are made; such are all created spirits, especially rational spirits. Material causes, therefore, which are made rather than make, are not to be considered among the efficient causes because they can only do what the wills of spirits do with them. In what way, therefore, does the order of causes which is certain in the foreknowledge of God necessitate that there should be nothing dependent on our wills when our wills have a large place in that very order of causes? . . .

Our wills, then, also have just so much power as God willed and foreknew that they would have. Therefore, whatever power they have, they possess with the utmost certainty, and what they are about to do, they are most surely about to do, for he whose foreknowledge is infallible foreknew that they would have the power to do it and would in fact do it. Thus, if I

---

5. The single Latin word *spiritus* means not only "spirit" but also "breath," "air," and "wind."

should choose to apply the name of "fate" to anything at all, I would say that the fate of the weaker is the will of the stronger, who has the weaker in his power, rather than say that the order of causes which the Stoics call "fate"—not by ordinary usage, but by their own custom—takes away the free choice of our will.

Chapter 11

The supreme and true God, with his Word and Holy Spirit who are three in one, the one all-powerful God, creator and maker of every soul and body, the God who bestows not vain but true happiness by allowing people to participate in himself, who made man a rational animal with soul and body, who, when man sinned, neither allowed man to go unpunished nor abandoned him without mercy; who gave, to both the good and the evil, being, which they share with stones, the vegetable life shared with trees, the sensitive life shared with the beasts, and the intellectual life shared with the angels alone; from whom is every kind, every species, every order; from whom are measure, number, weight; from whom is everything having existence in nature, of whatever kind and value; from whom are the seeds of forms and the forms of seeds, and the movements of seeds and of forms; who gave also to flesh its origin, beauty, health, fertility, disposition of parts, healthy balance; who also gave to the nonintellective soul memory, sense, appetite, and to the rational soul in addition to these mind, intelligence, and will; who has not neglected to give, not only to the heavens and the earth, not only to angels and men, but even to the entrails of the lowest, feeblest creature, to the bird's pinfeather, to the plant's tiny flower, and to the tree's leaf, a harmony of its parts and a certain peace—never should this God be thought to have wanted the kingdoms of human beings and their dominations and servitudes to be alien from the laws of his providence.

Chapter 15

God would not grant men such as these Roman heroes eternal life with his holy angels in his heavenly city. True piety leads to that society, but true piety does not offer that religious worship that the Greeks call *latreia* to any but the one true God. If he were not to grant the earthly glory of the most supreme empire to them, the reward for their good qualities, that is, the virtues with which they strained themselves to attain such great glory, would not be paid. Indeed, it is for that reason, so that they might receive glory from human beings, that such men are seen doing anything good. It was about them that the Lord said, "Amen, I say to you, you have received your reward" (Mt 6:2).

They scorned their own private goods for the sake of the common good, that is, for the republic, and for its treasury. They resisted avarice. They concerned themselves with their country's affairs through their generous advice. Crimes and vices were punished according to their laws. Through these qualities they sought, as if by a true path, honor, power, and glory. They were honored among nearly all peoples; they imposed the laws of their own empire on many peoples; and today they are glorified by the literature and history of almost all peoples. They have no reason to complain about the justice of the supreme and true God. "They have received their reward."

Chapter 16

Very different, however, is the reward of the saints. They have here endured reproaches for the sake of God's truth, which is hateful to those who desire this world. That city is everlasting. There none are born because none die. There exists true and complete felicity—not a goddess, but a gift from God. We have received from there the pledge of faith; while on our journey, we sigh for that city's beauty. There the sun does not rise on the good and the evil (Mt 5:45), but the Sun of Justice (Mal 4:2) protects the good alone. There no great industry will be needed to fill the public treasury by constricting private property, because there the common treasury is truth.

Therefore, it was not only for the sake of rewarding the citizens of Rome that the empire and glory had been so uniquely extended. It was also for the sake of the citizens of that eternal city, so that during their journeys here they might diligently and soberly contemplate these examples and learn what love they owe to the heavenly country on account of eternal life if the earthly country was loved so much by its citizens on account of human glory.

Chapter 17

Concerning this life of mortals, which is lived and ended in a few days, what difference does it make whose governance a man who is about to die lives under, so long as those who rule do not compel him to impiety and sin? Did the Romans harm those peoples on whom they imposed their laws when they conquered them, except insofar as there was a great slaughter in the wars? If it had been done with their consent, it would have been accomplished with greater success, but there would have been no glory of conquest. The Romans themselves lived under the laws they imposed on others. If this had been done without Mars and Bellona so that there would have been no place for Victory (there is no conquering where there is no fighting),[6] would not the condition of the Romans and the other peoples have been the same? Would this not have especially been the case if what was later done most humanely and acceptably had been done earlier; namely, that all who belonged to the Roman Empire were granted access to the society of the city and became Roman citizens? In this way, what was once the privilege of a few became the privilege of all, except that the lower classes, which had no lands of their own, lived at public expense. Under good public administration, their support might have been offered more willingly through agreement rather than, as was the case, through extorting it from conquered peoples. . . .

Consider what great things they scorned, what things they endured, the desires they conquered for the sake of human glory. Consider that they earned glory as a sort of reward for such virtue. Let this consideration be useful to us for suppressing our pride. That city in which it has been promised to us to rule surpasses this one as far as heaven is distant from the earth, eternal life from temporal joy, solid glory from empty praise, the company of angels from the company of mortals, the glory of he who made the sun and the moon from the light of the sun and the moon. The citizens of so great a country may not think themselves to have accomplished anything very great if, in order to attain it, they have done some good or suffered some evil, while these Romans did such great things and suffered such great harms for this earthly land which they already inhabited. Especially consider that the forgiveness of sins which gathers citizens into the eternal land has a shadowy resemblance in that asylum of Romulus, to which impunity for all sorts of crimes drew together the multitude from which that city was founded.[7]

Chapter 19

There is a great difference between the desire for human glory and the desire for domination. To be sure, one who takes excessive delight in hu-

6. Mars and Bellona were the Roman god and goddess of war. Victory was also personified as a goddess. The removal of her statue from the Senate in 385 caused a conflict between Symmachus and Ambrose, the bishop of Milan. Symmachus had been a patron of Augustine prior to the latter's conversion to Christianity.

7. On Romulus's creation of an asylum in Rome, see I. 34.

man glory can readily become one who ardently aspires to dominate; nevertheless those who desire true glory, even of human praise, will avoid displeasing those who think well of them. After all, many people are competent judges of many good moral qualities, even though they do not possess them. By means of these good moral qualities those men strive for glory, honor, and domination, and Sallust says of them, "They strive in the true way."[8] . . .

He who scorns glory and is avid for domination is worse than the beasts in the vices of cruelty and extravagance. Certain Romans were like this, for although they did not care about esteem, they were not without the desire to dominate. History testifies that many were like this. Nero Caesar was the first to reach the summit and, as it were, the citadel, of this vice.[9] So great was his extravagance that one would have thought that there was no manliness to be feared in him. So great was his cruelty that, had the contrary not been known, one would have thought there was nothing effeminate in his character.

Nonetheless, the power to dominate is not given even to these men except by the providence of the most high God, when he judges that the condition of human affairs is worthy of such masters. The divine voice speaks openly concerning this when the wisdom of God says, "Through me kings rule, and tyrants hold the earth through me" (Prv 8:15). To prevent our interpreting the word "tyrants" here not as "the worst and wicked kings" but in the old sense of "strong men" (as Virgil used it when he says, "There will be peace for me when tyrants join right hands"),[10] Scripture speaks most openly of God in another place: "He makes a hypocritical man to reign on account of the perversity of the people" (Jb 34:30).

Although I have demonstrated, to the extent of my ability, why the one true and just God assisted the Romans, who were good according to a certain earthly standard, to obtain the glory of so great an empire, there may be even another, more hidden cause, resulting from the diverse merits of the human race known better to God than to us. Let it be agreed, though, among all who are truly pious, that no one lacking true piety, which is the true worship of the true God, can have true virtue. Let it also be agreed that virtue is not true when it serves human glory. Nevertheless, those who are not citizens of the eternal city, which is called "the city of God" in the Sacred Scriptures, are more useful to the earthly city when

8. *Catiline* 11, 2.

9. Nero, emperor from A.D. 54–68, was famous for his profligacy. He was especially unpopular with the Christians because of his persecution against them in A.D 64.

10. *Aeneid* VII, 266.

they at least have that virtue which serves human glory than if they had none at all. Nothing, however, could be more felicitous for human affairs than that those living well and endowed with true piety, if they have the knowledge of ruling peoples, might also, by God's mercy, have the power. . . .

Chapter 24

We do not claim that certain Christian emperors were happy because they ruled a long time, or, in dying a peaceful death, left their sons to succeed them as emperor, or conquered the enemies of the republic, or were able to both guard against and suppress the attempts of hostile citizens rising against them. These gifts or other comforts of this sorrowful life were even earned by demon-worshippers who do not belong to the kingdom of God to which these emperors belong. All this happened through the mercy of God, so that those who believe in him would not desire these things as though they were the highest good. We do claim that the Christian emperors are happy if they rule justly and if, instead of being exalted by the praises of those who pay them the highest honors and by the groveling of those who salute them with excessive humility, they remember instead that they are human beings. We claim that they are happy if they make their power the servant of God's majesty by using it for the greatest possible extension of his worship; if they fear and love and worship God; if they love that kingdom in which they are not afraid to share power more than their earthly kingdom; if they are slow to punish and ready to pardon; if they apply that punishment as necessary to govern and defend the republic and not in order to indulge their own hatred; if they grant pardon, not so that crime should be unpunished, but in the hope of correction; if they compensate with the gentleness of mercy and the liberality of benevolence for whatever severe measure they may be compelled to decree; if their extravagance is as much restrained as it might have been unrestrained; if they prefer to rule evil desires rather than any people one might name; and if they do all these things from love of eternal happiness rather than ardor for empty glory, and if they do not fail to offer to the true God who is their God the sacrifices of humility, contrition, and prayer for their sins. Such Christian emperors, we claim, are happy in the present through hope, and are happy afterwards, in the future, in the enjoyment of happiness itself, when what we wait for will have come.

Chapter 25

The good God did not want men who believe that he is to be worshipped for the sake of eternal life to think that, since the evil spirits have great power over these high positions and earthly kingdoms, nobody could attain such things unless he called upon demons. Consequently, God gave the emperor Constantine,[11] who was not a worshipper of demons but of the true God himself, such earthly gifts as nobody would dare to wish for. God also granted to him the honor of founding a city, a partner in Roman rule, the daughter of Rome itself, but without any temple or likeness of demons. He reigned for a long time as sole augustus and held and defended the whole Roman world. In administering and waging wars he was most victorious, and in oppressing tyrants he was prosperous in every way. After a long life, he died of illness and old age, leaving sons to succeed him as emperor.

Yet, on the other hand, so that no emperor should become a Christian in order to earn the happiness of Constantine rather than for the sake of eternal life, God carried away Jovian far sooner than Julian.[12] He also permitted Gratian to be killed by the sword of a tyrant, though in a far less severe manner than Pompey the Great, who worshipped the so-called gods of the Romans.[13] Pompey could not be avenged by Cato, to whom he had left the civil wars as, in a way, an inheritance; Gratian, however—even though pious souls do not require such solace—was avenged by Theodosius.[14] Gratian had made Theodosius his associate in ruling the empire, even though Gratian had a younger brother of his own, because he

11. Constantine (c. 280–337) was the first Christian emperor. He founded the city of Constantinople in 330 as the capital of the eastern part of the empire.

12. Jovian was a Christian emperor who ruled for only about seven months (363–34). Julian, traditionally called "the Apostate" because of his repudiation of the Christian faith, ruled as emperor for about two years (361–363), although he ruled parts of the empire from 355.

13. Gratian (ruled 367–383) was killed by Maximus. Pompey was stabbed in the back; his head was cut off and brought to Julius Caesar, who is said to have wept at the sight. On Pompey, see the note on III. 30.

14. After Pompey's assassination, the leadership of the opposition to Julius Caesar passed to Cato and others, but Cato was unable to defeat Caesar and committed suicide rather than submit to his rule. Maximus, who murdered the Christian Gratian, was killed in battle by Theodosius in 388. Theodosius (ruled 379–395) actively promoted the cause of Catholic Christianity, as Augustine explains in the next chapter.

was more eager for a faithful alliance than excessive power.[15]

Chapter 26

Theodosius not only preserved during the lifetime of Gratian that faithfulness which was owed to him, but also after his death. Gratian's murderer Maximus expelled Gratian's younger brother Valentinian, but Theodosius, like a good Christian, took Valentinian, still a child, under his protection as a ward in his part of the empire and looked after him with fatherly affection. . . .

Later, when Maximus's success was making him dangerous, Theodosius, in the middle of difficult anxieties, was not drawn away to unlawful and sacrilegious curiosities, but contacted John, who lived as a hermit in Egypt. Theodosius had learned that this servant of God whose reputation was spreading was granted the gift of prophecy. John assured him of victory. At once Theodosius destroyed the tyrant Maximus and, with the greatest kindness and reverence, restored the boy Valentinian to his share of the empire from which he had had to flee.[16] . . .

Theodosius was unlike Cinna, Marius, Sulla,[17] and other such men, who did not wish civil wars to end even when they were finished. Instead of wanting to harm anyone when the wars were finished, he grieved that they had begun at all. Through all of these events from the beginning of his rule, he did not cease to help the church, laboring against the impious, by means of the most just and merciful laws. The heretical Valens,[18] favoring the Arians, vehemently afflicted the church; Theodosius, however, took more joy in belonging to the church than he did in being a king on earth. The idols of the pagans he ordered everywhere thrown down, understanding well enough that not even earthly gifts are in the power of demons, but in that of the true God.

15. Since Gratian's younger brother Valentinian was still too young to rule, Gratian made Theodosius ruler in the eastern part of the empire rather than attempting to rule the whole empire by himself.

16. After defeating and killing Gratian, Maximus forced Valentinian, only a boy, to flee from Italy to Theodosius's protection in the East. After defeating Maximus, Theodosius restored Valentinian to his place in the western part of the empire.

17. These three were leaders in the bloody civil wars that engulfed Rome in the first century B.C.

18. Valens ruled the eastern part of the empire in 364–378. He supported the Arians, a group of Christians who denied the full divinity of Christ.

Further, what could be more admirable than his religious humility? He was driven by the uproar of certain people who were close to him to avenge the most grievous crime of the Thessalonians, which, at the intercession of the bishops, he had previously promised to pardon. He was then corrected by the discipline of the church and did penance in such a way that the people, praying, wept more at the sight of the imperial highness prostrated on account of them than they feared his anger at their sin.[19] These and similar good works, which would take long to commemorate, he carried with him from this life, which, no matter what human summits and pinnacles are attained, is only a temporal mist (Jas 4:14). . . .

---

19. In 390, a riot broke out in Thessalonica in the wake of the imprisonment of a popular charioteer. Some Roman officials were killed. Theodosius apparently ordered reprisals and a massacre occurred. Ambrose, bishop of Milan, compelled Theodosius to do penance for his sin.

Book VI

Introduction

With Book VI, Augustine begins the second major section of The City of God, *a section that extends through Book X. His new target is the view that the traditional pagan gods should be worshipped for the sake of prosperity in the afterlife. The basic argument of Book VI is that the worship of the Roman gods does not provide a secure foundation for achieving immortality. In Chapter 6, Augustine returns to the division of theology into mythical, civil, and natural that he discussed in relation to Scaevola in Book IV, Chapter 27. Now, however, the adversary is Varro, who is criticized for refusing to state the whole truth about the gods out of fear of the opinions of the masses. Chapter 10 contrasts Varro's timidity with the attitude of the Stoic philosopher Seneca. Whereas Varro was willing to criticize the mythical theology of the theatres but not the civil theology of the temples, Seneca was willing to criticize both. In the end, though, he was also constrained by fear to observe the external customs of the civil theology.*

Chapter 6

O Marcus Varro![1] Although you are the sharpest and undoubtedly the most learned human being of all, you are still a human being, not God. Nor have you been carried up by the Spirit of God into truth and freedom in order to see and announce divine things. You do, indeed, see that the divine things must be separated from human trifles and lies. You are afraid, however, to offend the most vicious opinions and customs of peoples in their public superstitions. When you consider these superstitions from every angle, you yourself realize, and your writings echo, that they are inconsistent with the nature of the gods—even gods such as the feebleness

1. On Varro, see the note on III. 9.

of the human mind surmises to exist in the physical elements of this world. What does even the most excellent human intellectual power do with this problem? How does human learning, although complex and vast, help you in this predicament? . . .

Setting aside for the moment the theology called "natural," which must be treated later on,[2] is it acceptable to request or to hope for eternal life from the gods of poetry and theatre, the gods of stage shows and drama? Hardly! On the contrary, may the true God drive away such monstrous and demented sacrilege. What? Is eternal life to be sought from those gods who are pleased and appeased by the theatre, even though their crimes are performed for the crowd there? No one, I would judge, is mad enough to hold such extreme and furious impiety. Therefore, neither through the mythical, nor through the civil theology, does anyone obtain everlasting life. . . .

When this famous author, Varro, attempted to distinguish the civil theology from the mythical and the natural as a sort of third kind of theology, he wanted it to be understood more as a mixture of the other two than as separated from them, for he says that the things which the poets write are beneath what the peoples ought to follow, while the things which the philosophers write are above what is expedient for the multitude to investigate. He states,

> These two theologies are inconsistent with each other, but nevertheless not a few things from each of them may be appropriated for the principles of the civil theology. Because of this, we will describe the things it has in common with each of the others, together with the unique principles of civil theology. In doing this, we ought to be more closely associated with the philosophers than the poets.[3]

Notice that he does not say that we should have nothing to do with the poets. In another place he says that, concerning the generation of the gods, the people have been more inclined to the poets than to the natural scientists. In the first passage he said what ought to be done, in the second what is done. He said that the natural scientists had written in order to be beneficial, the poets in order to give pleasure. Accordingly, the peoples should not follow the crimes of the gods that are recorded by the poets—even though such things please both the people and the gods. As he says, the poets write not in order to be beneficial but in order to give pleasure. Nev-

2. Augustine will turn to this topic in Book VIII.
3. As is the case with almost all of Varro's writings, this work is not extant.

ertheless, they write about the things which the gods request and the peoples perform.

Chapter 10

Varro lacked liberty, and so he did not dare to criticize openly this theology of the city as he did that of the theatre,[4] which is very similar to it. Such liberty was certainly not lacking—or indeed not completely lacking but only partially—to Annaeus Seneca.[5] (We find some evidence that Seneca was a distinguished man in the times of our apostles.) That liberty was present in his writings; it was lacking in his living. In that book which he composed, *Against Superstitions*,[6] he himself refutes this civil theology of the city more abundantly and vehemently than Varro does the theatrical and mythical. . . .

How freely Seneca wrote about the cruel and shameful rites themselves! He says,

> This one amputates his own male parts. Another gashes his arms. Why do those who procure the gods' favor in this way fear their wrath? If that is what they want, the gods should not be worshipped at all. So great is the raving of a mind unsettled and driven from its own moorings that the gods are placated in ways in which not even the most hideous of cruel men described in myths vent their savagery. Tyrants have lacerated the body parts of some; they have commanded no one to lacerate their own. For the pleasure of royal lust, some men have been castrated, but no one, at the command of his master, has taken away his own manliness by his own hand. Yet they slice themselves to pieces in the temples, entreating the gods with their own wounds and blood. If one has the leisure to consider what they do and what they suffer, one will find deeds so disgraceful to honorable people, so unworthy of free people, so unlike sane people, that if fewer were involved in their ravings, no one would doubt that they were mad. As it is now, the only defense of their sanity is the tumultuous throng of the insane.

. . . Varro did not have this liberty. He dared to criticize the poetic

4. The rites of the civil theology were practiced in the temples; mythical theology flourished in the theatres.

5. Seneca (c. 4 B.C.–A.D. 65): Roman rhetorician and Stoic philosopher. He was the teacher of Nero (see the note on V. 19) and later an advisor to him. After Nero's profligacy became limitless, a rift developed between the two. This led first to Seneca's retirement and later to his death.

6. This work is not extant.

theology only so much; he did not dare to criticize the civil theology, which Seneca cut to pieces. However, if we attend to the truth, we see that the temples where these rites are actually performed are worse than the theatres where they are only acted out. Accordingly, with respect to these sacred matters of the civil theology, Seneca chooses for the wise man those parts that he need not have in the religion of his soul, but may pretend to have there through his actions. Thus he says, "The wise man will keep all these rituals as if they had been commanded by the laws, not as if they had been given by the gods." A little later he says,

> What about the fact that we even join the gods in marriages, and indeed not in pious marriages, but in marriages between brother and sister? We marry Bellona to Mars; Venus to Vulcan; and Salacia to Neptune. Nevertheless, we leave certain ones unmarried, as though no match could be arranged, especially when these are widows, such as Populonia, Fulgora, and the divine Rumina. I am not at all amazed that suitors have been lacking for these. We will adore this whole ignoble throng of gods, which a lasting superstition has accumulated over a long period of time, with this limitation: we will remember that their cult has more to do with customs than with reality.

Thus, neither law nor custom established in the civil theology what was pleasing to the gods or what pertained to reality.

Seneca was, in a sense, freed through philosophy. Nevertheless, because he was an illustrious senator of the people of Rome, he worshipped what he criticized, did what he was arguing against, and adored what he was condemning. Clearly, philosophy had taught him something great: not to be superstitious about the world. However, it also taught him, for the sake of the civil laws and customs of man, not indeed to act as an actor does when pretending in the theatre, but to imitate such an actor in the temple. This was the more reprehensible way to act, for in acting in this way he was acting mendaciously in order that the people might think he was acting sincerely. The stage actor, on the other hand, delights rather than deceives through his pretending.

Book VII

Introduction

In this book, Augustine considers a naturalistic interpretation of the traditional pagan gods that had apparently been advanced by Varro. According to this view, the Roman gods, or at least some of them, are representations or personifications of a part of nature. An example of this sort of interpretation is considered in Chapter 12, where Augustine ridicules Varro's view that Jove is a personification of the human desire for wealth. Augustine goes on to explain that Varro's naturalistic interpretation frequently glosses over many of the more embarrassing rites and practices of Roman religion, including the worship of the Great Mother (Ch. 26). Our author makes a frontal attack on Varro's theory in Chapters 29 through 31, arguing that natural causes and effects are better explained by reference to the one true God than by the tortuous reasonings of the naturalistic interpretation. Finally, in Chapter 34, Augustine returns to the figure of Numa Pompilius, the inventor of the Roman religious rites. Though Varro strives diligently to explain Numa's religion in terms of nature, in fact, says Augustine, it should be explained in terms of demons.

Chapter 12

How elegantly they produce an explanation for this name! "And Jove is called 'wealth,'" Varro says, "because all things belong to him." What a grand explanation for a god's name! In fact, the one to whom all things belong is most basely and insultingly named "wealth"! Compared to all the things contained in heaven and on earth, of what significance is absolutely everything that human beings possess and call "wealth"? Undoubtedly, greed gave this name to Jove, so that whoever loves wealth might not appear to himself to love just any ordinary god, but the very king of all things!

It would be quite different if he were called "riches," for riches are one thing; wealth another. We say that the wise, the just, and the good, are "rich," but wealth means little or nothing to them. Rather, they are rich through the virtues, which enable them to satisfy even their bodily necessities with whatever they have at hand. The truly poor are the greedy, always needy and craving. However much wealth they are able to possess and however great its abundance, they are not able not to crave. Moreover, we rightly call the true God himself "rich," not in wealth but in omnipotence. Certainly the wealthy are said to be rich, but if they desire, they are needy inside; likewise, the poor are said to be without wealth, but if they are wise, they are rich inside.

Therefore, what ought the wise to conclude about this theology in which the king of the gods receives his name from that "which no wise man desires"?[1] If anything pertaining to eternal life might profitably be learned through that teaching, how much more appropriate it would have been to call the god who rules the world not "wealth" but "wisdom," the love of which cleanses one from the filth of greed—that is, from the love of wealth.

Chapter 26

Up until yesterday, the effeminates consecrated to the Great Mother, in defiance of all modesty on the part of men and women, were sashaying through the streets and districts of Carthage with a womanly gait, perfume-drenched hair, whitened faces, and languid bodies, exacting even from the charlatans the means to live so foully. Varro was unwilling to say anything about them, nor do I recall having read about them anywhere else. Interpretation failed; reason blushed; speech was reduced to silence.

The Great Mother has surpassed her children the gods not in greatness of divine majesty but in crime. Not even the monstrosity of Janus compares to this monster![2] He was deformed only in his appearance; she by her cruelty in sacred rituals. He was deformed by additional body parts depicted in stone; she by missing body parts cut from human beings. The great and numerous outrages of Jove himself did not surpass this disgrace. He, the seducer of so many women, disgraced heaven by means of a single Ganymede;[3] she, by means of her numerous professed and public effeminates, has both polluted the earth and wronged heaven. . . .

The Romans did not accept the Carthaginian ritual of sacrificing their children to Saturn. However, this Great Mother of the gods has brought

---

1. Sallust, *Catiline* 11, 3. Jove was considered to be the king of the gods.
2. The "monstrosity of Janus" refers to that god's multiple faces.
3. Ganymede was Zeus's cup bearer as well as his lover.

her eunuchs even into the Roman temples and has preserved that savage custom—believed to strengthen the power of the Romans—of cutting off men's testicles. . . .

Chapter 29

Let us note that all the things which the philosophers refer to the world by means of natural explanations of the theological accounts of the gods may rather be attributed, without a single worry over irreligious conjectures, to the true God, the maker of the world and the author of every soul and every body. We worship God, not heaven and earth, of which two parts this world consists. We do not worship a soul or souls somehow diffused through all things, but God, who made heaven and earth and everything in them. He made every soul living in any way whatsoever: souls lacking sensation and reason, those with sensation, and also those with intelligence.

Chapter 30

I will begin now to list those works of the one and true God, the works on account of which, while attempting to interpret those disgraceful and wicked rites as if they were honorable, the philosophers have made for themselves many false gods. We worship that God who established for the natures created by him the first principles and the ends of their existing and moving. He possesses, knows, and orders the causes of things. He founded the power of seeds. He caused the rational soul which is called mind to be in those living things which he so willed. He gave the capacity and use of language. He has given the gift of foretelling future things to spirits whom he so willed, and he himself foretells future things and drives out sickness through those whom he wills. He controls the beginnings, developments, and endings of wars when the human race needs to be corrected and castigated in that way. He, in order to insure the proper balance of the whole of nature, both created and now rules the most furious and violent element of fire in this world. He is the creator and governor of the universal element of water. He made the sun the brightest visible light, and gave it fitting power and motion. He does not withdraw his own power and dominion even from those who have died. He has provided seeds and food, both dry and liquid, for mortal natures, assigning what is suitable to each. He establishes the earth and makes it fruitful. He bestows its fruits upon animals and human beings. He knows and orders not only first causes but also subsequent ones. He established the phases of the moon. He provides avenues in the heavens and on the earth for movements in space. He, to benefit life and nature, grants to human inventiveness, which he created, knowledge of the various arts. He instituted the joining of male and female to assist in the propagation of offspring. He gave the gift of earthly fire to those unions of human beings, who employ it most conveniently on their hearths and in their lights.

Assuredly, these are the works which Varro, the sharpest and most learned man of all, labored to distribute to selected gods through some strange interpretation belonging to natural philosophy—either one he received from others or one which he conjured up himself. However, the one true God makes and does these things, and he makes and does them as God, that is, as the God who is everywhere whole, not as a god who is enclosed in space, bound by chains, cut up into parts, or changeable in any part. As God, he fills the heavens and the earth through his ever-present power, not through a deficiency in his nature. He administers all the things that he has created in this way, even allowing them to initiate and to execute their own proper motions. Although no creatures could exist without him, they are not what he himself is. He also does many things through angels, but he does not make them happy except through himself. So, too, even though he might send angels to humans for certain reasons, he does not make men happy through the angels but, like the angels, through himself. From this one and true God, we hope for eternal life.

Chapter 31

We have already said something about benefits of this sort, which he lavishes on both the good and the wicked through the administration of nature. In addition to these benefits, however, we also have a great sign of his great love that is only for the good. To be sure, by no means may we sufficiently thank him for the fact that we are, that we live, that we perceive the sky and the earth, that we have a mind and reason through which we seek God himself, who established all these things. Yet even less could hearts and tongues suffice to give thanks to him who, even though we were oppressed and overwhelmed by sins and turned away from the contemplation of his light and blinded by the love of the darkness of iniquity, did not simply abandon us, but sent us his Word, who is his only Son. He did this so that, through Christ's taking on flesh and being born and suffering for us, we might know how much God cares for man, be cleansed by that singular sacrifice for all sins, and, overcoming all obstacles through the diffusion of his love in our hearts by his Spirit, come into eternal rest and into the indescribable sweetness of the contemplation of himself.

Chapter 34

We find that, as that most learned man Varro himself reports, the explanations of the sacred rituals offered in the books of Numa Pompilius could in no way be tolerated.[4] They were held to be unworthy not only of becoming known to religious people by being read, but even of being stored away in darkness by being written down. I will now relate what, in the third book of this work, I promised to relate in its appropriate place.[5] The same Varro, in his book entitled *On the Cult of the Gods*, says,

> A certain Terentius possessed property at the base of the Janiculum hill, and one day when his fieldman was ploughing near the tomb of Numa Pompilius, he turned up the books of Numa in which the explanations of the sacred institutions had been written. He carried them into the city to the praetor. When the praetor had inspected their introductions, he referred such an important matter to the senate. When the leaders of the senate had read certain of the explanations concerning why one or another sacred ritual had been instituted, the senators voted their agreement with the dead Numa and, just as if they were religious, decreed that the praetor should burn the books.

Let everyone believe whatever he thinks about this; indeed, let any distinguished defendor of great impiety say whatever his insane contentiousness might suggest. It is enough for me to point out that the explanations of the sacred rituals recorded by King Pompilius, the founder of the sacred rituals of the Romans, were not appropriate to be made known to the people, the senate, or even the priests themselves, and that Numa Pompilius himself, through illicit curiosity, attained the secrets of demons, which he wrote down so that he might be able to remind himself of them. Nevertheless, though he was a king and would least of all fear anyone, he did not dare to teach those secrets to anyone, nor to ruin the books by erasing or destroying them in any way. So that men would not be taught abominations, he did not want anyone to know about these things. Yet, he was afraid to damage the books for fear of enraging the demons. Conse-

4. On Numa, see the note on III. 9. An account of the recovery of Numa's works is also found in Livy XL. 29. The work of Varro that Augustine quotes in this chapter is not extant.
5. See III. 9.

quently, he buried them in a place he thought safe, not believing that a plow could come so close to his tomb.

The senate, however, terrified of condemning the religious rituals of their ancestors and thus compelled to agree with Numa, nevertheless judged those books to be so pernicious that it did not command that they be buried again, for fear that human curiosity would more eagerly seek them now that they had once been brought forth. Instead, it commanded that these abominable memoirs be destroyed by the flames. Because they deemed it necessary to perform the sacred rituals in those days, they thought it more tolerable to err by being ignorant of the explanations of the rites than to have the city in an uproar by learning of them.

Book VIII

Introduction

In Books VI and VII, Rome's mythical and civil theologies were examined and found wanting as a guarantee of immortality. With Book VIII, Augustine turns to natural or philosophical theology. The opening pages are primarily devoted to an analysis of the philosophy of Plato and his followers. Several chapters from this important section have been included here, including Chapter 10, in which Augustine explains his view of the relationship between Christian faith and human reason. Beginning with Chapter 13, Augustine embarks on a lengthy discussion of a topic on which the Christians and Platonists differ sharply: the worship of demons or intermediary beings that are superior to humans but still not divine.[1] This discussion fills up the remaining chapters of Book VIII as well as the next two books. Two selections from that discussion are included here. Chapter 19 considers the art of magic, which was said to have been practiced by the Platonic philosopher and poet Apuleius. In Chapter 27, Augustine treats the Christian cult of martyrs, which he distinguishes from the Egyptian cult of the dead.

Chapter 3

Socrates is remembered as the first to turn the whole of philosophy to the reforming and arranging of morals,[2] for all philosophers before him instead expended their greatest efforts on investigating physical—that is, natural—things. However, it does not seem to me to be possible to conclude for

---

1. For an introduction to the place of intermediate beings in later Roman thought, see J. Den Boeft, *Calcidius on Demons* (Leiden: E. J. Brill, 1977).

2. Augustine here discusses "the Socratic turn." See Cicero's *Tusculan Disputations* V. 4. 10; see also Leo Strauss, *The City and Man* (Chicago: University of Chicago Press, 1978), 13 ff.

certain just why Socrates did this. Was he turning his mind away from the weariness of obscure and uncertain things and toward the discovery of something clear and certain that was necessary for the happy life, since this is the single goal for the sake of which the industry of all philosophers is seen to have stayed up late and toiled? Or, as certain more benevolent people suspect of him, was he unwilling that minds made impure by earthly desire should strive to attain divine things? Indeed, he would see such minds inquiring about the causes of things, but, as he believed the first and highest of the causes to be only in the will of the one and highest god, he did not think they could be grasped except by a purified mind. Therefore, he recommended that one eagerly pursue the required cleansing of life through good morals. In this way the mind, unencumbered by the weight of lusts, might raise itself to eternal things by its natural vigor, and so contemplate with a purified intelligence the nature of immaterial and un-changeable light, where the causes of all created natures have their stable dwelling.

Nevertheless, it is known that he would agitate and manipulate the fool-ishness of ignorant men who believed that they knew something. He did this by means of a marvelous and pleasant style of discussion and a most cutting wit, either confessing his ignorance or dissimulating his knowledge even about questions concerning morals, to which it seemed that he had directed the whole of his attention. Because of this, he was condemned on a false charge by his enraged adversaries and punished by death.[3] After that, however, the city of Athens itself, which had publicly condemned him, publicly mourned him. The indignation of the people turned against his two accusors to such an extent that one of them perished due to the violence of the multitude and the other evaded a similar punishment by a voluntary and permanent exile.

So glowing were the reports of the life and death of Socrates that he left behind many followers of his philosophy. These eagerly engaged in debate about the moral questions which treat the highest good, the good by which man is able to become happy. Because all arguments are set in motion, defended, and destroyed in the disputations of Socrates, the position of Socrates himself on the highest good was not very clear. Each follower took what appealed to him and picked what seemed to him to be the ultimate good. The "ultimate good" is the name given to that which makes one happy when one attains it. In this way, the Socratics came to hold different opinions concerning this end among themselves, so that (what is scarcely

3. See Plato's *Apology*.

believable about the followers of a single teacher) some, such as Aristippus, said that the good was pleasure; others, such as Antisthenes, virtue.[4] Others have still other views, and it would be tedious to recount them all.

Chapter 5

If Plato said that the wise man imitates, knows, and loves this god, and is happy through participating in him, what need is there to examine the rest of the philosophers? No one comes closer to us than the Platonists.[5] Consequently, let not only the mythical theology, entertaining impious minds with the crimes of the gods, give precedence to them, but also the civil theology, in which impure demons, leading peoples given to earthly delights astray in the name of the gods, wanted to have human errors as their own divine honors. Such demons excite their worshippers through the filthiest cravings to treat the sport of watching their crimes as though it was their worship. The spectators themselves thus provide an even more delightful sport for the demons. Even if some honorable things are done in the temples, they are defiled by their being joined to the obscenities of the theatres, and whatever disgraceful things are done in the theatres are praised in comparison to the foulness of the temples.

The views of Varro, according to which the sacred rites are interpreted as if they refer to the sky, the earth, and the origin and progress of mortal things, must also give precedence to the Platonists. The reason for this is that the rites do not have the meanings that he attempts to suggest, and thus his attempt does not yield truth. Even if the rites did have these meanings, the rational soul still ought not worship as god those things which are placed beneath it by the order of nature, nor ought it place above itself as gods those things over which it has been placed by the true God. Also, those books that Numa Pompilius took care to hide by having them buried with himself, which were then turned up by a plough and ordered to be burned by the senate, in fact pertained to the same sacred rites and must likewise give precedence to the Platonists. . . .

4. Aristippus (fl. 370 B.C.) and Antisthenes (c. 445–c. 360 B.C.) were, as Augustine says, students of Socrates. Augustine also points out the disagreements among philosophers in XVIII. 41 and XIX. 1.

5. See also *Confessions* VII. 9–12. The relationship between Augustine's thought and the Platonic philosophical tradition has produced an enormous amount of debate in recent times. A summary of that debate may be found in James J. O'Donnell's "Introduction" to his edition of the *Confessions* (Oxford: Clarendon Press, 1993), vol. 1, xvii–lxxi.

Therefore, let these two theologies, the mythical and the civil, give way to the Platonic philosophers who said that the true God is the author of all things, the illuminator of truth, and the lavish bestower of happiness. Let also the other philosophers, who fancied the principles of nature to be material because their minds were surrendered to their bodies, give way to these great men who recognized such a great god. . . .

Some of them, such as the Epicureans,[6] believed that living things could come into being from non-living things. Others believed that both living and non-living things come into being from a living thing, but that material things still proceed from a material thing. The Stoics thought fire—one of the four material elements of which this visible world is composed—to be both living and wise, the maker of the world itself and everything in it: in short, they thought fire to be god.[7]

These and other similar philosophers were able to consider only what their hearts, entangled in the senses of the flesh, said to them. Certainly, they had within themselves something they did not see, and they pictured in their own minds what they had seen externally, even when they did not see it but only thought about it. Yet, what is viewed in such thinking is no longer a body, but the likeness of a body. Moreover, that whereby this likeness of a body is seen in the mind is itself neither a body nor a likeness of a body, and that whereby the likeness of a body is seen and judged to be beautiful or deformed, is surely better than what is judged. This thing by which the likeness of a body is seen and judged is the understanding of man and the nature of the rational soul. Certainly it is not a body, since that likeness of a body that is seen and judged by the thinking mind is itself not a body. Therefore, the mind is neither earth, nor sky, nor air, nor fire, which are the four material bodies called "elements," of which we see the material world to be constructed. Moreover, if our mind is not material, in what way is God, the creator of mind, material?

Therefore, as was said above, let these philosophers also give precedence to the Platonists. Those, too, who were embarrassed to say that God is material but still thought that our minds are of the same nature as God, must likewise give way. They did not take into account the great change-

6. Epicureanism: a school of philosophy founded by Epicurus (342–270 B.C.) in Athens. Epicurus followed the atomistic materialism of Democritus. The most important Latin representative of Epicureanism is Lucretius (c. 94–55 B.C.), whose poem *On the Nature of Things* provides an account of Epicurean cosmology. Overcoming materialism was a crucial aspect of Augustine's own intellectual development. See *Confessions* VII. 1. 1–2.

7. On Stoicism, see the note on V. 9.

ability of the soul, for it is an abomination to attribute such changeability to the divine nature. Yet, they respond that the nature of the soul is changed by the body, since in itself the soul is unchangeable. They could just as well say that flesh is wounded by some body, since in itself the flesh is not capable of being wounded! In a word, what cannot be changed can be changed by nothing, while what can be changed by a body is able to be changed by something and therefore cannot rightly be said to be unchangeable.

Chapter 6

Thus, those philosophers,[8] whom we see deservedly surpassing the rest in fame and glory, realized that no material body is God. In seeking God, then, they transcended all material bodies. They realized that whatever is changeable is not the highest God. Therefore, in seeking the highest God, they transcended every soul and every changeable spirit.

Next, they realized that, in any changeable thing, the form by which the thing is—no matter what it is, in what way it is, or what sort of nature it is—cannot exist except through him who truly exists, since he is unchangeable. Hence, the matter of the whole world—its shapes, qualities, and ordered movements; its elements arranged from heaven to earth and whatever bodies that are in them—cannot exist except through him who exists simply. Neither can any life exist except through him—whether it is the life of nutrition and preservation, such as the life which is present in trees; or the life which in addition also senses, such as is present in animals; or the life which does these things and also understands, such as is present in man; or the life which has no need of being sustained by nutrition but only preserves, senses, and understands, such as is present in angels.

The reason for this is that being and living are not distinct in him, as if he could exist without being alive. Neither are living and understanding distinct in him, as if he could live without understanding. Neither are understanding and being happy distinct in him, as if he could understand without being happy. Instead, his living, understanding, and being happy are his very being.

From this unchangeability and simplicity of God, the Platonists understood that he made all things and that he himself could not have been made by anyone. They considered that whatever exists is either body or life, and that life is something superior to body, and that the form of body is sensible

8. i. e., the Platonic school.

but that of life intelligible. Consequently, they placed the intelligible form higher than the sensible. By "sensible," we mean those things which can be sensed through the vision and touch of the body. By "intelligible," we mean those things which can be understood through the pondering of the mind, for there is no bodily excellence—whether in the condition of a body, such as in shape, or in the motion of a body, such as in song—that is not judged by the mind. Indeed, that would not be possible unless a superior form of these things existed in the mind without the bulging of mass, the clamor of voice, and the extension of space or time.

Yet, unless the mind was also changeable, one person would not be a better judge of sensible forms than another. In fact, though, a clever person is a better judge than a dullard, a skilled person than an unskilled, a well-trained person than one in training. Indeed, the very same person, when he improves, is certainly a better judge afterward than before. Whatever admits of more or less, however, is without doubt changeable.

From this argument, the Platonists, who were clever, learned, and trained in these matters, easily concluded that the primary form is not in those things which have been convincingly proven to be changeable. In their view, both body and soul admit of greater or lesser degrees of form, and thus, if they could lack all form, they would not exist at all. They saw that something exists in which exists the primary form, which is unchangeable and therefore not admitting of degrees of comparison. They quite correctly believed that the beginning of things is there, that it was not made, and that from it everything was made. Thus, "what is known of God, he himself made clear to them when they perceived and understood his invisible and everlasting power and divinity through created things" (Rom 1:19–20), for all visible and temporal things were created by him.

Let these remarks suffice for a discussion of that part of philosophy that the Platonists call "physics" or "natural philosophy."

Chapter 8

The remaining part of the Platonists' philosophy is morals, which is called "ethics" in Greek.[9] Here the supreme good is sought, the good to which we refer everything that we do, desiring it not for the sake of something else,

---

9. The Platonists divided philosophy into three parts: "physics" or "natural philosophy," which Augustine discussed in Chapter 6; "logic" or "rational philosophy," which is discussed in Chapter 7 (not included in this volume); and "ethics" or "moral philosophy," to which Augustine now turns.

but for its very own sake. Obtaining it, we require nothing further in order to be happy. It is truly called the "end," because we want everything else for the sake of this, but this we want only for itself.[10]

Some have said that this good which makes one happy comes from the body, others that it comes from the mind, and others that it comes from both. They saw that man himself consists of mind and body and they there-fore believed that well-being for themselves could come from one or the other of these two or from both together—from a sort of final good, through which they would be happy and to which they would refer every-thing they did, without seeking further for that to which everything must be referred. Thus, those who are said to have added a third class of goods called "extrinsic"—goods such as honor, glory, wealth, and things of that sort—did not add these things as though they were the final good. That is to say, they did not add these things as though they ought to be desired for their own sake, but for the sake of something else. This class of goods is good for good people but bad for bad people.

Thus, whether they sought the good of man from the mind, the body, or both, they thought that nothing other than what derives from man was to be sought. Those who sought the good of man in the body sought it in the inferior part of man; those who sought it in the soul in the better part; and those who sought it in both, in the whole of man. Yet, whether they sought it in either part or in the whole, they sought it nowhere except in man. Those three different views, however, have produced not only three, but many dissenting schools of philosophers, because different philoso-phers have held different opinions about the good of the body, the good of the mind, and the good of both together.

So then, let all these philosophers give precedence to those who have said that man is happy not by enjoying the body or the mind, but by enjoy-ing God, not as the mind enjoys the body or itself, nor as one friend enjoys another, but as the eye enjoys light, if an analogy can be made between those two things. If God will be my help, this analogy will be clarified, insofar as it is possible, in another place. For now, let it suffice to remem-ber that Plato determined that the final good is to live according to virtue and that this is possible only to one who knows and imitates God, and that there is no other cause of happiness. He did not doubt that to study phi-losophy is to love God, whose nature is immaterial. From this it certainly follows that the one who loves wisdom (for that is what "philosopher" means), will be happy when he begins to attain God. Although one who attains what he loves is not necessarily happy (for many, by loving the

10. See also Augustine's discussion of the final good or end in XIX. 1–4.

things that are unworthy of love, are miserable, and they are more miserable when they attain them), no one is happy who loves what he does not attain. Even those who love things unworthy of love think that they are happy not by loving but by attaining them. Who, therefore, except the most miserable, denies that anyone who attains what he loves, and loves the true and highest good, is happy? Plato says that God himself is the true and highest good. Thus, because philosophy reaches for a happy life, Plato wants a philosopher to be a lover of God, so that by loving God he might be happy in attaining him.

Chapter 10

A Christian educated only in ecclesiastical writings might perhaps be ignorant of the name of the Platonists and might not know of the existence of the two kinds of Greek-speaking philosophers, the Ionian and the Italian.[11] Nevertheless, such a person is not so deaf to human affairs that he does not know that philosophers profess either the enthusiasm for wisdom or else the actual possession of it. A Christian, however, is wary of those who philosophize according to the elements of this world and not according to God, who made the world. He is warned by the precept of the apostle and faithfully hears what has been said: "Be on your guard that no one deceives you through philosophy and the empty seduction of the elements of the world" (Col 2:8).

Next, in order that he does not judge all philosophers to be like those, a Christian hears the same apostle say about some of them, "Because what is known of God has been made clear to them, for God made it clear to them; from the creation of the world his invisible and everlasting power and divinity are perceived, having been understood through created things" (Rom 1:19–20). Furthermore, speaking to the Athenians, after he had said a great thing about God which few can understand—namely, that "in him we live and move and are"—the apostle added, "as even some of your own have said" (Acts 17:28).[12]

---

11. The Ionian school of philosophy was founded by Thales. Its most famous members are Anaximander, Anaximenes, and Anaxagoras. The Italian school of philosophy was founded by Pythagoras. Both of these philosophical movements originated prior to the time of Socrates. See XVIII. 37. See also Richard D. McKirahan, *Philosophy Before Socrates* (Indianapolis: Hackett Publishing Co., 1994).

12. Some have suggested that the source of the saying "in him we live and move and are" is Epimenides of Crete, who flourished in the sixth century B.C.

The Christian knows very well to be on guard even against these philosophers when they err on certain matters, for where it was said that God has made clear his invisible perfections through the perception and understanding of created things, it was also said that they have not correctly worshipped God himself because they offered the divine honors due only to him to other, unworthy things: "Knowing God, they did not glorify and give thanks to him as God, but they lapsed into empty speculation and their foolish hearts were darkened. Saying that they were wise, they became fools, and they exchanged the glory of the incorruptible God for an image bearing the likeness of corruptible man, or birds, or four-footed animals, or serpents" (Rom 1:21–23). In this passage, the apostle is referring to the Romans, Greeks, and Egyptians, who prided themselves on their famous wisdom.

We shall argue with them about that later on. Still, we prefer them to the rest of the philosophers, for they agree with us concerning the one God, the author of the universe, who is not only immaterial and above all material things, but also incorruptible and above all souls, our beginning, our light, and our good.

Perhaps a Christian, ignorant of their writings, does not use in argumentation words that he has not learned. Perhaps he does not use the Latin word "natural" or the Greek word "physics" to name that part of philosophy in which the investigation of nature is treated, nor the term "rational" or "logic" to name that part in which it is asked in what way one is able to comprehend truth, nor the terms "moral" or "ethics" to name that part which treats morals and the final good to be sought and the ultimate evil to be avoided. Yet he is not therefore ignorant that it is from the one, true, and supreme God that we have the nature by which we have been made according to his image, the teaching by which we know both him and ourselves, and the grace by which we are made happy by clinging to him.

This, then, is the reason why we prefer the Platonists to the rest. The other philosophers wore away their abilities and enthusiasm in inquiring after the causes of things and the manner of learning and living. These Platonists, having recognized God's existence, discovered there the cause of the ordered universe, the light of truth which we long to understand, and the fountain of happiness, made for drinking. Therefore, if either these Platonists or any other philosophers among the peoples think these things about God, they think as we do. It is better, however, to plead this cause with the Platonists, for their writings are better known. The Greeks, whose language is preeminent among the peoples, resoundingly praise their writings, and the Latins, persuaded either by their excellence or their glory, have studied them most enthusiastically and made them more well-known and illustrious by translating them into our language.[13]

Chapter 19

Shall I not summon the public itself as a clear witness against the arts of magic, on which some who are excessively wretched and impious even pride themselves? Why are those arts so harshly punished by the severity of law if they are the works of deities who should be worshipped? Is it perhaps because Christians instituted those laws which punish the magical arts?[14] . . . Did not Cicero relate that in the Twelve Tables, which are the oldest laws of the Romans, the magical arts were listed and a punishment established for those who practiced them?[15]

Finally, when Apuleius himself was accused of practicing the magical arts,[16] surely no one will claim his judges were Christians! If he knew that the practices with which he was charged were divine and pious and in accord with the works of divine power, not only should he have confessed them but professed them, accusing instead the laws which prohibited and condemned things which ought to have been considered admirable and venerable. Had he done so, either he would have persuaded the judges to his own opinion or, if they had ruled in accord with the unjust laws and had punished him with death for proclaiming and praising such things, the demons would have repaid him with gifts worthy of a soul which did not fear the loss of human life in order to proclaim their divine works. He would have been like our martyrs, who, when the Christian religion was charged against them as a crime, knew that salvation and the greatest eternal glory would be theirs through the Christian faith. They chose not to evade temporal punishment by denying their faith, but instead, by con-

---

13. Augustine also discusses the problem of faith and philosophy in XVIII. 41.

14. During the fourth century, there was an increasing volume of legislation against the practice of magic. For a sample, see the *Theodosian Code* IX. 16.

15. See *Twelve Tables* VIII. 8a. The passage in Cicero to which Augustine alludes does not seem to be extant.

16. Apuleius (born c. A.D. 123) lived in Roman Africa. His most famous work is his novel *The Golden Ass*. Although he was a Platonic philosopher of sorts, he also wrote extensively on the practice of magic. After marrying a wealthy, elderly widow, he was accused of using the art of magic to obtain her love. The apology he delivered in his defense, which Augustine mentions in the next paragraph, is still extant. He was acquitted of the charges.

fessing, professing, and proclaiming it, by enduring all things faithfully and courageously for it and by dying with the composure of piety, they compelled the laws to blush with shame and caused them to be changed.

There still exists, however, a most complete and eloquent oration by this Platonic philosopher in which he defends himself against the crime of practicing the arts of magic by claiming to be a stranger to them. He does not want to be judged innocent except by repudiating what an innocent person cannot commit. Moreover, he also says that all the miracles of the magicians, whom he rightly thinks ought to be condemned, result from the teachings and works of demons.[17] . . .

Chapter 27

We do not establish temples, priests, rituals, and sacrifices for the martyrs, for they are not gods but rather their God is our God. To be sure, we honor their memories, as they were holy men of God who struggled for the truth clear up until the death of their bodies. They struggled in this way in order that the true religion would become known and the false ones proven to be fabrications, for prior to those martyrs, even if some people realized that the fabrications were false, they restrained themselves from saying so because of fear. Yet, whoever heard a priest of the faithful standing before an altar, even one built above the holy body of a martyr for the honor and worship of God, at any time pray, "I offer a sacrifice to you, Peter," or "to you, Paul," or "to you, Cyprian"?[18] The sacrifice offered in their memory is offered to the God who made them both men and martyrs and who united them to his holy angels by means of celestial honor. He did so in order that, by renewing our memories of them, we might frequently give thanks to the true God for their victories, and so that we might be encouraged to imitate such crowns and palms by calling upon the same God for help.

Therefore, whatever services are conducted in the shrines of the martyrs are signs of respect to their memory, not sacred rites or sacrifices to the dead as if to gods. Some Christians bring food to the memorial. Indeed, this is not done by the better Christians and in many lands there is no such custom; nevertheless, those who do so, after setting it down and praying,

17. For Augustine's views on magic, see also X. 9 and 12.

18. Cyprian was a bishop of Carthage who became a venerated figure in North African Christianity after his martyrdom in 258. In Augustine's time there was a conflict between the Italian and African customs of honoring martyrs. See *Confessions* VI. 2. 2. See also, Peter Brown, *The Cult of the Saints: Its Rise and Function in Latin Christianity* (Chicago: University of Chicago Press, 1981).

carry it out to eat it or to distribute a portion of it to the poor. They want the food to be blessed on their behalf through the merits of the martyrs in the name of the Lord of the martyrs. Anyone, however, who knows the one sacrifice of the Christians that is offered there knows that these acts are not sacrifices to the martyrs.

We do not, then, worship our martyrs with divine honors or human crimes as the Egyptian pagans worship their gods. We do not offer sacrifice to our martyrs, nor do we turn their disgraceful conduct into sacred rites.

Thus, let those who are willing and able read, and let those who have already read recall, the kind and number of the evils recorded concerning the Egyptian goddess Isis, the wife of Osiris, and their ancestors, who are said to have all been kings. (Because this Isis, while sacrificing to her ancestors, discovered a field of barley and showed the ears to her husband the king and his counselor Mercury, she is said to be the same as the Roman goddess Ceres.) These evils are recorded not in poetry, but in Egyptian religious writings, such as those which the priest Leon showed to Alexander the Great, who then wrote about them in a letter to his mother Olympias. Let all who consider those texts observe which dead human beings and which of their deeds were commemorated by the institution of sacred rites as though they were gods.[19]

Let them not for an instant, however, dare to compare in any way the human beings whom they consider to be gods with our holy martyrs whom we do not consider to be gods! We do not appoint priests for our martyrs or offer sacrifices to them, because that is not proper, required, or permitted. Only to the one God are such things due. We do not amuse our martyrs with their own crimes or with those most shameful performances in which the Egyptian pagans celebrate either the disgraces of their gods (if their gods committed such disgraces when they were human beings) or (if they were not human beings) the amusing fabrications of harmful demons.

If Socrates had a god, he did not have this kind of a demon for a god.[20] Perhaps, though, those who wanted to excell at the art of making gods imposed such a god on that innocent man, to whom such an art was foreign.

What more should be said? No one of even moderate intelligence con-

---

19. In this paragraph Augustine attacks a collection of religious and philosophical writings known as the Hermetic Books. They were ascribed to Hermes Trismegistus of Egypt. Although they were probably composed after the time of Christ, it was claimed that they were very ancient. See also XVIII. 39.

20. Augustine refers to the "voice" that assisted Socrates. See *Apology* 31d.

tends that those spirits should be worshipped in order to obtain the happy
life which will exist after death. Perhaps, however, they could say that the
gods are all good but that some of the demons are bad and some are good,
and they might suggest that the good ones, through which we may be led
to a life of eternal happiness, should be worshipped. Such an opinion must
be examined in the following book.

Book IX

*Book IX continues the discussion of the status of intermediary beings begun in
Book VIII, Chapter 13. Its purpose is to show that the intermediary beings of
the Platonists are not necessary for eternal happiness. Though Book IX develops the theme of Books VI through X, namely, the relationship between pagan
religion and prosperity in the life to come, it is not directly relevant to the concerns of this volume, and hence no selections from the book have been included.*

Book X

Introduction

Book X completes the second major section of The City of God. *It also completes Augustine's lengthy discourse on intermediary beings. The principal question now is whether or not such beings ought to be worshipped. Chapter 3 is representative of Augustine's response: worship is owed exclusively to the one true God. Christian faith and worship, however, are based on revelation, and the evidence for revelation is miracles. Augustine is thus forced to distinguish between the miracles performed in support of true religion and the wonders of magic. This is the theme of Chapters 10 and 12. The revelation to which the miracles are a witness proceeded according to a certain order inasmuch as the human race needed to be instructed in a gradual manner. In Chapters 14 and 15, Augustine explains how the manner of God's revelation was consistent with his providence. Intermediary beings such as angels have a role to play in these matters, but their role is totally subservient to God's will.*

Chapter 3

If the Platonists, or anyone else who thought as they did, had, upon discovering God, glorified him as God and thanked him, not lapsing into empty speculations (Rom 1:21), neither becoming the authors of the errors of the people nor being afraid to resist them, then certainly they would admit that both those beings who are immortal and happy and we who are mortal and miserable must worship the one God of gods, who is both ours and theirs, so that we might be able to be happy.

To him we owe that service that is called *latreia* in Greek,[1] whether in the sacraments or in ourselves. Together, we are his temple, and individually, we are his temples, because he deigns to dwell in the union of all and

---

1. The word *latreia* means religious devotion or worship.

in every individual. He is not larger in the union than in the individual, for he is not increased through a large mass of people nor decreased by being separated in individuals. When lifted up to him, our heart is his altar. To him, by his priest, the only-begotten one, we are reconciled. To him we offer bleeding sacrifices when we struggle for his truth even to the point of martyrdom. To him we burn the sweetest incense when in his sight we are afire with pious and holy love. To him we dedicate and give in return his own gifts within us and our very selves. To him, in solemn feasts and established holy days, we affirm and consecrate the memory of his benefits, so that ungrateful oblivion might not steal that memory through the passing of time. To him we sacrifice the offering of humility and praise, burning with the fire of charity in the altar of our heart.

We are cleansed from every stain of sins and evil desires and consecrated to his name, because we must see him as he may be seen and because we must cling to him. He himself is the fountain of our happiness; he himself is the end of all our longing. In choosing him, or rather, since we had lost him through neglect, in re-choosing him (from which, it is said, the word "religion" comes),[2] we strive toward him by love, so that by attaining him we might rest, happy because we are perfected by him who is our end. Thus, our good, the end which is extensively disputed among the philosophers, is nothing other than to cling to him. Only in his immaterial embrace, if we may so speak, is the intellectual soul filled and made fruitful with true virtues.

We are commanded to love this good with our whole heart, our whole soul, and our whole strength. We must be led to this good by those who love us, and we must lead those whom we love to it. In so doing, those two precepts on which the whole law and the whole prophets depend are fulfilled: "You shall love the Lord your God with your whole heart and with your whole soul and with your whole mind," and "You shall love your neighbor even as you love yourself" (Mt 22:37–9; Dt 6:5; Lv 19:18). So that man might know how to love himself, an end was established for man, an end to which he directs everything that he does in order to be happy, for he who loves himself wants nothing other than to be happy. This end is to cling to God. Therefore, when one who knows how to love himself is commanded to love his neighbor as himself, what else is commanded except, as much as he can, to show his neighbor that it is good to love God? This is worship of God. This is true religion. This is correct piety. This is

---

2. Augustine points out that the Latin word *religio* is sometimes said to derive from the verb *relegere* (*re-eligere*), which means to choose again or "re-choose." See Cicero, *On the Nature of the Gods* II. 28. 72.

the service owed only to God.

Whatever immortal power there might be, endowed with whatever amount of strength, if it loves us as it loves itself, then, so that we might be happy, it wants us to be subordinate to him to whom it itself is subordinate and thus made happy. If such a power does not worship God, then it is miserable because it is deprived of God. If, however, it does worship God, then it does not want to be worshipped itself instead of God. It rather applauds and supports with all the forces of its love the divine decree which is written, "Anyone sacrificing to the gods, except only to the Lord, will be eradicated" (Ex 22:20).

Chapter 9

These miracles recorded in the Old Testament,[3] and many others of that kind (it would be exceedingly tedious to treat all of them), were done for the purpose of advancing the worship of the one true God and hindering that of the many false ones. Furthermore, they were done by the simple faith and trust of piety, not by the incantations and predictions constructed by the art of abominable curiosity. Some people refer to this art with the name "magic," or with the more detestable name of "witchcraft" or the more honorable one of "theurgy," as if they are attempting to distinguish with these latter terms those practitioners of the illicit arts who are damnable, whom the common call evil-doers (for they say that these are devoted to witchcraft) from those who are praiseworthy, to whom they attribute the practice of theurgy.[4] Both arts, however, are entangled with the fallacious rites of demons usurping the names of angels.[5] . . .

Chapter 12

Still, the deeds performed by these theurgic arts are so great and remarkable that they go beyond every measure of human ability. Therefore, what remains except to prudently conclude that those things which seem to be predicted and performed miraculously and divinely and yet are not di-

---

3. In the preceding chapter, which is not included here, Augustine comments on some miracles recorded in the Old Testament.

4. For a more complete discussion of theurgy and its history see E. R. Dodds, *The Greeks and the Irrational* (Berkeley: University of California Press, 1951), 283–311.

5. On Augustine's views on magic, see also VIII. 19.

rected to the worship of the one God—even the Platonists confess and testify at length that the only good which makes us happy is to cling to the one God—are tricks of malicious demons and seductive hindrances that true piety must guard against? Yet, it must also be believed that whatever miracles are divinely done, either by means of angels or in any other way, so that they advance the worship and the religion of the one God in whom alone our life is made happy, are done by those or through those who love us according to truth and piety, God himself working in them.

We must not listen to those who deny that the invisible God works visible miracles, because even according to them God made the world and they certainly cannot deny that the world is visible. Any wonder whatever that is worked in this world is surely a lesser marvel than the whole of this world, lesser than heaven and earth and everything that is in them, all of which God certainly made. Yet, just as he himself who made the world is hidden and incomprehensible to man, so is the manner in which he made the world. Thus, although the miracles of visible natures are not appreciated because they are constantly seen, nevertheless, when we consider them with wisdom we understand that they are greater than the most unusual and rarest miracles, for man is a greater miracle than any miracle that is done through man. Consequently, God, who made the visible heaven and earth, does not consider it undignified to perform visible miracles in heaven or on earth. Through such miracles he rouses the soul, now given to visible things, to worship his invisible self.

Where and when he performs such miracles, however, is part of the unchangeable plan belonging to God himself, in whose design all future times are already past. Moving temporal things, he is not moved temporally. He knows what will be done in the very same way that he knows what has been done, and he listens to those calling upon him for help in the very same way that he sees those who will call upon him for help. Even when his angels listen to those calling upon him, he himself listens in them, just as he listens in his true temple not made by hands, just as he listens in his holy human beings; and the eternal commands perceived in his law are executed in the course of time.

Chapter 14

The correct instruction of the human race, as it concerns the people of God, proceeded like the instruction of one person: it progressed through certain segments of time or ages, so that it advanced from grasping temporal things to eternal things, and from visible things to invisible. Nevertheless, at the same time that God was promising visible rewards, the worship of the one God was also commanded, in order that the human mind, even in seeking the earthly benefits of the transitory life, would not be subordinated to anyone except the true creator and lord of the soul.

Surely anyone is mad who denies that everything angels or human beings can offer to human beings is within the power of the one Almighty. Certainly the Platonist philosopher Plotinus discusses providence.[6] He holds that providence extends from the supreme God, whose beauty is intelligible and inexpressible, all the way down to the lowliest earthly things, and he proves it through the beauty of little flowers and leaves. He asserts that all such common and fleeting things could not have such harmoniously proportioned shapes unless they were fashioned from a source where an intelligible and unspeakable form continuously abides and yet dwells in all things at the same time. The Lord Jesus points this out when he says, "Consider the lilies of the field: they neither toil nor spin. Yet I say to you, not even Solomon in all his glory was arrayed as one of these. If God so clothes the grass of the field, which today is alive and tomorrow is thrown into the oven, how much more will he do for you, O you of little faith?" (Mt 6:28–30)

The human soul, still weak because of its earthly desires, longs in the course of time for the low, earthly goods necessary for this transitory life but contemptible in comparison with the everlasting benefits of that other life. It is best, therefore, that the soul not be accustomed to expect earthly goods except from the one God so that even in desiring such goods it does not withdraw from the worship of God, whom it may reach by scorning and turning away from those very same things.

Chapter 15

. . . Syllable by syllable, through the transitory moments of time, God spoke with the sounds of human speech. In his own nature he speaks, not materially but spiritually, not sensibly but intelligibly, not temporally but, if I may say so, eternally. He does not begin to speak, nor does he cease speaking. The servants and messengers in his presence, fully enjoying his unchanging truth in eternal happiness, hear purely, not by the ear of the

6. Plotinus (A.D. 205–269) was, in Augustine's eyes, the greatest interpreter of Plato's thought. His philosophical works were collected by his pupil Porphyry (233–c. 304) and published as *The Enneads*. Augustine is referring to *Enneads* III. 2. 13. Porphyry also composed works of his own, including an attack on Christianity.

body but of the mind. They hear in indescribable ways what must be done and what must be brought about in this visible and sensible world, and they accomplish it instantly and easily.

Furthermore, this law was given through the orderly intervals of time. As I have said, at first it contained promises of earthly goods. Through these, however, promises of eternal goods were signified, which many celebrated in visible sacraments but few understood.[7] . . .

Chapter 32

. . . Therefore, insofar as the true God and Lord thought fit to assist me, in these ten books I have satisfied the zeal of certain people, although less well than some were expecting of me, by refuting the contradictions of the impious who prefer their own gods to the founder of the holy city which I have undertaken to discuss. Of these ten books, the first five were written in response to those who think that the gods ought to be worshipped for the sake of the goods of this life. The last five were written in response to those who think that the worship of the gods must be preserved for the sake of the life which will exist after death. Next, as I promised in the first book, I shall explain, to the extent that I am assisted by God, what I think needs to be said concerning the origin, progress, and proper ends of the two cities, which, as I have said, are thoroughly entangled and interwoven with each other in this present age.

---

7. On the sacraments of the Old Testament, see the note on IV. 33.

Book XI

Introduction

Book XI marks the beginning of The City of God's *third major section. The ten books devoted to refuting the arguments of the pagans having been completed, Augustine now sets out to explain the origins of the heavenly and earthly cities. Book XI initiates this project with a discussion of the Christian view of creation. Augustine is especially concerned with the creation of angels, for the angels are the first citizens of the two cities and their division anticipates the division of the human race. The following selections also include an important discussion of the ordered levels of created being in the universe (Ch. 16) and a striking passage in which Augustine argues that human beings, in reflecting on themselves, are able to recognize within themselves the Triune image of the creator (Ch. 26).*

Chapter 9

I have undertaken to describe the origin of the holy city, first discussing the holy angels, who constitute a large part of it, and one that is all the more blessed as they have never journeyed from it. With God's help, I will devote myself to the task of explaining, as far as seems sufficient, the testimony of the Scriptures on this subject. Where Sacred Scripture speaks of the world's creation, it is not clearly explained whether or at what point the angels were created. If mention is made of them, it is implicitly, either under the name of "heaven" where it is said, "In the beginning God created heaven and earth" (Gn 1:1), or more likely under the name of "light" (Gn 1:3), which is what I am now discussing. I think, however, that they were not omitted, because it is written that God rested on the seventh day from all the works which he had made, yet the book begins, "In the beginning God created heaven and earth," so that before heaven and earth God seems to have created nothing. . . .

When God said, "Let there be light," and there was light, if we are right to understand this light to be the creation of the angels, then certainly they were created as sharers in the eternal light which is the unchangeable wisdom of God, by which all things were made and which we call the only-begotten Son of God. Illuminated by the light that created them, the angels themselves became light and are called "day," participating in that unchangeable light and day which is the word of God by whom they and everything else were made. Indeed, "The true light, which lights every man that comes into the world" (Jn 1:9), lights also every pure angel, that he may not be light in himself but in God. If an angel turns away from God, he becomes impure as are all those who are called impure spirits and are no longer "light in the Lord" (Eph 5:8) but darkness in themselves, deprived of the participation in eternal light.

Chapter 16

Among the beings that exist in some way and are not identical with God, by whom they were created, those which have life are placed higher than those which are not living, as, for example, those which have the capacity to reproduce, or even the desire, are placed higher than those which lack this movement. Among living things, the sentient are placed higher than those which have no sensation; animals, for example, are placed above trees. Among the sentient, the intelligent are placed higher than those which lack intelligence, as human beings are placed above cattle. Among the intelligent, the immortal are placed above the mortal, as angels are placed above human beings. These are the gradations according to the order of nature.

There are, however, other standards of evaluation according to the usefulness each man finds in a thing, so that we prefer some nonsentient to some sentient beings. In such cases this preference is so strong that, if we had the power, we would choose to remove from nature these things we find useless, either in ignorance of the place they hold in nature, or, if we did know it, still sacrificing them to our own convenience. Who would not rather have bread in his house than mice, or gold rather than fleas? Why is this not surprising, given that, in placing a value on human beings themselves, whose nature is certainly of such great dignity, more is often paid for a horse than for a male slave or for a jewel than for a female slave. The unenslaved judgment by which reason considers the value of things is very different from the necessity of the indigent or the pleasure of the lover. The first considers the value of a thing in itself with respect to the order of things, while necessity considers how a thing meets its need. Reason considers the truth that is clear to the light of the mind, while pleasure watches for what agreeably coaxes the senses of the body.

In considering rational creatures, however, will and love carry so much weight that even though in the order of nature angels are preferred to human beings, yet by the law of justice good men are preferred to bad angels.

Chapter 17

We should understand the saying, "This is the beginning of the works of the Lord" (Jb 40:19), as referring to the nature of the devil and not to his malice. This is because without doubt malice can be a defect only where a nature has first existed without a defect. A defect is so contrary to a nature that it can only harm it. Therefore, turning away from God would not be a defect except in a nature meant to be with God. Even an evil will, then, is proof of the goodness of the nature. Just as God is the supremely good creator of good natures, so he is the most just ruler of evil wills, so that even though evil wills make an evil use of good natures, God makes a good use of evil wills.

Accordingly, he caused the devil, who is good by God's creation but evil by his own will, to be ranked among inferior beings and to become the mockery of his angels. In other words, God causes the temptations with which the devil had sought to injure the saints to be a benefit for them. Because God was certainly not ignorant of the devil's future malice when he created him, and because he knew beforehand the good which he himself would bring out of the devil's evil, the psalm says, "This dragon whom you have made for their ridicule" (Ps 104:26). The psalm says this so that we might see that, while God in his goodness created the devil good, through his foreknowledge he was already devising some way of making use of the devil even after he would become evil.

Chapter 26

We recognize in ourselves the image of God, which is the image of the supreme Trinity. This image is not identical to God; rather, it is far removed from God because it is not co-eternal or, simply put, not of the same substance with him. Still, it is nearer to him by nature than any of his other works, though it needs to be further restored in order to become an even closer image. We are like the Trinity in that we exist, know that we exist, and delight in our existence and our knowledge of it.

Further, in these three things no deceptive illusion misleads us. This is because we do not come into contact with them by a bodily sense, as we perceive things outside of us: for example, colors through seeing, sounds through hearing, smells through smelling, tastes through tasting, hard and soft objects by touching. We also have images resembling these sensible things, but they are not material. We consider them in thinking, hold them in memory, and are excited by them to desire the things which they resemble. It is without any deceptive representation of images or phantasms, however, that I am most certain that I am, that I know, and that I delight in this.

With respect to these truths, I am not at all afraid of the arguments of the Academics who say, "What if you are deceived?"[1] If I am deceived, I exist. After all, he who does not exist cannot be deceived, and if I am deceived then I exist. Because I exist if I am deceived, how am I deceived in believing that I exist? It is certain that I exist if I am deceived. Therefore, because I, the one deceived, must exist even if I am deceived, then certainly I am not deceived in this knowledge about my existence.

It follows that neither am I deceived in knowing that I know. This is because insofar as I know that I exist, I know also that I know. When I love these two things, I add to them a certain third thing, namely my love, which is of equal value. Because I am not deceived in those things which I love, I am not deceived in saying, "I love." Even if these things I love were false, it would still be true that I loved false things. How could I justly be blamed and forbidden to love false things, if it were false that I loved them? As they are true and real, who can doubt that when they are loved, the love of them is itself true and real? Further, as there is no one who does not wish to be happy, so there is no one who does not wish to exist. How can one be happy, after all, if one is nothing?

Chapter 33

It is certain that angels sinned and were thrown down to the lowest parts of the world where they are imprisoned until their final damnation on the day of judgment, because the apostle Peter clearly says, "God did not spare the angels that sinned, but cast them down to hell and delivered them into

---

1. The Academics were a philosophical school which argued that human knowledge can never attain certitude but remains at best probable. Augustine's first work was a dialogue entitled *Against the Academics*.

chains of darkness to be held for judgment" (2 Pt 2:4). Therefore, who can doubt that God, in foreknowledge or in act, separated these from the others? Who will dispute that the others are justly called "light"? Even we who are still living by faith, only hoping and not yet enjoying equality with the angels, are already called "light" by the apostle: "You were once darkness; now you are light in the Lord" (Eph 5:8). However, those angels who deserted are fittingly called "darkness" by all who understand or believe them to be worse than unfaithful men.

Consequently, although it may be that another light should be understood where we read, "God said, 'Let there be light,' and there was light," and another darkness is signified in the passage, "God divided the light from the darkness," we nevertheless think that these two societies of angels are referred to. One of them enjoys God; the other swells with arrogance. To the one it is said, "Praise him all you his angels" (Ps 148:2); the prince of the other says, "All these things will I give you if you will fall down and worship me" (Mt 4:9). One blazes with the holy love of God, the other smolders with the impure love of its own exhaltation.

Since, as it is written, "God resists the proud, but gives grace to the humble" (Prv 3:34; Jas 4:6; 1 Pt 5:5), the one dwells in the heaven of heavens and the other is cast out and rages through the lower regions of the air. The one is tranquil in the brightness of piety; the other stormy with fogging desires. The one tenderly cares and justly avenges at God's bidding; the other boils in its own haughtiness with the lust for subduing and harming. The one is the minister of God's goodness to the fullest of its good will; the other is held in by God's power from doing all the harm it wills. The one laughs at the other when it does good unwillingly by its persecutions; the other envies the one when it gathers in its own pilgrims.

These two angelic societies, then, are dissimilar and contrary to each other. The one is both good by nature and righteous by will; the other is also good by nature but by will deformed. They are described in other and more explicit testimonies of Sacred Scripture, and we think that they are also spoken of through the terms "light" and "darkness" in this book which is called Genesis. Even if perhaps the author had a different meaning in mind, nonetheless our discussion of this obscure language has not been a waste of time, for even if we have been unable to discover his meaning, we have still held to the rule of faith[2] which is sufficiently confirmed for the faithful from other sacred writings of the same authority. . . .

2. On the "rule of faith," see Augustine's *On Christian Doctrine* II. 9. 14; III. 2. 2; 3. 6, *et passim*. Briefly put, the rule of faith demands that obscure passages of Scripture be understood in a manner consistent with passages that are more evident.

Book XII

Introduction

Book XII opens with a continuation of the discussion of angels initiated in Book XI, only now the fall of the wicked angels is the primary focus. In the selections from Chapters 1, 4, and 6, Augustine attempts to explain how the angelic nature, created good by God, became sinful through a defect in its willing. The discussion anticipates the analysis of human sinfulness in Book XIV. In Chapter 9, Augustine indicates that the city of God is composed not only of angels but also of human beings, and it is to the creation of man that he turns his attention (Chs. 23–24). Also included in this volume are selections from Chapters 27 and 28, which shed light on Augustine's understanding of the creation of the human body. There he harshly criticizes the dim views of the body taken by Plato and Porphyry, who had argued that the body was not created by the supreme God and that in order to be purified the soul must escape from the prison of the body.

Chapter 1

. . . The contrary tendencies in the good and evil angels do not come from a difference in their natures and sources, because God, the good author and creator of all substances, created them both. Rather, it cannot be doubted that they come from a difference in their wills and desires. The good angels remained in the good common to all things, which is God himself and his eternity, truth, and charity. The others were in love with their own power, as if they could be their own good, and they turned from the superior, beatific good common to all things to their own private good. They exchanged the most exalted eternity for puffed-up arrogance, most certain truth for inflated vanity, undivided charity for a love of factions. They became proud, error-prone, and envious.

Thus, the cause of the happiness of the good angels is clinging to God. The cause of the misery of the evil angels is the contrary: their not clinging to God. When the question is asked, "Why are the good angels happy?" it is correctly answered, "Because they cling to God." When it is asked, "Why are the evil angels miserable?" it is correctly answered, "Because they do not cling to God." It is clear, then, that there is no other good for the rational or intellectual creature except God alone.

Not every creature can be happy, for beasts, trees, stones, and things of that sort lack this capacity. Even so, the creature which has this capacity cannot be happy by itself, because it is created out of nothing. It can only have it through the one who created it. This is because the creature is happy through the possession of that which, if it is lost, makes it miserable. The one, therefore, who is happy through his own good and not through another, cannot be miserable because he cannot lose himself.

This is why I say that there is no unchanging good except the one, true, and blessed God. It is also why I say that the things he created are indeed good because they come from him, but changeable because they are created out of nothing and not out of him. Although changeable things are not the highest good because God is a greater good, still they are very good and they can cling to the unchangeable good and so be happy. This is because God is so completely their good that without him they cannot be anything but unhappy.

The other created things in the universe are not better because they cannot be unhappy. No one would say that the other parts of the body are better than the eyes because they cannot be blind. A sentient nature, even when it feels pain, is superior to the stone, which cannot feel anything. In the same way, a rational nature, even when it is unhappy, is better than that which lacks reason or feeling and so cannot experience unhappiness. The rational nature has been created so excellently that even though it is a changeable thing, it may still gain happiness by clinging to the unchangeable good who is God, the most high. Further, the rational nature is not satisfied unless it is perfectly happy and it cannot be happy except in God. Consequently, the failure of a rational nature to cling to God is clearly a defect.

Every defect harms a nature and is therefore contrary to the nature. The nature, therefore, that clings to God does not differ in nature but in defect from the one that does not. Nevertheless, this nature itself is shown to be praiseworthy and great by its very defect. Disdain for a defect in a nature is, to be sure, praise of the nature itself, because a defect is rightly disdained inasmuch as it degrades a praiseworthy nature.

We say that blindness is a defect of the eyes and thereby show that sight belongs to the nature of the eyes, and we say that deafness is a defect of the ears and thereby show that it is their nature to hear. In the same way, when we say that it is a defect of the angelic creature not to cling to God, we clearly demonstrate that it belongs to the nature of angels to cling to God. Who can worthily express how great a glory it is to cling to God and so live in him, to find wisdom in him, to delight in him, and to enjoy his great goodness without death, error, or worry? Therefore, because every defect is a harming of a nature, the very defect of the wicked angels, which is their turning away from God, is enough to show that God created their nature so good that it damages them to be apart from God.

Chapter 4

It is ridiculous to blame beasts, trees, and other mortal and changeable things lacking intelligence or sensation or life for their defects, which destroy their corruptible natures, for these creatures have received, by the command of the creator, a manner of existing in which, by passing away and being succeeded by others, they accomplish the lowest kind of beauty—a beauty of their own level, a beauty of the seasons in harmony with the elements of the world. Earthly things were not made to be equal to heavenly things, nor were they to be completely omitted from the universe, despite their inferiority.

Therefore, on those levels where such things are appropriate, some die to make way for others which are born in their place, and the lower gives way to the greater, and the things that are overcome are changed into the qualities of those that overcome. This is the order of transitory things. The beauty of this order does not delight us because, due to our condition of mortality, we are so much a part woven into it that we cannot perceive the whole into which the parts that offend us are harmonized in a most fitting and beautiful way. Accordingly, when we are not well-suited to contemplate the providence of the creator very adequately, we are still correctly commanded to believe in it so that we will not dare, out of the vanity of human rashness, to find fault with anything in the work of so great a creator.[1] . . .

It is not with respect to our comfort or discomfort but with respect to their own nature that creatures glorify their maker. Thus, even the nature of eternal fire, though it be a punishment to condemned sinners, is certainly worthy of praise. After all, what is more beautiful than flaming, blazing, bright fire? What is more useful than fire for heating, curing, and

---

1. On the various levels in the order of creation, see also XI. 16.

cooking, even though nothing is more destructive than fire when it burns and consumes? The same thing, applied in one way, is destructive; applied fittingly, it is very beneficial. Who is able to describe its uses throughout the whole world? Those who praise the light of fire, but blame it for its heat, should not be listened to, as they judge it according to their comfort or discomfort and not by its nature. They wish to see, but not to be burnt. They forget that this very light which pleases them so much is a discomfort to weak eyes and harms them. . . .

Chapter 6

. . . If someone should ask, "What was the efficient cause of an angel's evil will?" none will be discovered. What is it, after all, that makes the will evil when it is the will itself that makes the action evil? The evil will is the efficient cause of the evil act, but nothing is the efficient cause of the evil will. If anything is the cause, then this cause either has or lacks a will. If it has a will, its will is either good or evil. If it is good, then who would be foolish enough to say that a good will makes a will evil? If this were so, then a good will would be the cause of sin, which is absurd.

If, rather, this thing which supposedly makes a will evil has itself an evil will, then I ask: what made it evil? So that this mode of inquiry will reach an end, I will go on to ask: what made the first evil will evil? Whatever is corrupted by something else is not first, but whatever evil thing has not been made evil by something else is first. If it were made evil by something else which preceded it, then that will which made its successor evil was first. If, however, someone replies, "Nothing made it evil; it always was evil," then I ask whether it existed in some nature. If not, then it did not exist at all. If it did exist in some nature, then it marred, corrupted, and injured it, and consequently deprived it of good.

Therefore, an evil will could not have existed in an evil nature, but in a nature at once good and changeable which this defect then could harm. If it did no harm, there was no defect, and so the will in which it existed could not be called evil. If, however, it did harm, then it did so by removing or diminishing the good. It follows that there could not have been an eternal evil will in a thing in which there had previously been a natural good which the evil will was able to diminish by harm.

I ask, then, if it does not exist eternally, who made it? The only possible reply is that something which itself had no will made the will evil. Was this thing superior, inferior, or equal to it? If superior, then it is better; but how could it have no will and not instead a good will? It is the same if it is equal:

as long as two things have equally good wills, the one cannot make the other an evil will. There remains the possibility that an inferior thing with no will corrupted the will of the angelic nature which first sinned.

Such a thing, however, even if it is the lowest and most earthly thing, is without doubt good because it is a nature and an essence, having its own mode and species in its own genus and order. Given this, how can a good thing be the efficient cause of an evil will? How can good be the cause of evil? When the will abandons what is above itself and turns to what is lower, it becomes evil. This is true, not because what it turns toward is evil, but because the turning itself is a deformity. It is not, therefore, an inferior thing which makes the will evil, but it is the created will itself which has become evil by wrongly and inordinately seeking an inferior thing.

If two men who are the same in body and soul see the same beauty of a single body and one of them is moved to desire an illicit enjoyment of it while the other steadfastly maintains his chaste will, what do we think causes an evil will to be in the one and not the other? What makes it be in the one in which it was made? It cannot be the beauty of the body because that was equally available to the perception of both but did not bring about an evil will in both. . . .

Chapter 9

. . . Giving due praise to the creator, we must say of both holy men and holy angels that the charity of God is poured forth in them by the Holy Spirit who was given to them (Rom 5:5). It is truly written not only of men but especially of angels that "It is good for me to cling to God" (Ps 73:28). Those who share in this good have a holy fellowship with both him to whom they cling and with one another. Together they form one city of God, which is his living sacrifice and living temple.

This city has a part which is gathered from among mortal men and is to be united with the immortal angels. It now suffers the difficulties of this journey on earth, or, with respect to those who have died, is at rest in the secret receptacles and dwelling places of souls. I now see that I must explain how this part arose through creation by God, just as I did concerning the angels. According to the faith of the Holy Scripture, the human race came from one man whom God created first; that Holy Scripture rightly has a marvellous authority throughout the world and among all peoples—a fact which, among other truths, was divinely predicted by the Scriptures themselves.

Chapter 23

God was not ignorant of the fact that man would sin and, having sinned, would then be subject to death and would therefore give birth to human beings who would die. He also knew that mortals would commit such great sins that even the beasts, who lack rational will and were created from earth and water in great numbers, would live more peacefully among their own kind than men, who had originally been generated from one man as a means of commending concord. Even lions or dragons have never waged such wars among their own kind as men have waged against one another. God, however, foresaw that, by his grace, a holy people would be called into adoption (Gal 4:5) with their sins forgiven. He foresaw that they would be justified by the Holy Spirit and united in community with the holy angels in eternal peace, when the final enemy, death, was destroyed (1 Cor 15:26). God also knew that this people would benefit from the consideration that he built up the human race from one man in order to show them how pleasing unity even in the midst of plurality is to him.[2]

Chapter 24

God, therefore, made man in his own image. He created man with a soul gifted with reason and intellect, by which he might excel all the animals that move on land or fly or swim, and which do not have minds of this kind. Having formed man out of the dust of the earth he gave him a soul of the kind I have described. Either he had already made it and gave it to man by breathing it into him, or else he made it by breathing into him, so that God willed that the breath which he breathed into man would be his soul. . . . After his own manner, he also made a wife for man to aid him in the work of generating his kind, and he formed her from a bone taken out of the man's side.[3]

We should not think of this work in a carnal way, as if God worked in the way we usually see craftsmen work, using their hands and earthly matter of some sort, applying their skill to the production of some material object. God's hand is his power, and he, working invisibly, makes visible things. This, however, is judged mythical rather than true by those who

2. Augustine refers to Genesis 2, which describes the making of the woman from the rib of the man. See Chapter 28 below.

3. On the woman being created to aid in the generation of the species, see the section on "The Status of Women."

use common and everyday works to measure the power and wisdom whereby God understands and is able to produce without seeds the very seeds themselves. Because they do not know about the things that were first established, they find them unbelievable—as though what they do know about human conception and birth would not seem even less believable if they were told to someone who knew nothing about them. Yet, most people attribute the causes of these things as well to natural bodies rather than to the work of the divine mind.

Chapter 27

Plato attributed the creation of certain living things to minor gods who were made by the highest God, and he wished us to understand by this that their immortal part was taken from the highest God himself and the mortal part from the lower gods.[4] He did not want us to think of our souls as coming from these lower gods, but our bodies. Porphyry holds that in order to be purified the soul must escape from the body.[5] Plato and the Platonists agree with this and think that those who have lived an immoderate and dishonorable life must return to the mortal body to pay the penalty for such living. Plato thinks they must return even to the bodies of beasts,[6] but Porphyry thinks they must return only to human bodies. It follows that the gods they speak of, and which they wish us to worship as our parents and makers, are really nothing other than the makers of our shackles and chains. They are not our creators, but our incarcerators and jailers, who lock us up in a very bitter and burdensome prison. Therefore, let the Platonists either stop threatening us with our bodies as a punishment for our souls or stop urging us to worship those gods whose work in us the Platonists themselves exhort us to avoid and escape by all the means in our power! Indeed, both views are as false as can be!

Our souls do not return to this life to be punished, nor is there any other creator of anything in heaven or on earth than he who made heaven and earth. If there is no other cause for living in the body than to undergo punishment, how can it be that, as Plato himself says elsewhere, the world, in order to be most beautiful and most perfect, is filled with every kind of

4. *Timaeus* 41c.
5. On Porphyry, see the note on Plotinus and Porphyry on X. 14.
6. *Republic* X, 620a–c; *Phaedo* 81e–82a; *Phaedrus* 249b; *Timaeus* 42b–c; 91d–92c.

living being, both mortal and immortal?[7] Further, if our creation as mortal
beings with bodies is a divine gift, how can it be a punishment to return to
this body, that is, to a divine blessing? Even more, if God, as Plato constantly asserts, contains in his eternal intelligence all the forms of the whole
world and of all living beings, how can it be that he did not create them
himself?[8] Is it possible that he was unwilling to create those things, the plan
of which was contained in his ineffable and ineffably praiseworthy mind?

Chapter 28

True religion, then, properly acknowledges and proclaims that the creator
of the whole universe is also the creator of all living beings, that is, the
creator of both souls and bodies. For the reason that I have stated, and
perhaps for another greater albeit hidden reason, one single human being
was made by him in his image, preeminent among earthly things. However, that human being was not left alone, for nothing is so social by nature
and yet so full of discord by vice as is this race. Nothing more appropriate
could be spoken by human nature about guarding against the rise of the
vice of discord or about healing it once it has arisen, than the remembrance
that God willed to create as a single being the parent from whom the whole
multitude was to be propagated, in order that through this reminder the
concord of unity might be maintained even in multiplicity. Indeed, that
the woman was made for the man and from his side also clearly signifies
how affectionate the union of husband and wife ought to be.[9]

Because they were first, these works of God are for that reason unusual.
However, anyone who does not believe that they are marvels should not
believe that any deeds are marvels; nor would these works be called "marvels" if they had been produced in the usual course of nature. Yet does
anything arise without purpose under the great governance of divine providence, even though its reason may be hidden? A certain holy psalm says,
"Come and see the works of the Lord, what marvels he has placed upon the
earth" (Ps 46:8). . . .

Because this book must now be concluded, let us consider that in this

7. *Timaeus* 30c–d, 92c.

8. *Timaeus*, 30d.

9. On the union between husband and wife, see also the section on "The Status
of Women."

man who was made first there had arisen—not yet openly but already in the foreknowledge of God—two societies or cities among human beings. From him there were to be all human beings, some to be punished in the society of the wicked angels, others to be rewarded in the society of the good ones. Although the judgment of God is hidden, it is nevertheless just. Since it is written in Scripture, "All the ways of the Lord are mercy and truth" (Ps 25:10), his grace cannot be unjust, nor his justice cruel.

Book XIII

Introduction

In Books XIII and XIV, Augustine broaches a most difficult problem, that of human sinfulness. Book XIII considers in a very poignant manner the reality of death, for Christianity claims that death in all its forms is a result of human sinfulness. A brief sample of Augustine's reflections on this topic is included here. In the selection from Chapter 2, he explains the important distinction between the first and the second death, a topic to which he will return in Book XX. The tenth chapter of the present book is a reflection on how the temporal structure of human life continually and inexorably moves one closer to death, or at least closer to the first death.

Chapter 2

I see that it is necessary to speak a little more diligently about death. Although the human soul is correctly said to be immortal, it also has a certain death of its own. It is called immortal because it does not stop living and feeling in some way, however small. The body, though, is called mortal because it can lose all life and cannot live on its own. The death of the soul occurs when God leaves it, just as the death of the body occurs when the soul leaves it. Therefore, the death of both, which is the death of the whole man, occurs when the soul, abandoned by God, abandons the body. In this case, God is not the life of the soul nor is the soul the life of the body.

This death of the whole man is followed by what the authority of the divine pronouncements call "the second death" (Rev 2:11; 20:6 and 14; 21:8).[1] The Saviour referred to this when he said, "Fear the one who is able to destroy both the soul and the body in hell" (Mt 10:28). Because this does not occur before the soul is joined to the body in such a way that the two

1. On the "second death" of the wicked at the last judgment, see XX. 9.

cannot be separated, it may be wondered how the body can be said to be killed by a death in which it is not abandoned by the soul but rather remains alive and sensitive to pain. In that final and everlasting punishment, which we shall look at more closely in the proper place,[2] the soul is rightly said to die because it does not live from God. How, though, can we say that the body is dead, since it lives from the soul? After all, if it were not alive it could not feel the torments that will follow the resurrection. Is it because any kind of life is good but pain is evil, so that we should not say that the body lives when its soul is a cause of pain rather than of life?

The soul lives from God when it lives well, for it cannot live well unless God brings about good in it. The body lives from the soul when the soul lives in the body, whether the soul lives from God or not. The life in the bodies of the impious is not the life of the soul but of the body. It is a life that even dead souls, that is, souls abandoned by God, are able to bestow on their bodies, since the little life they have on their own, which makes them immortal, does not go away. In the final damnation, even though man does not stop feeling, there is good reason to call this "death" rather than "life" because his feeling is neither sweet with pleasure nor healthy with rest but painful with punishment. It is called a second death because it follows the first, which separates two conjoined natures, whether they be God and the soul or the soul and the body. Concerning the first or bodily death, therefore, we can say that it is good for the good and evil for the evil. The second death, however, because it belongs to none of the good, is without doubt good for no one.

Chapter 10

As soon as we begin to live in this dying body, each one of our actions hastens the approach of death. At every moment of this life (if it is to be called life) our mutability tends toward death. There is certainly no one who is not nearer to death this year than last, tomorrow than today, today than yesterday, a short time from now than now, and now than a short time ago. The amount of time that we have lived is subtracted from our whole life span and what remains is daily being shortened. Our whole life is nothing but a race toward death in which no one is permitted to stand still for a time or to go more slowly, for all men are driven forward with equal momentum and equal speed. One whose life was short lived through a day no more quickly than one whose life was longer. While equal moments

2. See Book XXI.

were snatched from both equally, one was nearer and the other more remote from the goal to which both were racing at equal speed. It is one thing to make a longer journey and another thing to walk at a slower pace. Accordingly, the one who lives longer on his way to death does not proceed at a slower pace but completes a longer journey.

Further, if each person begins to die—that is, to be in death—as soon as death has begun to act in him by taking away life (for when all life has been taken away a man will not then be "in" death but "after" death), then all begin to be in death as soon as they begin to live. What else is happening in all one's days, hours, and individual moments until death is completed? After this comes the time after death, rather than the time during which life was being withdrawn, which was the time in death. Man, therefore, is never in life from the moment he comes to be in this dying rather than living body—that is, if he cannot be in life and death at once. Or should we say that he is in both? Is he in life, a life which he lives until all is consumed, but in death too, which he dies as his life is consumed? If he is not in life, what is it which is consumed until all is gone? If he is not in death, what is this consumption itself? When the whole of life has been consumed from the body, the term "after death" would be meaningless unless that consumption were death. When life has been entirely consumed, if a man is not in death but after death, then when is he in death, except when life is being consumed?

Chapter 14

God, who is the author of natures and not of defects, created man upright. Man, however, was corrupted of his own accord and was justly condemned and gave birth to corrupted and condemned offspring. We were all in that one man, because we were all that one man, who fell into sin through the woman who was made from him before sin. The individual form was not yet created and distributed to us in which we would live as individuals. The seminal nature, however, from which we would be generated was present. This nature, though, becoming defective by sin and bound by the chain of death and justly condemned, could not be born in man in any other state. Thus, from the evil use of free choice, there originated that whole series of disasters in which the human race is led through a sequence of miseries from its deformed origin—as from a corrupted root—to the destruction of the second death, which has no end. Only those who are freed by the grace of God escape this death.

Book XIV

Introduction

This book concludes the third major section of The City of God, *which is devoted to the origins of the earthly and the heavenly cities. Augustine now sets forth his famous teaching on the human will, explaining that love is the most fundamental principle of human action. Our selections begin with his explanation of the crucial distinction between living according to God and living according to man (Chs. 4–6). This is the basic division separating the two cities. In Chapter 7, it is explained that living according to God, or willing and loving what one ought, is what Christians call "charity." Chapters 10 through 13 turn to a reflection on the difficult problem of how the human will originally became sinful. This section is followed by a lengthy discussion on the consequence of sin, which is disordered willing or "lust." Lust takes many forms, one of them being the disordered willing that now accompanies the human sexual impulses. This problem is treated in the selections from Chapters 15 through 24.*

Chapter 4

. . . I have said that two different and contrary cities have sprung up, because some live according to the flesh and others according to the spirit. To put this another way, some live according to man and some according to God. Thus, Paul says very clearly to the Corinthians, "When there is envy and conflict among you, are you not being carnal and walking according to man?" (1 Cor 3:3). To walk according to man, then, is to be carnal, because "flesh,"[1] which is part of a human being, stands for the whole human being.

---

1. The Latin adjective *carnalis* (translated as "carnal") is derived from the noun *caro* (translated as "flesh"). Augustine's point is thus easier to see in Latin: Paul identifies "walking according to man" with being "*carnalis*," but being "*carnalis*" means "to live according to *caro* or the flesh."

The very same people that he calls "carnal," he had earlier called "animal," saying,

> Among men, who knows what belongs to a man except the spirit of man which is in him? In the same way, nobody knows what belongs to God except the spirit of God. We have not, however, received the spirit of this world, but the spirit which is from God, so that we might know those things which are given to us by God. We speak of these things, not in the words taught by human wisdom, but in words taught by the spirit, likening spiritual things with spiritual. The animal man does not perceive what belongs to the spirit of God, for such things are foolishness to him" (1 Cor 2:11–14).

It is to such people—that is, the animal—that Paul later says, "I was not able to speak to you, brothers, as spiritual people, but only as carnal people" (1 Cor 3:1). With both "animal" and "carnal," Paul's manner of speaking is the same: the part represents the whole. Both the soul and the flesh,[2] which are parts of a human being, can signify the whole human being. Therefore, animal man and carnal man are not different, but the same— that is, man living according to man.[3] . . .

Chapter 5

There is no need to blame the nature of the flesh for our sins and defects and in so doing wrong the creator, because within its own kind and order the flesh is good. It is not good, however, to live according to a created good by turning our backs on the goodness of the creator. This is true whether we choose to live according to the flesh or according to the soul or according to the whole human being which is composed of flesh and soul (and which can be designated by either the word "flesh" alone or the word "soul" alone). Thus, he who praises the nature of the soul as the highest good and condemns the nature of the flesh as evil loves the soul in a carnal way and flees the flesh in a carnal way, for this view is based on human vanity not divine truth. Indeed, unlike the Manichaeans, the Platonists do not despise the nature of the earthly body as evil, because they attribute to God the creator all the elements of which this visible

2. The Latin adjective *animalis* (translated in this passage as "animal") is derived from the noun *anima* (translated here as "soul").

3. Augustine's point is thus that for Paul the crucial distinction within human nature is not the distinction between body and soul (between "carnal" and "animal"), but between man living according to man and man living according to God.

and tangible world is composed, and their qualities.[4] . . .

Chapter 6

The condition of the human will is of great importance, for if the will is twisted, its acts will be twisted. If, on the other hand, it is upright, not only will its acts be blameless but even praiseworthy. The will is in all the soul's acts. Indeed, these acts are nothing other than acts of the will. After all, what are desire and joy except the will consenting to the things that we will? What are fear and sadness except the will dissenting from the things that we do not will? When we consent to seeking the things that we will, this is called "desire." When we consent to enjoying the things we will, it is called "joy." In the same way, when we dissent from the things that we do not will to happen, such an act of will is called "fear." When we will to avoid the things that happen even though we did not will them to happen, this is called "sadness." In general, as the human will is attracted or repelled in accordance with the variety of things that are sought or shunned, so it is changed and turned into this or that attraction or repulsion.

Therefore, the human being who lives according to God and not according to man should be a lover of good and, consequently, a hater of evil. Because no one is evil by nature but only by defect, he who lives according to God ought to have a perfect hatred for evil. Thus, he will neither hate the man on account of the defect nor love the defect on account of the man, but hate the defect and love the man. Once the defect is healed, what will remain is everything that ought to be loved and nothing that ought to be hated.

Chapter 7

The one who proposes to love God and his neighbor as himself, not according to man but according to God, is without doubt said because of this love to be a man of good will. This good will is most commonly called "charity" in the holy scriptures, but the same sacred writings also call it "love."[5] Thus, the apostle says that the one chosen to rule the people must

4. The Manichaeans argued that the body was created not by the good God but by an evil power. On Manichaeism, see the note on I. 20 and the introduction to the section on "War."

5. In this chapter, Augustine is trying to explain the various Latin words used to describe Christian love. He discusses the nouns translated as "charity" (*caritas*) and "love" (*amor*), and the verbs "to love" (*amare*) and "to cherish" (*diligere*).

be a lover of the good (cf. Tt 1:8). When the Lord himself questioned the apostle Peter he asked, "Do you cherish me more than these?" Peter replied, "Lord, you know I love you." Again the Lord asked, not whether Peter loved him but whether Peter cherished him. Again, Peter answered, "Lord, you know I love you." On the third questioning, however, Jesus himself does not ask, "Do you cherish me?" but "Do you love me?" At this point the evangelist says: "Peter was saddened that he asked him a third time 'Do you love me?'" even though the Lord did not ask three times but only once, "Do you love me?" He did, however, ask twice, "Do you cherish me?" From this, we see that when the Lord asked "Do you cherish me?" he meant the same as "Do you love me?" Peter, however, did not change his word for this one thing but on the third occasion answered, "Lord, you know everything, you know I love you" (Jn 21:15–7).

I thought it necessary to mention this here because some think that cherishing or charity is one thing and love another. They say that "cherishing" is used in a good sense and "love" in a bad one. It is most certain, however, that the secular writers themselves have not spoken in this way. The philosophers will determine whether these are different and why; nonetheless, their books say enough to show that they prize love highly when it is directed toward good things and even God himself. It was necessary to point out, though, that the Scriptures of our religion, whose authority we place above that of all other writings, do not say that love is one thing and cherishing or charity another, for I have now shown that "love" is used in a positive sense.

If anyone thinks that "love" is said of both good and bad things while "cherishing" is only said of good things, let him attend to what is written in the psalm, "He who cherishes iniquity hates his own soul" (Ps 11:5), as well as to what the apostle John says: "If someone cherishes the world, the cherishing of the Father is not in him" (1 Jn 2:15). Note that "cherishing" is used in both senses, good and bad, in the same passage. If someone should demand an example of "love" in the bad sense (because I have already shown it used in the good sense), let him read the scripture, "Men, indeed, will be loving toward themselves and lovers of money" (2 Tm 3:2).

Therefore, an upright will is good love and a twisted will is bad love. A love, then, that longs to have what is loved is "desire." A love that possesses and enjoys what is loved is "joy." A love that flees what is opposed to what

---

Translating *diligere* as "cherish" may sound somewhat odd in contemporary English, but it is necessary in order to preserve the distinction between *amare* and *diligere* in this chapter.

is loved is "fear," and if that opposite should occur, what love feels is "sadness." Consequently, these feelings are evil if the love is bad and good if the love is good.

What I say here can be proved from Scripture. The apostle desires to die to be with Christ (Phil 1:23); and, "My soul desired to long for your judgments" (Ps 119:20); or it might be better to say, "My soul longed to desire your judgments"; and again, "The desire for wisdom leads to the kingdom" (Wis 6:20). Nevertheless, in customary usage, "desire" and "longing" can be understood only in a bad sense if their object is not specified. "Joy" is understood in the good sense: "Rejoice in the Lord and exult, you just ones" (Ps 23:11); and "You give joy to my heart" (Ps 4:7); and again, "You will fill me with joy in your countenance" (Ps 16:11). "Fear" is used in a good sense by the apostle when he says: "Work out your salvation with fear and trembling" (Phil 2:12); and "Do not be haughty, but fear" (Rom 11:20); and again, "I fear that, just as the serpent seduced Eve by his tricks, so your minds might be turned away from the chastity which is in Christ" (2 Cor 11:3). As for "sadness," Cicero usually calls it "sickness" and Virgil "suffering," as when he says, "they suffer and rejoice."[6] I, however, prefer to call it "sadness" because "sickness" or "suffering" are more usually said of the body. The question of whether it can be used in a good sense is more difficult to answer.

Chapter 10

It is not unreasonable to ask whether before the fall the first human being, or rather the first human beings (indeed, there was a marriage of two people), had in their animal bodies such sentiments as we will lack in our spiritual bodies when sin is at last purged and ended. If they did, how were they happy in that memorable place of bliss we call "paradise"? After all, who can be called absolutely happy if he is troubled by fear or suffering?

What could men fear or suffer in the midst of such an abundance of goods, where neither death nor sickness of the body was feared, where nothing was missing which a good will might want, and where nothing was present which might prevent a human being from living a happy life, both physically and mentally? Their love of God was undisturbed, as was their love for each other in marriage, living in a faithful and sincere partnership. From this love came great joy, because what they loved was always present. The avoidance of sin was tranquil, and as long as this lasted no evil from

---

6. See *Tusculan Disputations* III. 10. 22–23. *Aeneid* VI. 733.

any source capable of causing sadness could invade their lives.

Or could it have been that those first human beings did strongly desire to touch and eat the forbidden fruit but were afraid to die? Did desire and fear, then, already plague them, even in that place? By no means! We cannot consider this to have been true where there was no sin. Indeed, it is a sin to desire those things which God's law prohibits and to abstain from them out of fear of punishment rather than love of justice. By no means, I say, should we think that before the fall there was already the same sort of sin committed with respect to that forbidden fruit as the one of which the Lord speaks when he says: "If someone should look at a woman with lust, he has already committed adultery with her in his heart" (Mt 5:28).

Therefore, just as the first human beings were happy and free from mental distress and bodily discomfort, so the whole human society would have been happy if these first human beings had not transmitted this evil to their posterity and if each of their descendents had not committed in iniquity what they would receive in condemnation.

This happiness would have continued until, by that blessing which says, "Increase and multiply" (Gn 1:28), the number of predestined saints had been completed. They would have then been given that higher happiness which the most blessed angels have been given, where it would be certain that no one would sin and no one would die. Such would have been the life of the saints without the experience of labor, sorrow, and death. It is just this sort of life that the saints will enjoy when, after having experienced these evils, their bodies are resurrected from the dead and restored to incorruptibility.

Chapter 11

Yet, because God forsees everything, he knew that human beings would sin. We ought, then, to make our declarations about the holy city according to what God foresaw and planned, and not according to what cannot attain the status of knowledge for us since it was not in God's plan. Man could not alter the divine plan by his sin, as if God could be forced to change what he has established. God's foreknowledge anticipated how evil man, whom he created good, would become, as well as what good God himself would still draw forth from him. Even though God is said to change what he establishes (so that in a metaphorical way the Scriptures even say that God repented),[7] this is said with respect to what human beings had expected or

---

7. See, for example, Gn 6:6; Ex 32:14; 1 Sam 15:11.

with respect to the order of natural causes, and not with respect to what the Almighty foreknew he would do.

Therefore, God, as it is written, "made man upright" (Eccl 7:29) and hence possessing a good will. If man had not had a good will, he would not have been upright. A good will, therefore, is the work of God and he created man with it. The first evil will, which preceded all evil human works, was less a single deed than a falling away from the work of God to its own works. Thus, works are evil because they are done according to the will itself rather than according to God. The will, or the human being himself insofar as his will is evil, is like the bad tree producing bad fruit (Mt 7:17).

Further, although an evil will is not according to nature, but contrary to nature, since it is a defect, it nevertheless belongs to the nature of which it is a defect, for it cannot exist except in a nature. Moreover, it can only exist in a nature created from nothing and not in another the creator generates from himself, as he generated the Word through which all things were made. Even if God formed human beings from the dust of the earth, that same earth and all earthly materials come completely from nothing, as does the soul, which God made from nothing and gave to the body when he created man.

Even though evils are allowed to exist in order to demonstrate how the most provident justice of the creator can use them for good, they are nevertheless so overpowered by goods that goods can exist without them. This is the case with the true and highest God himself, as well as with every invisible and visible creature above the misty air of the heavens. Evils, on the other hand, cannot exist without goods, because the natures in which evils exist are good insofar as they are natures. Moreover, evil is removed not by removing any nature or part of a nature that evil brings to a thing, but by healing and correcting what evil has damaged and deformed.

The choice of the will, then, is truly free when it is not the slave of vices and sins. Such freedom was given by God. Lost through its own fault, it cannot be returned except by God, who is the only one who had the ability to give it in the first place. Thus, the Truth proclaims: "If the Son frees us, then we are truly free" (Jn 8:36). This is the same as saying: If the Son saves you, you are truly saved. Indeed, he is our liberator insofar as he is our savior.

Man once lived according to God in a corporeal and spiritual paradise. This was not simply a corporeal paradise for the good of the body and not a spiritual paradise for the good of the mind. Nor was it simply a spiritual paradise offering human beings enjoyment through the internal senses and not also a corporeal paradise offering them enjoyment through the external senses. . . .

Chapter 12

One might be disturbed by the question, Why is human nature not changed by other sins as it was by the sinful collusion of those first two human beings? The first sin subjected human nature to a corruption we see and feel, and thus to death also. Human nature was perturbed and tossed about by many and contrary emotions to which it was not subject in paradise before the fall, even though it existed in an animal body. If, as I said, anyone is troubled by this, he ought not suppose that the first sin was trivial and unimportant simply because it was about food—a food that was not evil and injurious except insofar as it was forbidden. Nor should one think that God would have created and planted anything evil in such a happy place.

Rather, obedience was commanded by God's precept. This virtue is, as it were, the mother and guardian of all the virtues in a rational creature. For such a creature, submission is advantageous, whereas exercising its own will against the one who created it is ruinous. The prohibition against eating this one kind of food where there was such an abundance of other kinds was such an easy precept to observe and such a brief one to remember, especially since the will was not yet opposed by desire, which only followed afterwards as the punishment for the sin! Hence, the injustice in violating the precept was all the greater given the extreme ease by which it might have been kept.

Chapter 13

The first human beings, having become evil in secret, openly fell into disobedience. After all, the evil work would not have been done unless an evil will preceded it. Further, how can the will begin to be evil except through pride? Thus, "The beginning of all sin is pride" (Sir 10:13). What, though, is pride, but the longing for wrongful exaltation? This exalting is wrong when the mind deserts the principle to which it ought to cling and becomes, as it were, its own principle. This happens when it takes too much pleasure in itself and falls away from that unchangeable good which ought to please it much more than it is able to please itself. This falling away comes from the will itself because, if the will had remained established in the love of the higher unchangeable good—through which it is illuminated so that it might understand and is inflamed so that it might love—then it would not have turned away to find satisfaction in itself, thereby making itself cold and dark. The woman would not have believed that the serpent spoke the truth; nor would the man have placed the will of his wife over the precept of God, thinking the transgression against this precept a venial matter and not abandoning the partner of his life, even though the partnership was one of sin.

It follows that the evil act—that is, the transgression involved in eating the prohibited food—was perpetrated by those who were already evil. That evil fruit could only come from an evil tree (Mt 7:18). That the tree should become evil was contrary to nature, because it could only come about through a defect of the will, which is contrary to nature. A nature, though, could not be deformed through a defect unless it were made from nothing. Thus, its existence as a nature results from its being created by God, but its falling away from God results from its being made from nothing. When human beings turned away from God in this way, they did not fall into pure nothingness. Rather, as a result of their being inclined to themselves they became less than they were when they clung to him who exists most perfectly. . . .

Therefore, humility is especially recommended in the city of God as it journeys in this world. The humility of the king of this city, who is Christ, is especially proclaimed. The opposite of this virtue, the defect of pride, especially dominates his adversary, who is the devil, as is said in Holy Scripture. Surely, this is the great difference that can be discerned between the two cities of which we are speaking. The one is a society of the pious and the other of the impious, each having its own angels associated with it. In the one prevailed the love of God; in the other, the love of oneself. . . .

Chapter 15

. . . Whoever thinks that this sort of condemnation is either excessive or unjust does not know how to judge the gravity of a sin that was so easy to avoid. Just as Abraham's obedience is rightly proclaimed to be great because what he was commanded to do—kill his son—was most difficult, so in paradise the disobedience was even greater because what was commanded was not at all difficult. Just as the obedience of the second man was more praiseworthy because he "became obedient even to death" (Phil 2:8),[8] so the disobedience of the first man was more detestable because he became disobedient even to death. Indeed, where the penalty laid down for disobedience is great and the matter commanded by the Creator is easy,

---

8. By "the second man," Augustine means Christ.

who can sufficiently explain how evil it is not to obey in an easy matter the command of so great a power threatening so great a punishment?

To put it briefly, in the punishment of that sin, what was the retribution for disobedience if not disobedience itself? What else is man's misery if not his disobedience to himself? Because he was unwilling to do what he could, now he wants to do what he cannot. Even though he could not do everything in paradise before the fall, he did not want to do what he could not do and so was able to do everything he wanted. . . .

Bodily pain is nothing but an aversion of the soul arising from the flesh and a sort of dissenting from what happens to the flesh, just as the mental pain called "sadness" is a dissenting from those things which happen to us against our will. Sadness, however, is most often preceded by fear, which is in the soul, not in the flesh. Bodily pain is not preceded by any sort of fear that would be experienced in the flesh before the pain.

Pleasure, on the other hand, is preceded by a certain craving that is felt in the flesh as its own desire, as in hunger thirst, and what with respect to the genital organs is usually called "lust"—although this is also the general term for all desire.[9] The ancients, for example, defined anger as nothing other than the lust for revenge, even though a man is sometimes angry even at inanimate things, which do not feel his vengeance, as when he smashes a style or breaks a pen which writes badly. Although irrational, this is still a sort of lust for revenge and, so to speak, a strange shadow of the notion of retribution, according to which those who do evil should suffer it.

Therefore, there is a lust for revenge that is called "anger." There is a lust to possess money called "greed." There is a lust to overcome in any way whatsoever called "stubbornness." There is a lust for glory called "bragging." There are many and various lusts, some having names of their own and some not. Who, indeed, can easily say what we should call that lust to dominate, which is often so strong in the souls of tyrants, as civil wars testify?

Chapter 16

Therefore, there are lusts for many things, but when "lust" is used without specifying the object, then what usually occurs to the mind is almost always the lust involving the arousal of the private parts of the body. This

---

9. In this passage Augustine distinguishes between two senses of the Latin word *libido* or "lust." On the one hand *libido* can mean sexual lust; on the other it can mean desire in general or *cupiditas*. In this volume, *libido* is always translated as "lust."

lust overcomes not only the whole body, nor only outwardly, but also inwardly; it carries away the whole human being with a conjunction and mixture of mental emotion and bodily craving, so that the resulting pleasure is the greatest of all bodily pleasures. Indeed, at the moment when it reaches its high point, almost all sharpness and, one could say, alertness of thought are overwhelmed.[10]

What friend of wisdom and holy joy, living the married life but, as the apostle warns, "knowing that he possesses his vessel in holiness and honor, not in the affliction of desire, as do the peoples who do not know God" (1 Thes 4:4–5), would not prefer, if he could, to procreate children without this lust? If this could be done, then in performing the duty to procreate the bodily parts created for this purpose would not be excited by the agitation of lust, but would function at the command of the will, as do other parts of the body in the exercise of their functions.

In fact, not even lovers of this pleasure, whether they seek it in marital intercourse or in shameful impurity, are moved to it whenever they might wish. Rather, sometimes the impulse troubles them when they do not want it and sometimes it deserts them when they do, the mind seething with the desire while the body is cold. Thus, astonishingly, lust not only fails to serve the will to bring forth children, but also the lust for lascivious gratification. Although it is often completely opposed to the resisting mind, it is sometimes opposed to itself, moving the mind, but leaving the body unmoved.

Chapter 18

The act itself to which one is impelled by such lust is always done in secret, not only in the case of rape, which requires a hiding place to escape human law courts, but also in the use of prostitutes, which the earthly city disgracefully allows. Although the law of that city does not punish this act, even lust that is permitted and unpunished avoids public scrutiny. On account of a natural sense of shame, secrecy is provided even in brothels, and it was easier for lewdness to eliminate the restrictions of legal prohibitions than for shamelessness to remove the privacy surrounding that foulness. Indeed, even the disgraceful call this prostitution disgraceful; though they love it, they dare not indulge it openly.

What about marital intercourse, which, according to the matrimonial

---

10. The words translated here as "sharpness" and "alertness" (*acies* and *vigilia*) also have military overtones. Thus, the phrase could be translated as ". . . almost the whole front line and sentries of thought are overrun."

code of law, is done for the procreation of children? Although it is right and honorable, is not even it performed in a private room away from witnesses? Before the bridegroom even begins to caress the bride, does he not send out all the servants and even the groomsmen and anyone else who had been permitted to enter the bridal chamber on account of kinship? Since, as "the greatest Roman authority on eloquence" said,[11] all right acts wish to be placed in the light—or in other words, wish to be known—this right act wishes to be known yet blushes to be seen.[12] Who does not know what a married couple do in order to bear children? Is this not why wives are married with such celebration? Nonetheless, when this act which brings about children is performed, not even those children who have already been born are allowed to witness it. Thus, this right act seeks to be known by the light of the mind but hides from the light of the eyes. Why is this so if not because that act, which by nature is fitting and decent, is done with shame, which is the penalty for sin?

Chapter 22

I have no doubt that, according to the blessing of God, to increase, multiply, and fill the earth is the gift of marriage as God established it from the beginning, before the fall. He created a male and a female, a sexual difference quite evident in the flesh. It was to this work of God that the blessing was attached, for when the scripture says, "Male and female he created them," it continues, "God blessed them saying, 'increase and multiply and fill the earth and dominate it'" (Gn 1:27–28), and so on.

Although all of this can be appropriately understood in a spiritual way, male and female cannot be understood as a metaphor for two things existing in a single human being simply because there is plainly in him one thing which rules and another which is ruled.[13] Rather, it is a great absurdity to deny that, as is most evident, human beings were created male and female with bodies of different sexes in order that they might increase, multiply, and fill the earth by generating offspring. When the Lord was asked whether it was permitted for someone to divorce his wife for any reason, since Moses permitted a decree of divorce to be given on account of the hardness of the hearts of the Israelites, his answer was not about the spirit which commands, nor about the flesh which obeys, nor about the

---

11. The Roman poet Lucan (A.D. 39–65) says this of Cicero in *Pharsalia* 7, 62.

12. See Cicero's *Tusculan Disputations* II. 26. 64.

13. On this metaphor, see the section on "The Status of Women."

rational soul which rules, nor about irrational desire which is ruled, nor about contemplative virtue which is higher, nor about active virtue which is subordinate, nor about the understanding of the mind, nor about the senses of the body, but clearly about the union of marriage by which both sexes are mutually bound to each other. He said, "Have you not read that he who created them in the beginning, created them male and female and said to them: "for this reason a man will leave his father and mother and cling to his wife and the two will become one flesh?" So they are not now two, but one flesh. Therefore, what God has joined, man must not separate" (Mt 19:4–5).

It is certain, then, that the first human beings were created male and female, as we see and know two human beings of different sexes to be now. They are called "one" either because of the marriage union or because of the origin of the woman who was created from the side of the man. Through this original example, a precedent which God established, the apostle admonishes everyone that men should love their wives (Eph 5:25; Col 3:19).

Chapter 24

When, and as often as, it was necessary to produce offspring, the man would have planted the seed and the woman would have received it, their genital organs being moved by the will, not by the excitement of lust. We not only move at will those parts of the body composed of rigid and jointed bones—such as hands, feet, and fingers—but also the nonrigid parts having pliant tendons. When we want, we can move them by shaking, extend them by stretching, bend them by twisting, and harden them by constricting, as we do with the mouth and face. The lungs, which are the softest of the internal organs except for the marrow—and because of this are protected in the cavity of the chest—serve the will by inhaling and exhaling and by emitting or modifying sounds, like the bellows of blacksmiths or organists. They do this in breathing, blowing, speaking, shouting, and singing. I omit here discussion of certain animals who are naturally able to move a particular place on the hide that covers their whole bodies if they feel something there that they want to drive away. This ability is so developed that by a quivering of the hide they can not only shake off flies that have settled on them but also spears that have pierced them.

Could it be true that, because human beings lack this ability, the creator was not able to give it to whatever living things he wished? Thus, human beings, too, might have been able to have the obedience of their lower parts had they not lost it through their own disobedience. Indeed, it was not difficult for God to form them in such a way that those parts of the body which are now moved only by lust should have been moved only by the will. . . .

Chapter 25

No one lives as he wishes save the happy, and no one is happy save the just. Even the just man himself does not live as he wishes until he has reached that place where he cannot in any way die, be deceived, or be hurt, and until he is certain that these things will never happen to him. Indeed, his nature requires this, and he will not be fully and perfectly happy until he attains what his nature requires.

What human being is now able to live as he wishes when life itself is not in his power? Though he wants to live, he is compelled to die. In what way, then, does he live as he wishes when he does not live as long as he wishes? If he wishes to die, in what way is he able to live as he wishes when he does not wish to live? Furthermore, if he wishes to die, not because he does not wish to live, but so that after death he might live a better life, he is still not yet living as he wishes, but will do so when, by dying, he has attained what he wishes.

Look at a man living as he wishes because he tortured and commanded himself not to wish what he cannot have and to wish only what he can. As Terence says, "Because you cannot do what you want, want what you can do."[14] Is a person like this happy because he is patiently miserable? One does not possess the happy life if one does not love it. Further, if the happy life is loved and possessed, it is necessary that it be loved more than anything else, because everything else that is loved must be loved for the sake of that happy life. Moreover, if the happy life is loved as much as it deserves to be (for he is not happy who does not love the happy life as it deserves to be loved), then he who loves it in this way cannot but wish it to be eternal. Therefore, life will be happy only when it is eternal.

Chapter 28

The two cities, therefore, were created by two loves: the earthly city by love of oneself, even to the point of contempt for God; the heavenly city by the love of God, even to the point of contempt for oneself. The first glories

14. *Andria* 305–6. Terence (195–c. 159) was a famous comic playwriter.

in itself, the second in the Lord. The first seeks glory from human beings; God, who is the witness of the conscience, is the greatest glory of the other. The first lifts its head in its own glory; the second says to its God, "You are my glory and the one who raises my head" (Ps 3:3). The first, its princes and the nations that it subjugates, is dominated by the lust to dominate; in the second, all mutually serve one another in charity, the leaders through their counsel and the subjects through their obedience. The first, in its princes, loves its own strenth; the second says to its God, "I will love you, Lord, my strength" (Ps 18:1).

Therefore, the wise of the first city, living according to man, have sought the goods of the body or of the soul or of both. Those among them who were able to know God "did not honor him as God or give him thanks, but they disappeared into their own thoughts and their foolish hearts were darkened, and all the while they were telling themselves they were wise"— that is, dominated by pride, they exalted themselves in their own wisdom—"and became fools, changing the glory of the incorruptible God into the images of corruptible man, birds, four-footed animals, and serpents"—for in adoring images of this sort they were either leaders or followers of the people—"and they honored and served creatures more than the creator, who is blessed forever" (Rom 1:21–25). In the other city, there is nothing of human wisdom except the piety by which the true God is rightly worshipped, for it expects to find its reward in the company of the holy ones, not only of human beings, but also of angels, "so that God may be all in all" (1 Cor 15:28).

Book XV

Introduction

Having finished his treatment of the origins of the two cities, Augustine now takes up a discussion of their development or progress. This discussion constitutes the fourth major section of The City of God *and will require four books for its completion. Book XV is devoted to an analysis of the development of the two cities during the period from Cain through Noah. The analysis begins with an explanation of how the struggle between the earthly and heavenly cities was foreshadowed in the relationship between the free woman Sarah and the slave woman Hagar, as discussed by Paul in his letter to the Galatians (Ch. 2). Also included in our selections from Book XV are Augustine's profound reflections on the story of Cain and Abel (Gn 4) and on the strange story about the love of the sons of God for the daughters of mankind, found at the beginning of Genesis 6.*

Chapter 2

When the time came for the heavenly city to be manifested, there appeared on earth a certain shadow and prophetic image of it by which it was signified rather than openly exhibited. The shadow itself was also rightly called the "holy city," not because it was the complete reality destined to exist in the future, but because it was a signifying image of it. In the Letter to the Galatians, Paul speaks of this subservient image and the free city that it prefigures:

> Tell me, you who want to be under the law, do you not hear the law? It is written that Abraham had two sons, one with a slave woman and one with a free woman. However, the son of the slave woman was born according to the flesh; the son of the free woman was born through the promise. These things are an allegory. They are the two covenants. One is from Mount Sinai, giving birth into slavery; that is Hagar. Sinai is a mountain in Arabia, which

corresponds to what is now Jerusalem, which is enslaved with her children. That Jerusalem which is above, however, is free; she is our mother, for it is written:

> Rejoice, you who are barren, who do not bear,
> break forth and cry out, you who are not in labor.
> For many are the children of the abandoned,
> more than she who has a husband (Is 54:1).

We, brothers, are children of the promise, after Isaac. However, as in those days, he who had been born according to the flesh persecuted him who was born according to the spirt, so is it now. Yet what does Scripture say? "Cast out that slave woman and her son, for the son of the slave woman will not inherit with the son of the free woman" (Gn 21:10). We, brothers, are not children of the slave woman, but of the free woman, by means of the freedom by which Christ has made us free (Gal 4:21–31).

This kind of interpretation,[1] handed down with apostolic authority, shows us how we ought to understand the writings of the two covenants, the old and the new. A certain part of the earthly city has been made into an image of the heavenly city. It stands not for itself, but for that other city, and that is why it is its slave. It was established not for its own sake but for the sake of representing the other city.

Moreover, this image was itself preceded and prefigured by another image, for Hagar, Sarah's slave, and her son were an image of this image. Because with the coming of the light the shadows were about to pass away, the free Sarah—who represented the free city, and of whom Hagar, the shadow, was also the slave in this other manner of signifying—said, "Cast out that slave woman and her son, for the son of the slave woman will not inherit with my son Isaac" (Gn 21:10), or, as the apostle said, "with the son of the free woman" (Gal 4:30).

Therefore, we find in the earthly city two things: one is its own clear and immediate existence and the other is its enslavement to the heavenly city of which it is the image. Citizens of the earthly city are produced through a nature corrupted by sin, but citizens of the heavenly city by

1. By "this kind of interpretation," Augustine means the interpretation which seeks the figurative or allegorical sense of the text. In this sort of interpretation, it is asserted that the historical or literal events described in the Old Testament also refer to later historical events or realities. Another example of Augustine's use of this sort of exegesis, which was very common among Christians, can be found in XVI. 41.

grace, which liberates nature from sin. Thus, the former are called "vessels of wrath"; the latter "vessels of mercy" (Rom 9:22–23). This was also pre-figured in the two sons of Abraham. Ishmael was born to the slave woman called Hagar according to the flesh; Isaac was born to the free woman Sarah according to the promise. Indeed, both are from the seed of Abraham. However, custom, reflecting nature, produced the one; a promise, signify-ing grace, gave the other. In the former case, human practice is displayed; in the latter, divine kindness is shown.

Chapter 4

The earthly city will not last forever, for when it is condemned to final punishment, it will cease to be a city. It possesses its own good here and now, and it is made joyful through its association with the joy that may be derived from such things. Because its good is not the sort of good that causes no difficulties for its lovers, this city is most often divided against itself by lawsuits, wars, and conflicts, and by victories that either cause death or are themselves subject to death. Out of whichever part of itself that has risen up to wage war against another part of itself, this city seeks to be the conqueror of peoples while being itself the captive of vices. If indeed its pride is elevated because it conquers, then its victory causes death. If, however, considering the common circumstances and vicissitudes of hu-man life, the earthly city is troubled by possible adversities more than it is inflated by the successes that have already occurred, then its victory is itself subject to death, for it will not be able to dominate permanently those whom it was able to subjugate through conquest.

Nevertheless, it is not right to say that the things this city desires are not good, because, in its own human way, it is better by desiring them, for in order to obtain these base things, it desires a certain earthly peace. This peace it strives to obtain through war. If it triumphs and there is no one left to resist, there will be peace, which the parts of the city struggling against each other did not have before, for they were struggling miserably in a condition of scarcity in order to obtain the things they could not all have. Exhausting wars try to obtain this peace, and whatever achieves it is con-sidered a glorious victory.

When, however, those fighting with the more just cause triumph, who doubts that the victory should be celebrated and that the hoped-for peace has arrived? These things are good and without doubt they are gifts of God. If, however, to the neglect of better goods, the ones pertaining to the city on high, where victory will be secure in the eternal and highest peace, these lower goods are desired in such a way that they are believed to be the only goods, or else are loved more than the goods believed to be better, then misery necessarily follows and the misery that was already present increases.[2]

Chapter 7

. . . What all people do who follow their own will rather than God's, and who live by a twisted rather than an upright heart, is to offer God a gift, thinking they can buy him off so that he will serve them, not by healing their deformed desires, but by fulfilling them. This is typical of the earthly city. It worships God or the gods by whose assistance it may reign in victory and in earthly peace, not with the charity of caring but with the desire for dominating. Truly, the good use this world in order to enjoy God, but the wicked, on the other hand, want to use God in order to enjoy the world—at least those wicked people who still believe that God exists and cares about human affairs do so. There are many who do not even believe that and are thus worse.

Thus, when Cain learned that God had looked favorably upon the sacrifice of his sibling and not upon his own, he should have changed and imitated his good brother, and not have become envious and proud. Yet he became depressed and his face fell. God greatly reprimands this sin, the sin of being sad because of another's good—and a brother's good at that.

Indeed, God asked Cain an accusing question, "Why are you sad, and why did your face fall?" (Gn 4:6), for God saw that Cain was envious of his brother and he reprimanded Cain. Human beings, from whom the heart of another is hidden, could be uncertain and quite unsure whether, through this sadness, Cain was grieving because of his own wrongdoing, which he had learned had displeased God, or because of the good of his brother, which God, in looking with favor on his sacrifice, had found pleasing. God, however, explained that he had not been willing to accept Cain's oblation so that Cain would be displeased with himself, as was proper, rather than with his brother, as was wrong. In doing so he showed Cain that, although he was unjust in "not distinguishing correctly" (Gn 4:7), that is, in not living correctly, and although he was unworthy of having his oblation accepted, he was even more unjust in hating his just brother without cause. . . .

2. This discussion of peace should be compared with XIX. 11–13.

Chapter 22

As the human race advanced and grew, the free choice of the will brought about a mixing of the two cities, and even, by their participation in iniquity, a sort of blending of them. Evil once again found its cause in the female sex, though not in the same way as originally, for these women were not seduced by anyone's tricks, nor did they persuade men to sin.[3] From the start, however, there were women with deformed morals in the earthly city, that is, in the society of the earthborn. For the sake of their beautiful bodies, they were loved by the sons of God, that is to say, by the citizens of the other city who were journeying in this world (Gn 6:1–2).

To be sure, the good of bodily beauty is a gift of God, but he lavishes it even upon the wicked so that it will not seem to the good to be a great good. Abandoning the great good that was peculiar to the good resulted in a fall to the lowest good, which was not peculiar to the good but common to the good and the wicked. In this way, the sons of God were ensnared by their love of the daughters of men, and in order to enjoy them in marriage they stooped to the morals of the society of the earthborn, abandoning the piety they had observed in the holy society.

The beauty of the body, then, was indeed made by God, but it is a temporal, carnal, and lower good. When placed above God, who is the eternal, internal, and everlasting good, it is loved wrongly. It is just like the case of the greedy man. When he abandons justice for the love of gold, it is not the gold that sins but the man. So it is with everything created. Although it is good, it can be loved both rightly and wrongly. It is loved rightly when the correct order is preserved; wrongly when that order is violated. I have expressed this briefly in these verses in praise of a candle:[4]

> These things are yours, and they are good, because you who have
>   created them are good.
> Nothing in them is ours, except our sin in neglecting your order
> By loving what you have established instead of loving you.

---

3. Augustine is referring to the story recorded in Gn 6:1–3, in which the sons of God lust for the beautiful bodies of the daughters of man.

4. It is generally surmised that the candle to which Augustine refers in these beautiful verses must be a votive candle of some sort, or perhaps even the Easter candle.

Book XVI

Introduction

Augustine now concentrates his efforts on explaining the development of the heavenly city from Noah to David. Relatively early in Book XVI, while tracing the lines of descent of the human race after the flood, he considers the monstrous races recorded by pagan authors. This leads him to raise the important question about whether or not the human species has a common origin (Ch. 8). The following selection is taken from Augustine's discussion of the life of Abraham. Augustine there considers God's judgment on Sodom and Abraham's perhaps deceitful practice of passing Sarah off as his sister rather than his wife (Ch. 30). In the selection from Chapter 35, which may be compared with Book XVIII, Chapter 46, our author comments briefly on relations between Jews and Christians. Chapter 41 of the present book contains Augustine's interpretation of Jacob's blessing of Judah as recorded in Genesis 49. This is a good example of the Christian practice of interpreting the Old Testament according to its figurative or allegorical rather than its merely literal or historical sense. One basis for this procedure was given by Paul himself in the passage from Galatians that Augustine discussed in Book XV, Chapter 2. Also included in this volume is the final chapter of Book XVI, in which Augustine recounts the events pertaining to the life of Moses.

Chapter 8

. . . It is not necessary to believe in the existence of all the races of human beings that are said to exist.[1] Yet, whoever anywhere is born a human being, that is, a rational, mortal animal, however unusual to our senses the form, color, movements, or sounds of his body might seem, whatever the

---

1. In the omitted portion of the chapter, Augustine has been discussing accounts of various bizarre and fabulous races of human beings.

power, parts, or quality of his nature might be, none of the faithful should
doubt but that he stems from that one original human being. Nevertheless,
what nature maintains for the most part can be clearly distinguished from
what is, by its very rarity, extraordinary.

The sort of reason that is given to explain monstrous births among us
can be given to explain monstrous peoples: God is the creator of all things.
He himself knows where and when something ought to be created or to
have been created. Knowing the beauty of the universe, he weaves together
both likenesses and differences out of its parts. Nevertheless, anyone who
is unable to view the whole is on that account offended by the deformity of
the part, since he is ignorant of its fitness or proper relationship to the
whole. . . .

Who would be able to recount all the human offspring so completely
different from those who are most certainly their parents? Hence, just as it
cannot be denied that these offspring stem from that one first man, so it is
concerning any peoples who are reported to have deviated through bodily
differences from the usual course of nature to which most, indeed nearly
all, human beings hold. If they are defined as rational and mortal animals,
then it must be acknowledged that they derive from that very same, single,
first father of all.

In saying this, we assume that the things which are reported about the
diversity of those races and the great differences that separate them from
one another and from us are in fact true. Indeed, if we did not know that
the various apes and monkeys are not human beings but beasts, the historians[2] who pride themselves on their curiosity could, through unrestrained
vanity, fabricate for us new races of human beings! Suppose that those who
are described by means of such wonders are in fact human beings. Perhaps
then God wanted also to create some peoples in that way to keep us from
thinking that the wisdom by which he fashioned human nature had blun-
dered in the case of the monstrosities that would be born among us from
human beings, like the art of some less than perfect craftsman. Therefore,
it ought not seem absurd to us that, just as within individual races of human beings there are monstrous births, so within all of humankind there
are monstrous races.

Therefore, I conclude this discussion with care and caution: either
these beings concerning which such things have been written do not
exist; or, if they do exist, they are not human; or, if they are human,

2. Presumably Augustine has in mind Pliny's *Natural History* (VII. 2), in which
many stories about such races of human beings are reported.

they are descended from Adam.

Chapter 30

Once the promise had been made to Abraham and Sarah (Gn 18) and once Lot had been liberated from Sodom (Gn 19:12–22), a firestorm from heaven came down upon the whole region of that impious city and turned it into ashes (Gn 19:23–25). In Sodom, debauchery among males had grown into a custom so widespread that the laws permitted it just like any other activity. Surely their punishment was an image of the divine judgment to come.

Those who were being liberated by the angels were forbidden to look back. To what does this fact refer? It can only signify that the mind, regenerated through grace, must not return in spirit to the old life that it has laid aside if we intend to avoid the final judgment. Finally, Lot's wife remained where she was when she looked back, having been changed into salt (Gn 19:26). She provides faithful people with a seasoning by which they might taste something that will warn them against following her example.

Abraham repeated at Gerar (Gn 20), with Abimelech, the king of that city, what he had done in Egypt concerning his wife (Gn 12), and, as before, she was returned to him unharmed. When the king reproached Abraham with having said that she was his sister and passing over in silence the fact that she was his wife, Abraham admitted that he had been afraid and added, "In fact, she is my sister, the daughter of my father, but not of my mother," for she was Abraham's sister through their father and was thus closely related to him.[3] So beautiful was she that even in her old age she could inspire feelings of love.

Chapter 35

. . . Almost none of our authors have understood the saying, "The older will serve the younger (Gn 25:23)," to mean anything other than that the older people, the Jews, will serve the younger people, the Christians. In truth, this prophecy might seem to be fulfilled in the Idumaean race, which

---

3. In passing off Sarah as his sister rather than his wife, Abraham might seem to have come close to lying. In pointing out that Sarah was in fact Abraham's sister, Augustine seems to want to protect Abraham's veracity as much as possible. See the section below entitled "On Lying."

was born of the elder brother who had two names (for he was called both Esau and Edom, whence comes the name "Idumaeans"), since later on the Idumaeans were surpassed by the Israelites, a people whose origin is from the younger brother, and to whom the Idumaeans were subjected.[4] Nevertheless, it is preferable to believe that this prophecy, which states that "One people will surpass another, and the older will serve the younger" referred to something greater. And what would that be, except what is clearly fulfilled in the Jews and the Christians?

Chapter 41

If, therefore, for the sake of the Christian people, in which the city of God journeys on earth, we look for the flesh of Christ in the descendants of Abraham, by setting aside the sons of Abraham's concubines we come to Isaac; if we set aside Esau, who is also Edom, from the descendants of Isaac, we are left with Jacob, who is also Israel; if we set aside the rest of the descendants of Israel, we are left with Judah, for Christ was born of the tribe of Judah. Let us then hear how Israel, blessing his sons when he was about to die in Egypt, blessed Judah prophetically:

> Judah, your brothers will praise you. Your hands will be upon the backs of your enemies. The sons of your father will adore you. The cub of a lion is Judah. From a shoot, my son, you have arisen. Lying down, you have slept like a lion and like a lion's cub. Who will wake him up? A ruler will not be lacking from Judah nor a leader from his thighs, until those things arrive which are preserved for him. And he himself the peoples await. Tying his colt to the vine and the offspring of his ass with a tether, he will wash his robe in wine and his clothing in the blood of the grape. His eyes will be dark with wine and his teeth whiter than milk (Gn 49:8–12).

I have explained this passage in arguing against Faustus the Manichaean,[5] and, to the extent that the truth of this prophecy shines forth, I judge that explanation to be sufficient. The death of Christ is foretold by the word about his sleeping, and not the necessity of his dying but his power even in death is foretold by the use of the noun "lion." He himself predicts this power when he says in the Gospel, "I have the power to lay down my life and I have the power to take it up again. No one takes it from me, but I lay it down and take it up again" (Jn 10:17–18). Thus did the lion

---

4. As Augustine says, the Idumaeans were neighbors of the Israelites. They were reputed to be descended from Esau.

5. See *Contra Faustum* XII. 42.

roar! Thus did he fulfill what he had said! This is clear since what comes next in the passage—"Who will wake him up?"—concerns his resurrection and pertains to this power. No human being will do this except he who also said of his own body, "Destroy this temple and in three days I will renew it" (Jn 2:19). Moreover, the kind of death that would be his, namely, being lifted up on a cross, is understood by the single phrase, "You have arisen." The evangelist expounds what is next—"lying down, you have slept"— when he says, "And he bowed his head and handed over his spirit" (Jn 19:30). Or at least the passage refers to his sepulchre, in which he lay sleeping, and from which no human being raised him, as the prophets raised some or as he himself raised others, but as from sleep he himself arose.

Furthermore, there is his robe, which he washes in wine, that is, which he cleanses from sin in his own blood (the baptized know the sacrament of this blood), and also the phrase that comes next, "and his clothes in the blood of the grape". What else are his robe and his clothes but the church? "His eyes dark with wine" are the spiritual people who have drunk of his cup, of which the psalm sings, "And your cup that inebriates, how excellent it is!" (Ps 23:5). "And his teeth are whiter than milk": this milk refers to the nourishing words, that, according to the apostle, the little ones drink who are not yet ready for solid food (1 Cor 3:2). Therefore, it is he himself in whom the promises of Judah were preserved, and until they arrived no ruler—that is, no kings of Israel—were lacking from that line. "And he himself the peoples await" is clearer by simply reading it than it could be made by commenting upon it.

Chapter 43

After the deaths of Jacob and Joseph, 144 years remained until the Israelites went out of the land of Egypt. During those years, that people reproduced in incredible fashion despite being depleted by persecutions so great that, at one time, when the enormous increase of the people terrified the astonished Egyptians, their male infants were murdered. Then Moses was taken away from the murderers of the little ones through trickery and reached the house of the king, for God was preparing to do great things through him. He was raised and adopted by the daughter of the Pharaoh (as kings were called in Egypt) and became so great that he delivered the wondrously increased people from the exceedingly harsh and heavy yoke they had been bearing—or rather God, who had promised it to Abraham, brought them out through Moses.[6]

6. The events which Augustine mentions in this paragraph may be found in Ex 1:1–2:10.

First Moses fled Egypt in fear because, while defending an Israelite, he had killed an Egyptian. Afterwards he was sent back by God, and by the power of the spirit of God he overcame Pharaoh's magicians, who were resisting him. Then, when the Egyptians refused to let God's people go, ten memorable plagues were inflicted on them through Moses: the changing of the water into blood, frogs, gnats, flies, the death of the cattle, boils, hail, locusts, darkness, and the death of their firstborn sons. The Egyptians, broken at length by so many and such great plagues, allowed the Israelites to leave but were destroyed in the Red Sea when they pursued them. Indeed, the sea divided, making a passage for the fleeing, and then returned to its own place to drown the pursuers.[7]

Next, the people, led by Moses, wandered in the desert for forty years. This was when the "tabernacle of testimony," where God was worshipped through sacrifices foretelling future events, was given its name (Ex 27:21). The law had already been given on the mountain in a terrifying fashion, for the divine power, most plainly present, bore witness to it through wondrous signs and pronouncements.[8] This happened soon after the exodus from Egypt and marked the beginning of their time in the desert, on the fiftieth day after the pasch was celebrated with the sacrifice of a lamb.[9] This lamb is so much a prefiguration of Christ announcing his passing over to the Father from this world through the offering of his suffering (indeed the Hebrew word *"pasch"* is translated as "passover") that when the new covenant was revealed after Christ, our pasch, was offered, the Holy Spirit came down from heaven on the fiftieth day. In the Gospel, the Holy Spirit is called the "finger of God" (Lk 11:20) in order to remind us of the earlier, prefiguring events, for the tables of the law were also described as having been written by the finger of God (Ex 31:18).

After Moses' death, Jesus,[10] the son of Nun, ruled the people and led them into the land of the promise and divided it among the people.[11] Wars were also waged most successfully and wondrously by these two amazing leaders, with God bearing witness that the victories were achieved not so much on account of the merits of the Hebrew people as on account of the

7. These events are recounted in Exodus 2–15.

8. See Exodus 19–24.

9. See Exodus 12.

10. "Jesus" is the Greek name for the Hebrew "Joshua." Augustine's Latin text uses the Greek name.

11. This is recounted in Joshua 1–21.

sins of the peoples whom they defeated.[12] After those leaders, there were judges.

The people were already settled in the promised land, so that the first promise made to Abraham, that is, the promise about the one people, the Hebrews, and the land of Canaan, was beginning to be fulfilled. However, the promise about all the peoples and the whole earth was not yet fulfilled.[13] That promise would be fulfilled not by the observances of the Old Law but by the coming of Christ in the flesh and the faith of the Gospel. This was prefigured by the fact that it was not Moses, who had received the law for the people on Mount Sinai, but Jesus the son of Nun, whose name was changed by divine command so that he was called Jesus (Nm 13:16), who led the people into the promised land. In these times of the judges, prosperity and adversity in war alternated in accord with the sins of the people and the mercy of God.

Next came the era of the kings.[14] The first king to reign was Saul. He was rejected and laid low by a military disaster, and his line was abandoned so that no kings would rise from it. David succeeded to the throne, and Christ is especially said to be his son. With David, a new epoch is inaugurated. He marks the beginning, so to speak, of the young adulthood of the people of God, who had been led through a kind of adolescence from Abraham all the way up until David. Not without reason did the evangelist Matthew record the generations so that he recognized in this first interval fourteen generations from Abraham to David.[15] Indeed, in adolescence a human being first develops the capacity to reproduce. For this reason, the beginning of the generations is taken from Abraham, who was also established as the father of the peoples when he received his new name. Therefore, before this, from Noah to Abraham, the people of God were in a kind of childhood, and thus they are found to have had a language then, which was Hebrew, for man begins to speak in childhood, after infancy, which is so termed because he cannot yet speak.[16] Truly, this first age of infancy is swallowed up by forgetfulness, just as the human beings of the first age

12. For further discussion of the wars of Moses, see the section on "War."

13. The promise about all the peoples and the whole earth was made in Gn 12:3; the promise about the one people and the land of Canaan especially in Gn 15 and 17.

14. This era is discussed more fully in Book XXVII.

15. See Mt 1:17. Augustine will come back to this division of the ages at the very end of *The City of God*, in XXII. 30.

16. The Latin word *infans* literally means "not speaking."

were wiped out by the flood. Indeed, how many people are there who remember their own infancy?

Accordingly, in our survey of the progress of the city of God, just as the preceding book contained only one age, the first, so this one contains two ages, the second and the third.[17] In the third age, in accord with the three-year old heifer, the three-year old she-goat, and the three-year old ram, the yoke of the law was imposed, an abundance of sins appeared, and the earthly kingdom made its first appearance. Still, spiritual men were not lacking, as the the turtle-dove and the pigeon mysteriously prefigure.[18]

17. Thus, Book XV covered infancy, the period up to Noah. Book XVI covers both childhood and adolescence, the periods from Noah to Abraham and from Abraham to David.

18. In Gn 15:9, these animals are used in the making of the covenant between God and Abraham. Augustine suggests tentatively in XVI. 24 (not included here) that the heifer, the she-goat, and the ram are all three years old in order to signify to Abraham what would happen in the third period of the life of the people, that of adulthood. He also wonders whether the heifer might not refer to the people being placed under the yoke of the law, the she-goat to the people being subject to the proliferation of sin, and the ram to the the establishment of rule among the people. Against these carnal symbols, he adds, the turtle-dove and pigeon prefigure spiritual blessings.

Book XVII

Introduction

Book XVII continues the discussion of the development of the city of God, covering the period from David to the coming of Christ. Much of the book is concerned with the Israelite monarchy. The basic history of the kings of Israel is well-known to most readers from the biblical sources: The first king was Saul, but he offended God and lost the kingdom to David, to whom the remarkable promise recorded in 2 Samuel 7 was delivered through the prophet Nathan. Although David's son Solomon was wise, rich, and powerful, he also began to worship other gods. As a result, the kingdom was divided between his two sons, Rehoboam and Jeroboam, after his death. The northern part of the kingdom was named "Israel"; the southern, which included Jerusalem, was called "Judah." In the selections included here, Augustine emphasizes the many ways in which Christ was prefigured in the history of the political leaders of ancient Israel. The history of the Israelite monarchy thus bears witness to the Incarnation and to God's providence.

Chapter 6

... The kingdom of Saul, who was certainly rejected and cast aside, was in the same way a shadow of a future kingdom that would last forever. In truth, the oil with which he was anointed, the chrism on account of which he was called "the Christ," must be taken mystically and understood as a great sacrament.[1] David himself revered it greatly. Trembling and with troubled heart, hidden in the darkness of a cave which Saul had entered to satisfy a pressing necessity of nature, David secretly cut off a small piece of

---

1. As a sign that he had been chosen to be king, Saul was anointed with oil or "chrism" by the prophet Samuel (1 Sam 10:1). The Greek word "Christ" means "the anointed one"; it translates the Hebrew word "Messiah."

Saul's robe from behind. He did this so as to be able to prove that he had
spared Saul even though he could have killed him. David wanted to remove any suspicion from the mind of Saul, who, thinking David his enemy, was pursuing him relentlessly.

Since he had handled Saul's garment in this way, David was terrified
that he might be accused of violating such a great sacrament in the person
of Saul, for in the Scriptures it is stated, "David's heart was troubled because he had cut off the tail of Saul's mantle" (1 Sam 24:6). To the men
who were with him and who were urging him to kill Saul since he had been
delivered into their hands, David said, "The Lord has not granted it to me
to do such a thing to my lord, the anointed of the Lord, to lay my hands
upon him, for he is the anointed of the Lord" (1 Sam 24:7). Such great
reverence, then, was shown to this shadow of the future, not on account of
itself, but on account of what it prefigured.

These words of Samuel to Saul should also be understood in the same
way:

> Because you have not kept my commandment which the Lord gave to you,
> as the Lord once planned your kingdom to last forever over Israel, now
> your kingdom will not remain for you. The Lord will seek for himself a
> man according to his own heart, and the Lord will command him to be the
> ruler over his people, for you have not kept what the Lord commanded you
> (1 Sam 13:13–14).

This passage must not be taken as though the Lord had prepared for Saul
an eternal kingdom but that once Saul had sinned the Lord abandoned his
plans, for he was not unaware that Saul would sin. Rather, the passage
means that God had planned that Saul's kingdom would prefigure the
eternal kingdom. Thus, Samuel added, "now your kingdom will not remain for you." Hence, what was signified in that kingdom did remain, and
will remain; however, it will not remain for Saul, for Saul himself would
not rule forever. Nor would Saul's offspring rule forever and so insure the
fulfillment of the word "forever" at least through his posterity, one de-
scendent succeeding another.

Samuel continues, "the Lord will seek for himself a man." This signifies either David or "the mediator of the new covenant" (Heb 12:24) himself, who was also prefigured in the chrism with which David and his
offspring were anointed. However, it was not as if God, not knowing where
this man was, had sought him for himself. Rather, in this passage God
speaks through a human being after the manner of human beings, and in so
speaking he "seeks" us, for we were already so thoroughly known not only

to God the Father, but also to his only-begotten Son, who came to seek what was lost (Lk 19:10), that we were chosen before the foundation of the world (Eph 1:4). Consequently, Samuel said, "he will seek for himself," meaning "he will have his own." Hence, in Latin the verb "to seek" (*quaerere*) with the addition of a prefix means "to acquire" (*adquirere*). . . .

Chapter 7

. . . In recounting Samuel's prophecy to Saul, the Scripture does not say "The Lord has torn the kingdom of Israel from your hand" (1 Sam 15:28), which is what is read in most of the Latin manuscripts, but, as I put it, "He has torn the kingdom from Israel, from your hand," which is what is found in the Greek, so that we are given to understand that "from Israel" means the same as "from your hand."[2] That man, then, prefigured the people of Israel, who would in the future lose the kingdom when, through a new covenant, our Lord Jesus Christ came to rule not in the flesh but in the spirit. When it is said of him, "and he will give it to your neighbor" (1 Sam 15:28), the reference is to bodily kinship, for like Saul Christ was from Israel according to the flesh.

What follows in the text, "to one who is good above you," can indeed be understood as meaning "to one better than you," and some have interpreted it in this way. It is better, however, to take "to one who is good above you" as meaning "because he is good, therefore he should be above you," which is in accord with that other prophetic passage, "Until I place all your enemies under your feet" (Ps 110:1). Among those enemies is also Israel, the persecutor whose kingdom Christ took away. Yet even here there was also the Israel "in whom there was no guile" (Jn 1:47), as wheat among the chaff, for certainly the apostles were from Israel, and so were many martyrs, of whom Stephen was the first, and so were many churches which Paul mentions as glorifying God because of his conversion (Gal 1:24).

I do not doubt that what follows in the text—"And Israel will be divided in two"—ought to be understood as referring to Israel the enemy of Christ and Israel clinging to Christ, to Israel the slave woman and Israel the free woman.[3] At first these two lines of descent were together, just as Abraham still clung to the slave woman until the barren woman, made

2. Augustine's argument is that the reading of the Septuagint, the Greek translation of the Hebrew Scriptures, is to be preferred to the Latin translation. The Greek text reveals that the phrase actually refers to the people of Israel also, not just to Saul.

3. See XV. 2.

fruitful through the grace of Christ, cried out, "Cast out that slave woman and her son" (Gn 21:10). . . .

Of course, we know that, on account of Solomon's sin, Israel was divided in two during the reign of his son Rehoboam. The division persisted, each individual part having its own king, until that whole people suffered a terrible disaster at the hands of the Chaldeans and was deported. But what does that have to do with Saul? If a threat of this sort was necessary, it should rather have been addressed to David, for Solomon was his son. Finally, the Hebrew people are not now divided but indiscriminately dispersed throughout the world with only their common error to unite them.[4]

Yet the division foretold by God to that kingdom and people through the person of Saul, who figuratively signified the same kingdom and people, is eternal and unchangeable. This is the meaning of the next part of the passage: "And he will not change his mind nor will he repent, for he is not like a human being who repents; he threatens and does not follow through" (1 Sam 15:29). That is to say, a human being threatens and does not follow through, but God, who does not repent like a human being, does follow through. When the Scriptures say that God repents (Gn 6:6, Jer 18:7–10, etc.), a change in temporal things is signified, while the divine foreknowledge remains immutable. Therefore, when it is said that he does not repent, the meaning is that he does not change.

Absolutely incontrovertible and utterly unremitting is the sentence concerning the division of the people of Israel divinely published in these words. All those who have passed over to Christ, or who are passing over, or who will pass over, did not belong to that people according to the foreknowledge of God or according to the one, common nature of the human race. In a word, all those among the Israelites who cling to Christ and persevere in him will have no part with those Israelites who persist as his enemies clear up to the end of this life. The people of Israel will remain in the perpetual division which is here foretold. The old covenant of Mount Sinai, which "gives birth into slavery" (Gal 4:24), is of no use except to bring forth testimony to the new covenant. To put it another way, as long as Moses is read, a veil is put over their hearts, but when anyone of them passes over to Christ, the veil will be lifted (2 Cor 3:15–6). Truly, the very intention of those passing over is changed from old to new, so that now each one intends to grasp not carnal but spiritual felicity.

---

4. Augustine's point is that the scriptural phrase "and Israel will be divided in two" cannot refer to the division of the nation after the death of Solomon or to the present state of the Jews as dispersed throughout the world, but only to the division between the Israel that accepts Christ and the Israel that rejects him.

Consequently, when the great prophet Samuel himself, before he had anointed Saul king, cried out to the Lord on behalf of Israel, the Lord heard him. He offered a holocaust while the foreigners approached to attack the people of God, but the Lord sent thunder upon them and confused them, and they fell before Israel and were overcome. Samuel then took a single stone and stood it between the new and the old Mizpah, and named it Ebenezer, which means "stone of the helper," and he said, "To this point, the Lord has helped us" (1 Sam 7:9–12). Mizpah is understood to mean "intention." That stone of the helper is the mediation of the Savior, through whom one must pass over from the old Mizpah to the new. That is, one must pass over from the intention which hopes for a false bodily happiness of the flesh in a material kingdom to the intention which, through the new covenant, hopes for the truest happiness of the spirit in a heavenly kingdom. Because there is nothing better than this happiness, God helps us to this point.

Chapter 13

Whoever hopes for so great a good as is promised to David in this world and on this earth shows all the understanding of a fool.[5] Does anyone really think that the promise of such a good was fulfilled in the peace that existed during the reign of Solomon? Through that excellent proclamation Scripture surely prizes the peace of Solomon as a shadow of a future event. Still, the idea that the promise to David was fulfilled in the reign of Solomon is carefully precluded when, after the passage says, "And the son of iniquity will not approach to humiliate him", it immediately adds, "as he has done from the beginning, from the days in which I established judges over my people Israel" (2 Sam 7:10–1). Now, judges had been established over that people from the time that they received the land of the promise, before there began to be kings in Israel. Also, the son of iniquity—that is, the foreign enemy—certainly did humiliate them during the intervals of time of which we read that peace alternated with war. Yet, longer periods of peace are found than the one enjoyed by Solomon, who reigned for forty years. Under that judge called Ehud there were eighty years of peace.[6]

5. Augustine refers is to the promise delivered to David through the prophet Nathan. He especially has in mind 2 Sam 7:10–11, in which respite from enemies is promised.

6. Augustine's argument in this paragraph is designed to show that the promise given to David cannot refer to Solomon but only to Christ. The oracle states that the promised peace will be greater than any that has existed since the time of the

Thus, dismiss the thought that this promise given to David predicts the reign of Solomon, much less that of any other king, for none of them reigned in peace as long as Solomon. Never did that people possess the kingdom so securely that it did not have to worry about being overrun by enemies, for due to the great vicissitudes of human events no people has ever been granted such security that they did not dread attacks hostile to this life. Therefore, that place which is promised to be such a peaceful and secure dwelling is eternal, and is owed to the eternal ones in Jerusalem, the free mother. In that place will dwell those who are truly the people of Israel, for the name Israel is understood to mean "seeing God." In this journey full of hardships, the pious soul must be led, through faith, by a longing for that reward.

Chapter 23

Prophets were not lacking in the kingdom of Judah, which belonged to Jerusalem, even during the reigns of the kings which succeeded Solomon's son Rehoboam. It pleased God to send them either for the purpose of delivering a necessary prediction or of rebuking sins and commanding justice. Even there, although much less than in Israel, kings arose who gravely offended God with their own impieties, and they, along with the people who were like them, were punished with moderate scourges. Clearly, the merits of the pious kings, which were not small, are praised. In Israel, however, we read that all the kings were wicked to a greater or lesser degree. Thus, both parts, as divine providence commanded or allowed, were alternately lifted up by prosperity and knocked down by adversity. In this way they were weakened not only by wars against foreigners but also by civil wars among themselves, so that, through definite and immediate causes, either the mercy or the wrath of God was made clear.

His indignation grew until that entire people was conquered by the Chaldeans. Not only were they overthrown in their own territory, but the greater part of them were also carried off into the lands of the Assyrians. First, that part composed of the ten tribes, which was called Israel, was carried off;[7] afterwards, with Jerusalem and that most noble temple having been demolished, Judah also was deported.[8] In those

---

judges, but there were eighty years of peace under the judge Ehud and only forty during the reign of Solomon.

7. The northern kingdom was conquered by Assyria in 721 B.C.; see 2 Kgs 17.

8. The southern kingdom was conquered by Babylon in 586 B.C., at which time the temple of Jerusalem was destroyed. See 2 Kgs 25.

lands they lived quietly as captives for seventy years.

After those years they were allowed to leave, and the temple which had been demolished was restored.[9] Even though most of them lived in foreign lands, they did not any longer have two kingdoms and two different kings, one in each part. Instead, they had one prince in Jerusalem, and at fixed times all of them, wherever they were and from wherever they could, came altogether to the temple of God that was there. Yet they did not lack enemies and conquerers from other peoples even then, for Christ found them again tributaries, this time of the Romans.[10]

9. The exilic period in Israel's history, its Babylonian captivity, came to an end when Cyrus, the Persian king, conquered Babylon and released the Israelites. The rebuilding of the temple is the dominant theme of the book of Ezra.

10. Pompey conquered Judaea for Rome in 63 B.C.

Book XVIII

Introduction

Books XVI and XVII traced the progress of the city of God from Noah to the coming of Christ; Book XVIII traces the progress of the earthly city during the same period. In the selection from Chapter 2, Augustine returns to a theme initially raised in Book IV, explaining that the inordinate desires of the earthly city have led to the rise of empires. For all its flaws, the earthly city has its own accounts of miraculous events, and it is necessary to distinguish those stories from the miracles performed by the true God. This is the subject of Chapter 18; it should be compared with Book X, Chapters 9 and 12. Besides accounts of miraculous deeds, the earthly city also has its own wisdom, represented preeminently by philosophy. Augustine devotes an extensive portion of Book XVIII to arguing for the superiority of the wisdom of the city of God, which is imparted to human beings not through philosophy but through God's prophets (Chs. 37, 39, and 41). In a noteworthy chapter towards the end of the book, Augustine criticizes the view of those Christians who, like his former student Orosius, think that the church will not suffer any more persecutions at the hands of the earthly city (Ch. 52). In rejecting the position of Orosius, Augustine refuses to simply identify the welfare of the city of God with its present dominant position within the Roman empire.

Chapter 2

The society of mortals, scattered everywhere throughout the earth in a vast diversity of places, was bound in a sort of unity of one and the same nature, though all pursued their own advantages and desires. Now that which is desired in this way either satisfies no one or does not satisfy everyone, for it is not the very object of desire, and so the society of mortals is generally divided against itself, and the part which prevails oppresses the rest. The conquered part surrenders to the victorious part, preferring any sort of peace and safety at all to domination, of course, and even to liberty, so that those who have chosen to perish rather than to be enslaved have caused great astonishment. In almost all peoples this voice of nature somehow proclaims that those who happen to have been conquered choose to be subjugated to their victors rather than to be obliterated totally by the devastation of war. Hence, some have been placed over empires and some have been placed under emperors—not, though, without the control of the providence of God, whose power determines who subjugates and who is subjugated in war.

Among the many empires of the world into which the society of earthly advantages or desires has been divided—we have given these empires the general name of "the city of the world"—we perceive two to have succeeded much more brilliantly than the rest: first, the Assyrian, then the Roman. They have been as ordered and distinct from each other in time as in place, for the first arose early on, the second later, and the first arose in the East, the second in the West. Finally, the end of the first was followed immediately by the beginning of the second. I could say that all other empires and all other emperors were, in a sense, appendages of these two.[1]

Chapter 18

. . . Accounts of men being transformed into animals are either false or so uncommon as to be disbelieved with good reason.[2] On the other hand, it must be believed most firmly that the omnipotent God can do everything that he wills, whether it is to punish or to bestow benefits. It must likewise be believed that the demons do nothing through the power of their own nature (for although they were created angelic, by their own defect they are wicked), except what he, whose judgments are frequently hidden but never unjust, has permitted. If the demons do some such deeds of the sort under question, clearly they do not create natures, but change only the appearance of things which have been created by the true God, so that they seem to be what they are not. Therefore, I would not by any means believe that the mind or even the body can actually be changed by the art or the power of demons into the body parts and features of beasts.

1. This chapter on empire should be compared with IV. 4, 6, and 15.

2. Augustine is referring to pagan literature and mythology, which are replete with instances of human beings being changed into beasts. In the omitted section of this chapter, he mentions *The Golden Ass* of Apuleius, in which a human being is changed into a donkey, and also reports that he himself has heard tales about such things occurring in a particular section of Italy.

I would rather believe the following explanation: The imaginative faculty of a human being is varied through innumerable kinds of things, even by thinking and dreaming. Though it is not a body, it grasps with an amazing quickness forms that are likenesses of bodies. It can be led, when the bodily senses are asleep or overwhelmed, to the senses of others in a material form in some ineffable way that I do not know. Thus, the bodies of human beings might lie resting somewhere, living indeed, but with their senses having been closed up much more deeply and firmly than by sleep. That imaginative faculty, however, might appear to the senses of others as being embodied in the likeness of some animal, and it might even seem to be so to the man himself, just as this sort of thing can seem to him to be so in his sleep. Also, it might seem to him that he carries burdens, but if these burdens are material, then demons carry them in order to dupe human beings into perceiving partly the true bodies of the burdens and partly the false bodies of the beasts of burden. . . .

These things have not come to us from the sort of people whom we think to be unworthy of being believed, but they have been referred to us by those whom we would not judge to be liars. Consequently, when it is said and put down in writing that men frequently are changed into wolves by the Arcadian gods—or rather demons—and that "Circe changed the friends of Ulysses by charms,"[3] it would seem to me that, as I have said, such things could have happened in this way—if they happened at all. . . .

Chapter 22

To be brief, the city of Rome was founded as another Babylon and as the daughter of the first Babylon. Through the city of Rome, God was pleased to subdue the world and to make it peaceful far and wide in the single society of that republic and its laws. By now there were peoples powerful and strong and practiced in arms, and they did not yield easily. To overcome them required enormous dangers, and not a little devastation on both sides, and horrendous struggles. When the empire of the Assyrians subjugated almost all of Asia, although they did so by war, the wars were not very harsh or difficult, for at that time the peoples were still unskilled at resisting. Also, when Ninus subjugated all of Asia except India,[4] the peoples were not so numerous or so great—if indeed not more than one thousand years had gone by after that greatest universal flood when only

3. Virgil, *Eclogues* 8. 70.
4. Ninus: the legendary king of the Assyrian empire.

eight human beings escaped in Noah's ark. Rome, however, did not so quickly and easily tame all the eastern and western peoples that we see have been conquered by the Roman empire. Expanding little by little, she found them robust and warlike no matter which way she spread.

At the time when Rome was founded, the people of Israel had possessed the land of the promise for 718 years. Of this, 27 years were during the time of Jesus, son of Nun. The next 329 pertain to the time of the judges. From the time when the kings began to reign, there had been 362 years. At that time there was a king in Judah named Ahaz, or, as others compute, his successor Hezekiah.[5] He was indeed the best and the most pious king; it is established that he reigned in the time of Romulus. In that part of the Hebrew people called Israel, Hoshea had begun to reign.[6]

Chapter 37

In the age of our prophets, whose writings were already known to almost all peoples, and especially in the era following the prophets, lived the gentile philosophers who were first called by the name of "philosopher." The name begins with Pythagoras of Samos, who was distinguished and well-known at the time when the Jews were freed from their captivity.[7] Much more so, then, are the rest of the philosophers found to have lived after the prophets. Socrates of Athens himself, the teacher of all who were most illustrious at that time, pre-eminent in that part of philosophy called "moral" or "practical," is found after Esra in the *Chronicles*.[8] Not long after, Plato, who far surpassed the rest of the disciples of Socrates, was born.[9]

Even if we count the earlier philosophers, who were not yet called such—namely, The Seven Wise Men, and then the physicists who succeeded Thales and imitated his zeal in scrutinizing the nature of things, such as Anaximander, Anaximenes, and Anaxagoras, and not a few others

5. Ahaz reigned in Judah from 735 to 715 B.C.; Hezekiah from 715 to 687 B.C. Ahaz is discussed in 2 Kgs 16; Hezekiah in 2 Kgs 18–20.

6. Hoshea ruled the northern kingdom from 732 B.C. until its collapse. His reign is discussed in 2 Kgs 16:1–6.

7. The captivity ended in 538 B.C. Pythagoras lived c. 571–497 B.C.

8. Augustine refers to a work of the early Christian historian Eusebius (264–c. 340).

9. Socrates is thought to have been born in 469 B.C. and to have died seventy years later. Plato lived from 428 to 349 B.C.

prior to Pythagoras, the first philosopher to profess the name—they did not, regarded as a group, precede our prophets in time. Indeed, Thales, after whom came the rest, is reported to have been prominent during the reign of Romulus, when the river of prophecy burst forth from the fountains of Israel in the writings which would flow across the whole world.[10]

Therefore, only those theological poets Orpheus, Linus, Musaeus, and any others that there may have been among the Greeks, are found to have been prior to these Hebrew prophets, whose writings we hold as authoritative. None of those poets, however, temporally preceded Moses, our true theologian, who truly proclaimed the one true God, whose writings are now first in the authoritative canon. Thus, the Greeks, in whose language the literature of this world has most streamed forth, have no reason to brag about their own wisdom if it does not seem to be superior to or at least older than our religion, which is the true wisdom. . . .

Chapter 39

. . . Accordingly, let no people vainly pride itself about the antiquity of its own wisdom being superior to our patriarchs and prophets, in whom there is divine wisdom. Egypt is accustomed to glory falsely and inanely about the antiquity of its own teachings, yet its wisdom, such as it is, is found not to have preceded in time the wisdom of our patriarchs. Nor will anyone dare to say that the Egyptians were expert in their wonderful learning before they knew letters, that is, before Isis arrived and taught them such things.

Furthermore, what is that memorable teaching of the Egyptians, which is called "wisdom," except primarily astronomy and other such learning that is customarily used more to exercise wittiness than to illuminate minds with true wisdom? Insofar as this Egyptian learning pertains to philosophy, which professes to teach something whereby human beings might be made happy, studies of that sort became illustrious in Egypt around the time of Mercury, whom they have called Trismegistus.[11] This was certainly long before the wise men or the philosophers of Greece, but nevertheless after Abraham, Isaac, Jacob, and Joseph, and long after Moses

10. The dates of the philosophers mentioned here are: Anaximander, c. 610–546 B.C.; Anaximenes, c. 585–528 B.C.; Anaxagoras, c. 500–428 B.C.; Thales, c. 624–546 B.C. Romulus's founding of the city of Rome was traditionally dated to 753 B.C.

11. In discussing the wisdom of Egypt, Augustine is referring to the Hermetic Books, on which see the note on VIII. 27.

himself, for Atlas, the great astronomer, is found to have lived in the time in which Moses was born, and Atlas was the brother of Prometheus and the maternal grandfather of Mercury the elder, whose grandson was this Mercury Trismegistus.

Chapter 41

However, let us now set aside the study of history. The philosophers themselves, from whom we have digressed to consider that subject, do not seem to have labored in their own studies for any other reason than to discover in what manner one must live in order to be fit to embrace happiness. Why then did the students disagree with their teachers, and why did the fellow students disagree among themselves, if not because those human beings have sought happiness by means of human sensation and human reason? To be sure, it might have been a zeal for self-aggrandizement, by which everyone desires to be seen as wiser and smarter than others and in no way bound by the thoughts of others, but the inventor of his own teachings and opinions. Nevertheless, I concede that some or even most of them broke with their teachers or fellow students because of a love of truth, so that they might argue for that which they thought—either correctly or incorrectly— to be the truth.[12]

What does human misery do, to what extent and in what manner does it reach out to attain happiness, if divine authority does not lead it? Far be it from our authors, to whom the canon of sacred writings is not without reason fixed and limited, to disagree among themselves in any way! Thus, it is not without merit that so many and such numerous peoples, both on farms and in cities, both learned and unlearned—and not merely a few babblers in contentious disputations in schools and gymnasia—have believed that God has spoken to or through our authors as they were writing those canonical books. There ought to have been only a few of these authors, in order that what ought to be dear to religion not become cheap by being abundant. Nevertheless, they ought not be so few that their agreement not be astonishing. Among the multitude of philosophers who have also left behind a monument of their teachings through their literary labors, it is not easy to discover any two who are in agreement with each other about everything. It would take too long, however, to prove that in this work. . . .

On the other hand, that race, that people, that city, that republic, those

---

12. On the disputes among the disciples of Socrates, see VIII. 3.

Israelites, to whom the eloquence of God was entrusted, in no way mixed together pseudo-prophets with true ones by tolerating them all as though they were the same. Those, however, who were in accord with each other and were without any dissent were recognized and known to be truthful authors of sacred writings. These authors were "philosophers"—that is, lovers of wisdom. They were their wise men, their theologians, their prophets, their teachers of righteousness and piety. Whoever thought and lived according to them thought and lived not according to man but according to God, who spoke through them. If a sacrilege is prohibited in their writings, God has prohibited it. If it is said, "Honor your father and your mother," God commands it. If it is said, "You shall not commit adultery, you shall not kill a human being, you shall not steal," and so forth, such things are not uttered by a human mouth but by a divine oracle.

Among their false opinions, certain philosophers were able to discern some truth: the truth that God made this world and that he administers it through the greatest providence, the truth about the honorable character of the virtues, about the love of one's country, about the faithfulness of friends, about good deeds and everything pertaining to upright morals. Even though these philosophers did not know to what end and in what manner all these things needed to be directed, they struggled through laborious disputations to persuade people of them. These truths were commended to the people of Israel by prophetic—that is, by divine—voices, although through human beings; they were not inculcated through the strife of argumentation. This was so that those who would learn of these truths would be afraid to scorn not the wittiness of human beings but the eloquence of God.[13]

Chapter 46

When Herod was king in Judea and Caesar Augustus emperor in Rome— for the constitution of that republic had already changed and the world had been made peaceful through that emperor—then, in accord with an earlier prophecy, in Bethlehem of Judea Christ was born, manifestly human from a human virgin, invisibly God from God the Father. The prophet had foretold his coming in this way: "Behold, a virgin will conceive in her womb and bear a son and he will be named 'Immanuel,' which means 'God with us'" (Is 7:14). In order to make his divinity more acceptable, he performed many miracles, some of which—as many as seemed to be sufficient

13. This chapter should be compared with VIII. 10.

to make him known—the Gospel writings contain. The first of these was that he was born so miraculously; the last, that he ascended into heaven with his own body, which was revived from death.

Also, the Jews who killed him and were unwilling to believe in him (for it was necessary that he die and rise again) were then devastated miserably by the Romans and utterly rooted out from their own kingdom, where foreigners were already dominating them, and were dispersed throughout the earth so that there is no place lacking them. These very Jews are themselves witnesses on our behalf through their own scriptures, showing that we have not fabricated the prophecies about Christ. . . . If they lived with that testimony of their scriptures only in their own land, and not everywhere, then surely the church, which is everywhere, could not have had them among all the peoples as witnesses of the prophecies sent beforehand about Christ. . . .

Chapter 52

Some have thought, or do think, that the church will not suffer any more persecutions than it has already suffered—that is, ten—until the time of the Antichrist, so that the eleventh and last persecution will be that of the Antichrist.[14] I do not think that this view should be rashly asserted or believed. They count the persecution of Nero as first; Domitian's as second; Trajan's third; Antoninus's fourth; Severus's fifth; Maximinus's sixth; Decius's seventh; Valerian's eighth; Aurelian's ninth; and Diocletian's and Maximian's as tenth.[15] They hold that the plagues of the Egyptians must be understood as referring to these persecutions since there were ten such plagues before the people of God began the exodus from Egypt. Thus, they hold that the last persecution of the Antichrist seems similar to the eleventh plague, in which the Egyptians perished in the Red Sea while chasing the Hebrews, whereas the people of God passed through on dry ground. I, however, do not think that those events in Egypt prophetically signified these persecutions. Even though those who hold this view would seem to have compared the individual plagues and persecutions carefully and cleverly, they have done so not through the prophetic spirit but through the conjectures of the human mind, which sometimes reaches the

14. Augustine clearly has in mind his former student Orosius. See *Seven Books against the Pagans* VII. 27.

15. These persecutions occurred intermittently in the years between 64 (Nero) and 313 (Diocletian and Maximian).

truth and sometimes is led astray.

What will the proponents of this view say about the persecution in which the Lord himself was crucified? To which number will they assign it? If they hold that this should not be counted, as though only those persecutions which fall upon the body should be counted and not the persecution in which the head itself was attacked and killed, then what will they do about the persecution that happened in Jerusalem after Christ ascended into heaven? That was when the blessed Stephen was stoned, when James the brother of John was slaughtered with the sword, when the apostle Peter was jailed so that he might be killed but was freed by an angel, when the brothers fled Jerusalem and scattered, when Saul, who later became the apostle Paul, was devastating the church.[16] Saul himself, while proclaiming the faith which he had persecuted, also suffered what he had perpetrated, whether in Judea or among other peoples, wherever this most zealous man was preaching Christ. Why, therefore, does it seem necessary to them to begin with Nero, when the church reached the age of Nero by growing amidst the harshest persecutions, which would take too long to describe completely? If they think that only persecutions waged by kings ought to be counted, Herod was the king who waged the most severe persecution, even after the ascension of the Lord.

Furthermore, what will they say about Julian,[17] whom they do not enumerate in the ten? In prohibiting Christians from teaching or learning the liberal arts, did he not persecute the church? During his reign, the elder Valentinian (who became the third emperor after him) stood out as a confessor of the Christian faith and was banned from the military.[18] I will omit what Julian set out to accomplish at Antioch and would have accomplished except for a single young man of the utmost fidelity and constancy. Many people were arrested in order to be tortured. This young man was first and he was tortured for a whole day. Yet, amidst the claws and tools of torment, he sang psalms. Julian, awestruck at his cheerfulness and boldness, was shaken and afraid that he would be embarrassed even more shamefully by the others who had been arrested.

Finally, in times we remember, did not Valens the Arian,[19] brother of the Valentinian mentioned above, devastate the Catholic church in the

16. See Acts 6:8–8:3.

17. On Julian, see the note on V. 25.

18. Valentinian I ruled from 364 until his death in 375. Jovian ruled between Julian and Valentinian. He is not to be confused with the Valentinian II discussed in V. 25–26.

19. On Valens, see the note on V. 26.

eastern regions with a great persecution? Is it not odd to fail to consider that the church, bearing fruit and growing throughout the whole world, can suffer persecution at the hands of kings among some peoples even when it does not suffer persecution among others? Should it not be counted as a persecution when the king of the Goths persecuted Christians with astonishing cruelty in Gothia itself,[20] even though there are only Catholics there? Many of them were crowned with martyrdom, as we have heard from some brothers who were boys there at that time and who instantly remembered having seen these events themselves. What about the recent events in Persia?[21] Did not a persecution boil so hotly against the Christians (if indeed it has quieted down even now) that some fled all the way to Roman towns?

Upon considering these and similar events, it does not seem to me to be proper to limit the number of persecutions by which the church ought to be troubled. On the other hand, it is no less rash to affirm that there will be future persecutions by kings in addition to the last persecution, concerning which no Christian has any hesitations.[22] Thus, I leave this matter undetermined, neither building up nor tearing down either side of this issue, but only calling both sides back from making assertions about it through audacious presumption.

Chapter 54

. . . Let us at last conclude this book. To this point we have discussed and shown, as much as seemed sufficient, the mortal development of the two cities, the heavenly and the earthly, which are mixed together from the beginning to the end. One of them, the earthly city, has made for itself the false gods that it wanted from any source whatsoever—even from human beings—and it serves them with sacrifices. The other city, the heavenly city journeying on earth, does not make false gods, but is itself made by the true God, whose true sacrifice is that very city. Both alike use temporal goods and are attacked by temporal evils, though with different faiths, different hopes, and different loves, until they are separated by the last judgment and each one will reap its own end, of which there is no end. These ends of the two cities must be discussed next.

20. According to Orosius VII. 32, this occurred in approximately 367.

21. A persecution occurred in Persia in 420.

22. The last persecution is discussed in XX. 11, which should be compared with this chapter.

Book XIX

Introduction

Book XVIII marks the end of the section of The City of God *devoted to the progress or development of the two cities. With Book XIX, Augustine turns to their respective ends. He initiates the discussion with a consideration of Varro's enumeration of the manifold and diverse views held by the philosophers on the subject of the end of human life (Chs. 1–2). In a key chapter, he rejects all such views because they overestimate the ability of either natural goods or virtue to secure happiness (Ch. 4). Among other things, the philosophers recommend pursuing a social and political life, but our author points out that such a life necessarily involves many evils. In the selections included here, he laments the predicaments in which human judges often find themselves (Ch. 6) as well as the problems posed by the diversity of languages and the miseries of war (Ch. 7). The next section of the book contains the city of God's answer to the question about the supreme good. This leads Augustine into his famous meditations on the nature of peace in Chapters 12 and 13. He then turns to a series of reflections on temporal existence in light of that notion of peace. Included here are important comments on slavery (Ch. 15), the household (Chs. 16–17), and the relative merits of the active and contemplative lives (Ch. 19). In Chapter 21, Augustine returns to the discussion of Cicero's* Republic *that he had begun in Book II, Chapter 21. Now, however, he argues that if the implications of Cicero's arguments are spelled out completely, then one must admit that the Romans never really were a people. In the end, the only true people, the only true city, is the city of God.*

Chapter 1

Because I see that I must next discuss the proper ends of the two cities—namely, the earthly and the heavenly—I must first explain, insofar as the limits imposed by the plan of this work allow, the arguments by which mortals have struggled to make themselves happy in the misery of this life. This is necessary in order to clarify the difference between their futilities and our hope, which God has given us, and its object, namely true happiness, which God will give us. This will be done not only through divine authority, but also, for the sake of unbelievers, through reason.

Concerning the ends of goods and evils, philosophers have engaged in many and varied disputes among themselves; but the question they have pursued with the greatest effort, turning it over in their minds, is, What makes man happy? Indeed, our final good is that for the sake of which other things are desired, but which is itself desired for its own sake; and the final evil is that on account of which other things are avoided, but which is avoided on its own account. Hence, we now call the "final good" not that through which good is destroyed, and so ceases to exist, but that through which it is perfected, and so exists fully; and we call the "final evil" not that through which evil ceases to be, but that through which it produces its greatest harm. Thus, these ends are the supreme good and the supreme evil.

As I said, many who have professed the study of wisdom in the futility of this age have worked hard to discover these ends, as well as to obtain the supreme good and to avoid the supreme evil in this life. Although they wandered off in different directions, nevertheless the limit of nature did not permit them to deviate from the path of truth so far that they failed to place the final good and final evil in the soul, in the body, or in both. To this tripartite division of schools Marcus Varro,[1] in his book *On Philosophy*, directed his attention, diligently and subtly scrutinizing a large number of different teachings. By applying certain distinctions he easily arrived at 288 possible—though not necessarily actual—schools.[2] . . .

1. 1. On Varro, see the note on III. 9.

2. Varro's book *On Philosophy*, like most of his other works, is not extant. In an omitted section, Augustine explains that Varro arrived at the figure of 288 in the following way: he reasoned that there are four things which human beings seek (pleasure, repose, a combination of the two, or the primary goods of nature). These four things may be desired for the sake of virtue, or virtue may be desired for their sake, or both might be desired for their own sakes. There are also two possible positions concerning whether one seeks the good only for oneself or for one's fellows as well. Next, one could hold his position as certain or, like the New Academics, as probable. Then, one could accept the traditional dress of philosophers as appropriate or follow the view of the Cynics on dress. Finally, one could hold that the life of leisure is best, or that the active life is best, or that a combination of the two is best. Multiplying $4 \times 3 \times 2 \times 2 \times 2 \times 3$, Varro arrived at no fewer than 288 possible philosophical schools.

Chapter 2

Then there are those three kinds of life: the first is the leisurely—but not slothful—life, devoted to contemplating or seeking the truth; the second is the busy life devoted to conducting human affairs; and the third is the life which mixes both of these kinds. When it is asked which of these three ought to be chosen, the final good is not being disputed. What is considered by that question is which of these three brings difficulty or assistance for seeking or preserving the final good. When anyone attains the final good, he is forthwith made happy. However, the life devoted to learned leisure, to public business, or to performing both alternately does not necessarily make one happy. Certainly, many are able to live in one or another of these three ways, but err with respect to desiring the final good by which man is made happy.

Therefore, it is one thing to ask about the final good and the final evil, and the answer to that question distinguishes every single one of the philosophical schools. It is quite another thing to ask questions about the social life, the hesitation of the Academics, the dress and diet of the Cynics, and the three kinds of life—the leisurely, the active, and the combined. The final good and evil are not disputed in any of these questions.

By using these four distinctions—that is, the distinctions derived from the social life, the new Academics, the Cynics, and the three kinds of life—Marcus Varro reaches 288 schools. If there are other distinctions, they could be added in the same way. By removing all of those four distinctions, because they do not bear upon the question of pursuing the supreme good and thus do not give rise to what can properly be called "schools," he returns to those twelve in which it is asked, What is the good of man, the pursuit of which makes man happy? From these twelve, he shows that one is true and the rest false.[3] . . .

To Varro, it seemed proper that these three schools be treated carefully. He asked, Which ought to be chosen? True reason does not permit more than one to be true, whether it is among these three or—as we will see later on—somewhere else.[4] In the meantime, we will examine, as briefly and

---

3. Varro reduces the twelve to three in the following way: pleasure, repose, and the combination of the two are all included in what the Stoic philosophers call the "primary goods of nature." Hence, those four possible positions are reduced to one. The three possible positions left are that virtue is to be desired for the sake of the primary goods of nature, that the primary goods of nature are to be desired for the sake of virtue, and that both should be desired for their own sakes.

4. In Chapter 4, it will become evident that Augustine thinks the supreme good lies in none of these three positions of the philosophers but somewhere else.

clearly as we can, how Varro chooses one of these three. Certainly, these three schools arise as follows: either the primary goods of nature[5] are chosen for the sake of virtue, or virtue is chosen for the sake of the primary goods of nature, or both—that is, both virtue and the primary goods of nature—are chosen for their own sakes.[6]

Chapter 4

If, then, we are asked what the city of God would reply to each of these questions, and, most importantly, what it thinks about the final good and final evil, it will reply that eternal life is the supreme good and eternal death the supreme evil, and that in order to attain the one and avoid the other, we must live rightly. That is why it is written, "The just man lives by faith" (Gal 3:11), for we do not at present see our good and thus must seek it through believing, nor does our living rightly derive from ourselves, except insofar as he, who gave the very faith through which we believe ourselves to be in need of help from him, helps us in our believing and praying.

Those, however, who have held that the final good and evil are in this life, whether they place the supreme good in the body, in the soul, or in both—and indeed, to express it more explicitly, whether they place it in pleasure or in virtue or both; whether in rest or virtue or in both; whether in pleasure and rest simultaneously or in virtue or in all these; whether in the primary things of nature or in virtue or in all these—they wanted to be happy here and now and, through an astonishing vanity, they wanted to be made happy by their own actions. The Truth ridiculed them through the prophet, saying, "The Lord knows the thoughts of men" (Ps 94:11), or, as the apostle Paul puts this testimony, "The Lord knows the thoughts of the wise, that they are vain" (1 Cor 3:20).

Indeed, who is able, however great the flood of his eloquence, to expound the miseries of this life? Cicero lamented them, as well as he was able, in the *Consolation* on the death of his daughter,[7] but how much was he

5. This phrase was used by the Stoic philosophers to refer to the basic goods of both mind and body, such as health, strength, beauty, perception, understanding, and so forth.

6. In an omitted section, Varro chooses the latter position, since it properly aimed at both what is good for the soul and for the body. As will become clear, in Chapter 4 Augustine attacks the idea that the primary goods of nature could contribute to the final good and then ridicules the idea that moral virtue could do so.

7. Cicero composed this work after the death of his daughter Tullia in 45 B.C. Unfortunately, it survives only in fragments.

able to do? In truth, when, where, and in what way can those things called the primary goods of nature be so well possessed in this life that they are not tossed about under the sway of unforeseen accidents? What pain contrary to pleasure, what restlessness contrary to rest, could not befall the body of a wise man? Certainly, the amputation or the debility of a man's limbs destroys his soundness, deformity his beauty, feebleness his health, exhaustion his strength, numbness or slowness his mobility. Which of these is it that cannot overcome the flesh of a wise person? The postures and movements of the body, when they are fitting and harmonious, are likewise numbered among the primary goods of nature. Yet what if some state of ill health causes the limbs to shake and tremble? What if the spine is so curved that the hands are forced to touch the ground, making the man a sort of quadruped? Is not every type of posture and movement of the body distorted?

What about the primary things of the mind itself, which are called goods? Sense and intellect are placed first since on account of them perception and comprehension of the truth are possible. Yet what sort of and how much sensation remains if, to say nothing of other things, a man becomes deaf and blind? Indeed, if reason and intelligence recede from someone rendered insane by some illness, where would those faculties slumber? The mad, when they speak or act, do many absurd things, for the most part unrelated—indeed, even opposed—to their own good intentions and inclinations. When we either reflect on or observe what they say and do, if we consider them properly, we are barely—if at all—able to contain our tears. What shall I say of those who suffer the assault of demons? Where is their own intelligence hidden or buried when an evil spirit uses both their soul and their body according to its own will? Who is confident that this evil cannot befall a wise man in this life? Next, how well and to what extent do we perceive truth in this flesh, when, as we read in the true book of Wisdom, "The corruptible body weighs down the soul and the earthly dwelling oppresses the intelligence as it considers many things" (Wis 9:15)? An "impulse" or "appetite for action," if in this way Latin rightly names that which the Greeks call *hormē*, is counted as one of the primary goods of nature. Yet is it not precisely this which also produces those miserable motions and deeds of the insane which horrify us when sense is distorted and reason is put to sleep?

Further, virtue itself, which is not among the primary goods of nature because it is added afterward through education, claims to be the highest of human goods; and yet what does it do except conduct perpetual wars with vices, not external but internal ones, not those of others but our very own?

Is this not the particular struggle of that virtue which in Greek is named *sōphrosynē*, in Latin "temperance," by which the carnal passions are curbed so that they do not drag the mind into consenting to every sort of shameful action? Vice is never absent when, in the words of the apostle, "The flesh desires in opposition to the spirit." To this vice there is a contrary virtue, when, as the same apostle says: "The spirit desires in opposition to the flesh. For these," he says, "are at war with each other, so that what you will is not what you do" (Gal 5:17). What, however, do we will to do when we will to be perfected by the supreme good? It can only be that the flesh not desire in opposition to the spirit and that this vice opposed to what the spirit desires not be in us. We are not strong enough to do this in this life, however much we will, but with the help of God, let us at least not surrender the spirit and so yield to the flesh warring against the spirit, and be dragged into sinning by our own consent. Therefore, let us not believe that, as long as we are in this internal war, we have already attained our happiness, which we will to attain by conquering the flesh. And who is so utterly wise as to have no conflict at all with his lusts?

What about the virtue called prudence? Does not its total vigilance consist in distinguishing goods from evils, so that in seeking the former and avoiding the latter no error sneaks in? Yet in this way does not prudence itself give evidence that we are among evils or that evils are within us? Prudence teaches that evil is consenting to the desire to sin and that good is withholding consent to that desire. Nevertheless, that evil, to which prudence teaches us not to consent, and to which temperance enables us not to consent, is not removed from this life by either prudence or temperance.

What about justice, whose function is to render to each his due, thereby establishing in man a certain just order of nature, so that the soul is subordinated to God, and the flesh to the soul, and consequently the flesh and the soul to God? Does it not demonstrate in performing this function that it is still laboring at its task instead of resting in the completion of its goal? Surely, the less the soul keeps God in its own thoughts, the less it is subordinated to him; and the more the flesh desires in opposition to the spirit, the less is it subordinated to the soul. Therefore, as long as there is in us this weakness, this plague, this weariness, how shall we dare to say that we are already made well? If we are not yet made well, how shall we dare to say that we are already happy in the attainment of final happiness?

As for the virtue called courage, no matter how wise one may be, it bears the clearest witness to human evils, which it is forced to endure patiently. I am astonished to see with what boldness the Stoic philosophers contend that such evils are not evils, yet they allow that if evils become so great that a wise man cannot or ought not endure them, he may be driven to bring about his own death and leave this life.[8] So great is the stupid pride of these men that, while holding that the final good is found in this life and that they are made happy by their own efforts, their wise man (that is, the man whom they describe with an amazing inanity) is one who—even if he is made blind, deaf, dumb, and lame, even if he is tormented by pain and assailed by any other such evils that could be spoken or thought, so that he is driven to bring about his own death—is still not ashamed to call this life so composed of evils "happy"!

O happy life, which seeks the help of death in order to be ended! If it is happy, he should remain in it. In what way are those things not evils? They conquer the good of courage and not only compel the same courage to yield to themselves, but also to rave, so that it both calls the same life happy and persuades one to flee it! Who is so blind that he does not see that if it is happy, one ought not flee it? In saying that such a life must be fled, they openly admit the weakness of their position. The neck of their pride having been broken, why do they not also admit that such a life is miserable? I ask, did Cato kill himself because of endurance or lack of endurance? He would not have done it, except that he could not bear to endure the victory of Ceasar.[9] Where is the courage here? Truly, it yielded; truly, it surrendered; truly, it was so completely overcome that it abandoned, deserted, and fled the happy life. Or was it not then happy? Clearly, it was miserable. In what sense, then, were there no evils which made life miserable and something necessary to flee? . . .

If virtues are true—and true virtues cannot exist except in those who possess true piety—they do not profess to be able to protect the men who have them from suffering miseries. True virtues are not such liars as to profess this. They do, however, profess that human life, which is compelled by the great number and magnitude of evils in this world to be miserable, is happy through hope in a future world, and in the same way made well. Indeed, how can it be happy until it is made well? And thus the apostle Paul, speaking not of imprudent, impatient, intemperate, and unjust men, but of men living according to true piety and thereby having true virtues, says: "By hope we are made well. However, hope that is seen is not

8. The Stoics argued that suicide was appropriate, at least under some conditions. On the Stoics, see the note on V. 9.

9. Rather than endure what he considered to be the tyranny of Caesar, Cato of Utica killed himself in 46 B.C. The Stoics considered Cato to be a hero for this.

hope, for how can one hope for what one sees? However, if we hope for what we do not see, we look forward to it with patience" (Rom 8:24–25).

Therefore, as we are made well by hope, so we are made happy by hope; and as we do not presently possess well-being, but look forward to it in the future "with patience," so it is with happiness. This is because we are now among evils, which we must endure patiently, until we arrive at those goods in which we will find only indescribable delight and none of the things which we must now endure. Such well-being, which we will find in the future world, will itself be final happiness. Because they do not see this happiness, the philosophers refuse to believe in it, but struggle to fabricate for themselves in this life an utterly false happiness through a virtue as dishonest as it is proud.

Chapter 6

What about the legal judgments of men concerning other men? No matter how much peace abides in cities, they cannot be eliminated. How wretched, how sad we think they are! Those judging are unable to discern the consciences of those whom they judge. Consequently, they are frequently compelled to investigate the truth by torturing innocent witnesses concerning a case that is not even their own.[10] What about when someone whose own case is at stake is tortured? He is asked whether he is guilty while he is being tortured. Even an innocent person, then, pays a most certain penalty for an uncertain crime, and not because it is discovered that he committed it, but because it is not known that he did not commit it. Thus, the ignorance of the judge is frequently the calamity of the innocent.

What is much more intolerable, what must be lamented and washed, if it were possible, by fountains of tears, is this: a judge, on account of ignorance, tortures an accused in order not to execute an innocent person mistakenly, yet it happens that the judge does execute, through wretched ignorance, one who is both innocent and tortured, one whom the judge had tortured in order that he might not execute an innocent person. If, following the "wise," the accused has chosen to flee this life rather than endure the tortures any longer, he says he has committed what he did not commit. Though he is condemned and executed, the judge still does not know whether the person he tortured in order that he might not mistakenly execute an innocent person was innocent or not. Thus, he both tortures an innocent man in order to know and kills him though he does not know.

10. Torture was an accepted and even required practice for Roman judges.

In this darkness of the social life, will a judge who is "wise" sit in judgment or not?[11] Certainly he will, for human society, which he considers it a crime to desert, binds him and drags him to this duty. These things he does not consider to be crimes: that innocent witnesses are tortured in the cases of others; that the innocent who are accused are frequently overcome by the power of pain when they are tortured, and are then punished on account of falsely confessing; that, although not punished by death, they frequently die while being tortured or as a result of being tortured; or that sometimes the accusers, perhaps desiring to be beneficial to human society by seeing to it that no crimes go unpunished, are unable to prove the charges even though they are true, since the witnesses lie and the defendant himself fiercely endures the torture without confessing, and are themselves mistakenly condemned by a judge. This great number and magnitude of evils he does not consider to be sins, for a wise judge does not do them because of a will to harm, but because of the necessity imposed by not knowing, and also because of the necessity of judging imposed by human society.

Accordingly, even if they are not the malice of the wise, these evils are certainly what we call the misery of man. If indeed it is through the necessity of not knowing and of judging that he tortures and punishes the guiltless, is it not enough for him that we do not hold him to be guilty? Must we call him "happy" besides? How much more thoughtful and appropriate it is for man to recognize misery in this necessity, and to hate himself because of it, and if he is wise in the manner of the pious, to cry out to God, "Deliver me from my necessities!" (Ps 25:17)

Chapter 7

After the city or municipality comes the world, which they regard as the third level of human society. Beginning with the household, they progress to the city and then to the world. Like converging waters, as the world is larger, so is it more dangerous. In the first place, the diversity of languages in the world alienates one man from another. Imagine that two people meet and are compelled by some necessity not to pass by but to remain together. If neither knows the language of the other, although they are both human beings, speechless animals—even if they are of different species—will associate with each other more easily. When human beings realize that they

---

11. Augustine is chiding the philosophers who hold that the happy life is a social life. His point is that social life can never truly be happy in this world.

cannot communicate between themselves solely because of the difference of language, nothing promotes their association despite their similarity of nature. A man would rather be with his own dog than a foreigner.

Yet it might be said that, by taming peoples through the peace of society, the imperial city attempts to impose not only its yoke but also its language, so that there is no lack of interpreters, but indeed a great abundance. This is true. Yet how does it compensate for the numerous and immense wars, the great slaughter of men, the tremendous effusion of human blood? Even though those evils are now settled, the misery of them is not yet finished. Although bordering, hostile nations have never been and are not presently lacking, and although wars always have been and continue to be waged against them, nevertheless the very size of the empire has given rise to wars of a worse kind; namely, social and civil wars. The human race is shaken by these more miserable wars, either when they are waged so that there might eventually be calm, or when a fresh outbreak of them is feared. If I wanted to speak appropriately of these evils, great and immense destructions, and hard and dire necessities, even though I could by no means do so as the subject demands, where would this lengthy discussion end?

They say, however, that the wise man will wage only just wars—as if, mindful that he is human, he would not much rather lament that he is subject to the necessity of waging just wars.[12] If they were not just, he would not be required to wage them, and thus he would be free of the necessity of war. It is the iniquity on the part of the adversary that forces a just war upon the wise man. Even if it did not give rise to the necessity of war, such iniquity must certainly be lamented by a human being since it belongs to human beings. Therefore, let anyone who reflects with sorrow upon these evils so great, so horrid, and so savage, confess that he is miserable. Anyone, however, who either permits or considers these things without sorrow in mind is certainly much more miserable, since he thinks himself happy because he has lost human feeling.

Chapter 11

Because the name "peace" is also frequently used with respect to things which are subject to death, where there certainly is no eternal life, we prefer to call the end of this city, where its highest good will be, "eternal life" rather than "peace." Of this end the apostle says, "Now, indeed, having been liberated from sin and having become servants of God, you will have

12. For Augustine's views on war, see the section on "War."

your reward in sanctification, your true end in eternal life" (Rom 6:22).

On the other hand, "eternal life" could be taken by those who are not familiar with the Sacred Scriptures to include also the life of the wicked. One might think this either because certain philosophers profess the immortality of the soul, or also because our faith professes the unending punishment of the impious, who certainly could not be eternally tormented unless they also lived eternally.

So that it can be understood more easily by all, it must be said that the end of this city, in which it will have its highest good, is either "peace in eternal life" or "eternal life in peace." Peace is such a great good that even with respect to earthly and mortal things, nothing is heard with greater pleasure, nothing desired more longingly, and in the end, nothing better can be found. If I wish to speak of it at somewhat greater length, I will not, I think, be burdensome to readers, both because my subject is the end of this city and because of the very sweetness of peace, which is dear to all.

Chapter 12

Anyone who pays any attention to human affairs and our common human nature recognizes as I do that just as there is no one who does not wish to be joyful, so there is no one who does not wish to have peace. Indeed, even those who want war want nothing other than to achieve victory; by warring, therefore, they desire to attain a glorious peace. What else is victory, unless triumphing over the opposition? When this has happened, there will be peace. Therefore, even those who are eager to exercise the military virtues by commanding or fighting wage war with the intention of peace. Consequently, the desired end of war is peace, for everyone seeks peace, even by waging war, but no one seeks war by making peace.

Even those who want the peace they now have to be disturbed do not hate peace, but they desire to change the peace according to their own wishes. Thus, they are not unwilling that there be peace, but they want it on their own terms. Furthermore, even if they have separated themselves from others through sedition, when they conspire or plot amongst themselves they do not achieve what they intend unless they have some sort of peace. Likewise, robbers themselves want to have peace with their partners, so that they might more violently and safely attack the peace of others. Perhaps one person is so strong and so wary of conspiring with others that he does not ally himself to any partners. Waiting in ambush and prevailing alone, he gains plunder by crushing and annihilating whom he can. Still, with those whom he cannot kill and from whom he wants to hide what he does, he certainly has some sort of a shadow of peace.

In his home, with his wife and children and anyone else who might be there, he surely strives to be at peace. Their complying with his command is no doubt pleasing. If they do not do so, he is enraged; he rebukes and punishes them. He establishes peace in his own home, if it is necessary, even by brutality. He thinks that peace is not possible unless the rest of the household is subject to a ruler, and in his own home he himself is that ruler. That is why, if the service of a great multitude, or of cities, or peoples is offered to him, so that they would serve him in the same manner as he wanted to be served in his own household, then he would no longer conceal himself like a bandit in a hideout, but raise himself up like a visible king, although the same desire and malice would abide in him. Thus, all desire to have peace with their own associates, whom they want to live according to their own decree. Indeed, they want, if they are able, to make even those against whom they wage war into their own associates, and to impose on them, when conquered, the laws of their own peace.

Let us imagine someone of the sort sung about in poetry and myth, someone whom, perhaps because of his unsociability and savageness, they have preferred to call "semihuman" rather than "human." His kingdom was the solitude of his horrible cave. So extraordinary was his malice that a name was invented from it, for in the Greek language evil is called *kakos*, which is what he was named.[13] He had no wife with whom to carry on endearing conversation, no little children to play with, no older children to give orders to, no friends with whom to enjoy speaking. He did not even enjoy the society of his father Vulcan, compared to whom he was happier simply because he had not generated such a monster as himself. He gave nothing to anyone, but took from whomever he could whatever and whenever he wanted.

Nevertheless, in the very solitude of his own cave, in which, as is said, "the ground was always reeking with fresh carnage,"[14] he wanted nothing other than peace—a peace in which no one would molest him, in which the quiet was not disturbed by the violence of anyone or the fear of it. Further, he desired to be at peace with his body, and to the extent that he was at peace with it, all was well with him. When he commanded, the limbs of his body submitted. Yet, his own mortality rebelled against him out of need and stirred up sedition through hunger, aiming to dissociate and exclude the soul from the body. In order to make peace with that mortality as quickly as

13. The story of Cacus is related by Virgil in *Aeneid* VIII. 184–305.
14. *Aeneid* VIII. 195.

possible, he plundered, he killed, and he devoured. Though monstrous and savage, he was nevertheless monstrously and savagely providing for the peace of his own life and well-being. Moreover, if he had been willing to make peace with others while he was striving to make peace in his cave and in himself, he would not have been called evil or a monster or semihuman. Also, if the appearance of his body and his breathing horrible fire frightened human society, possibly he was not so much savage because of a desire for harming but because of the necessity of his staying alive.

He might not, however, have even existed, or, what is more believable, he might not have been the same as the description given by the vanity of poetry, for if Cacus were not blamed too much, Hercules would be praised too little.[15] Therefore, it is better, as I have said, to believe that a human or semihuman of that sort never existed, as is the case with many of the imaginings of the poets.

Even the most savage wild animals, from whom Cacus got part of his wildness (for he was even said to be half-wild), care for their own species by means of a certain peace. They do this by associating, begetting, bearing, cherishing, and nourishing the offspring, even though they are for the most part insociable and solitary. I do not mean those animals such as sheep, deer, doves, starlings, and bees, but those such as lions, wolves, foxes, eagles, and owls. Indeed, what tigress, pacifying her wildness, does not gently purr and caress her young? What kite, however much it circles its prey alone, does not unite with a mate, put together a nest, warm the eggs, nourish the young birds, and, as if with the mother of his family, keep peace in his domestic society as much as he can? How much more is man brought by the laws of his nature, as it were, to enter into society and keep peace with all men to the extent that he is able?

After all, even the evil wage war for the sake of the peace of their own associates, and they would want to make everyone their own, if they could, so that everyone and everything would be enslaved to one individual. How would that happen if they did not consent to his peace, either through love or fear? In this manner, pride imitates God in a distorted way. It hates equality with partners under God, but wants to impose its own domination upon its partners in place of God. Consequently, it hates the just peace of God and loves its own iniquitous peace. Nevertheless, it is not able not to love some sort of peace. Truly, there is no defect so contrary to nature that it wipes away even the last vestiges of nature. Accordingly, he who knows to prefer the upright to the deformed, and the ordered to the distorted, sees that the peace of the iniquitous, in comparison to the peace of the just,

15. Cacus was eventually slain by Hercules.

should not be called "peace" at all. However, it is necessary that even what is distorted be at peace in some way with a part of the things in which it exists or from which it is established. Otherwise, it would not exist at all.

This is just like if someone were to hang with his head downward. The position of the body and the order of the limbs would certainly be distorted, because what nature demands to be above is below, and what it wants to be below is above. This distortion disturbs the peace of the flesh and for that reason is painful. It is nevertheless true that the soul is at peace with the body and is busy struggling for its well-being, and thus there is someone suffering. If the soul departs, having been driven out by the pain, as long as the structure of the limbs remains, so does a certain amount of peace, and thus there is still something hanging there. Because the earthly body tends toward the earth and is resisted by the chain by which it is suspended, it tends to the order of its own peace and requests in a weighty voice, as it were, a place where it might rest. Now lifeless and without any sense, nevertheless it does not depart from the peace of its own natural order, either when it has it or when it reaches toward it.

If embalming potions and treatments are applied, which do not allow the form of the cadaver to break up and dissolve, a sort of peace still unites certain parts to other parts and connects the whole mass in its suitable and therefore peaceful place in the earth. If no one applies the treatment for burying, however, then the cadaver disintegrates in the course of nature. It is in a state of disturbance due to dissenting vapors which are disagreeable to our senses (for this is what is smelled in putrefaction), until it is assimilated to the elements of the world and gradually, little by little, separates into their peace. Nevertheless, in no way is anything withdrawn from the laws of the supreme creator and governor by whom the peace of the universe is administered, for even if tiny animals are born from the cadaver of a greater animal, by the same law of the creator each little body serves its own little soul in the well-being of peace. Even if the flesh of the dead is devoured by other animals, wherever it is carried, whatever the things to which it is joined, whatever the things into which it is changed and altered, it finds those same laws diffused throughout all things for the well-being of every mortal species, making peace by harmonizing suitable elements.

Chapter 13

Thus, the peace of the body is the ordered proportion of its parts. The peace of the irrational soul is the ordered repose of the appetites. The peace of the rational soul is the ordered agreement of knowledge and action. The peace of the body and the soul is the ordered life and well-being of a living thing. The peace between a mortal man and God is an ordered obedience, in faith, under the eternal law.

The peace among human beings is ordered concord. The peace of the household is an ordered concord concerning commanding and obeying among those who dwell together. The peace of the city is an ordered concord concerning commanding and obeying among the citizens. The peace of the heavenly city is a fellowship perfectly ordered and harmonious, enjoying God and each other in God. The peace of all things is the tranquility of order.

Order is the arrangement of things equal and unequal, alloting to each its own position. Hence, the miserable indeed lack the tranquility of order in which there is no disturbance, since insofar as they are miserable, they certainly are not at peace. Nevertheless, since they are deservedly and justly miserable, they are not, in their very own misery, able to be outside that order. They are surely not united to the happy, but, by the law of order, are separated from them. When they are free from disturbance, they are adjusted to the circumstances in which they find themselves by a harmony of some degree. Thus, some tranquility of order belongs to them, and so some peace. Therefore, the reason they are miserable is because, even if they have some freedom from concern and are not suffering, they are still not in a position where they ought to be exempt from concern and suffering. They are more miserable, however, if they are not at peace with the very law by which the order of nature is administered.

Moreover, when they suffer, they suffer in that part in which a disturbance of peace occurs, but there is still peace in that part not disturbed by suffering and in the structure itself, which is not dissolved. As, therefore, there is a kind of life without suffering, but suffering cannot exist without some life, so there is a kind of peace without any war, but war cannot exist without some peace. This does not follow because of what war itself is, but because it is waged by those or in those who are natural beings in some way. They would not exist at all, unless they remained in a peace of some sort.

Accordingly, there is a nature in which there is no evil, or even in which there can be no evil, but there cannot be a nature in which there is no good. Thus, not even the nature of the devil himself, insofar as it is a nature, is evil. Rather, it is the distortion of that nature that makes it evil. Hence, he did not stand firm in the truth, but he did not escape the judgment of the truth. He did not remain in the tranquility of order, but he nevertheless did not avoid the power of the one who orders. The goodness of God, which is in the devil's nature, does not remove him from the justice of God, which orders by punishing him. God did not then reproach the good that he created, but the evil that the devil has committed. Neither does God take away all that he gave to the devil's nature, but some he takes and some he leaves, so that there might be something to suffer the loss of what was taken away. That very suffering is a witness to the good taken away and the good left behind, for unless good were left behind, the devil could not suffer because of the good lost. . . .

Therefore, God, who founded all natures most wisely and ordered them most justly, who established the mortal human race as the greatest embellishment of the earth, gave to mankind certain goods suitable for this life. These goods include a temporal peace proportional to the short span of a mortal life, a peace involving health, preservation, and the society of one's own kind. They also include the things necessary for guarding or recovering this peace (such as what is appropriately and fittingly present to the senses: light, sound, breathable air, drinkable water, and whatever is suitable for feeding, covering, healing, and adorning the body). All this was given through the most equitable stipulation, that he who uses such mortal goods rightly, adapting them to the peace of mortals, would receive more and better goods; namely, the peace of immortality and the glory and honor suitable to it, in an eternal life which is for enjoying God and one's neighbor in God. He, however, who uses mortal goods wrongly, would lose them and would not receive eternal ones.

Chapter 15

God said, "Let him have dominion over the fish of the sea and the winged things of the heavens and all the crawling things which crawl upon the earth" (Gn 1:26). He did not will that the rational being, having been made according to his own image, dominate any except the irrational beings; he did not will that man dominate man, but that man dominate the beasts. Therefore, the first just men were established as shepherds of beasts rather than as kings of men, so that even in this way God might suggest what the order of creatures requires and what the reward of sinners drives away. Surely it is understood that the condition of slavery is rightly imposed on the sinner. Accordingly, nowhere in the scripture do we read the word "slave" before the just Noah punished the sin of his son with this word. Thus, he earned the name through fault, not through nature. . . .

The first cause of slavery, then, is sin, with the result that man is placed under man by the bondage of this condition. This does not happen except through the judgment of God, in whom there is no iniquity, and who knows how to distribute the various punishments according to the merits of the delinquent. Yet, as the Lord above says, "Anyone who sins is a slave of sin" (Jn 8:34), and thus indeed many religious people enslaved to iniquitous masters are nevertheless not enslaved to the free: "For by whatever one has been conquered, to that one has also been made a slave" (2 Pt 2:19). And it is certainly a happier condition to be enslaved to a man than to a lust, since the very lust for dominating—not to mention others—ravishes the hearts of mortals by a most savage mastery. In that order of peace by which some are subordinated to others, humility is as beneficial to the enslaved as pride is harmful to the dominating.

Nevertheless, by the nature in which God first established man, no one is a slave of man or of sin. It is also true that penal slavery is ordained by that law which commands the preservation and prohibits the disturbance of the natural order, because if nothing had been done contrary to that law, there would have been nothing requiring the restraint of penal slavery. That is why the apostle also warns slaves to be subject to their masters and to serve with good will and from the heart (Eph 6:5), so that if they are not able to be freed by their masters, they might make their slavery in a certain sense free, by serving not with the cunning of fear, but with the faithfulness of affection, until iniquity is transformed and all human rule and power are made void, and God is all in all (1 Cor 15:24, 28).

Chapter 16

. . . Those who are true "fathers of their families" are concerned that all in their family—the slaves as well as the children—should worship and be reconciled to God.[16] Such fathers desire and long to come to the heavenly household, where the duty of ruling mortals is not necessary because the duty of being concerned for the welfare of those already happy in that immortality will no longer be necessary. Until that home is reached, fathers ought to endure more because they rule than slaves do because they serve.

If, however, anyone in the household opposes the domestic peace through disobedience, he is disciplined by word or by whip or by any other kind of just and legitimate punishment, to the extent that human society allows. Such discipline is for the profit of the one being disciplined, so that he is readjusted to the peace from which he had departed. After all, just as it is not kindness to help someone when it would cause him to lose a greater good, so it is not innocence to spare punishment and permit someone to fall

---

16. The phrase "fathers of their families" refers to the Roman institution of the *paterfamilias*.

more grievously into wickedness.[17] Therefore, in order to be innocent, duty demands not only that one not bring evil to anyone, but also that one restrain another from sin or punish his sin, so that either the person who is punished might be set straight by the experience or others frightened by his example.

Hence, because the human household ought to be the beginning or the building block of the city, and because every beginning is directed to some end of its own kind and every part to the integrity of the whole whose part it is, the consequence is clearly that domestic peace is directed to civic peace. That is to say, the ordered concord concerning commanding and obeying of those dwelling together is directed to the ordered concord concerning commanding and obeying of the citizens. Accordingly, the father of the family should obtain the precepts by which he rules his household from the laws of the city, so that his household might be adapted to the peace of the city.

Chapter 17

The household of those who do not live by faith chases an earthly peace consisting of the affairs and advantages of this temporal life. The household of human beings living by faith, on the other hand, looks forward to the future, to those things which are promised as eternal, and makes use of temporal and earthly things like a traveller. Those things do not seize such a person and turn him away from the path to God. They do not increase the burdens of "the corruptible body which weighs down the soul" (Wis 9:15), but sustain him for more easily enduring them. Consequently, both sorts of men and both sorts of households use the things necessary for this mortal life, but the end of such use is unique to each and varies greatly. So also the earthly city, which does not live by faith, desires earthly peace, and it secures a concord concerning the commanding and obeying of the citizens, so that there might be a certain orderly arrangement of human wills concerning the things pertaining to mortal life. The heavenly city, however, or rather the part of it which journeys in this mortal life and lives by faith, necessarily uses this peace, too, until the very mortality which makes such a peace necessary might pass away.

Because of this, so long as it leads the life of a captive, as it were, journeying within the earthly city, already having received a promise of redemption and a spiritual gift as a pledge of it, the heavenly city has no

17. This passage should be compared with the selection from *Letter 93* in the section on "The Use of Persecution."

doubts about conforming to the laws of the earthly city which administer the things required for the sustainance of the mortal life. Because mortality itself is common to both of the cities, concord between them is preserved with respect to those things pertaining to the mortal life. . . .

So long as this heavenly city journeys on the earth, it calls forth citizens from all peoples and gathers a society of foreigners speaking all languages. It is not troubled at all about differences in customs, laws, and institutions by which the earthly peace is either sought or maintained. So long as they do not impede the religion which teaches the worship of the one, supreme, and true God, the heavenly city abrogates or destroys none of them, but indeed observes and follows them, for whatever the diversities of different nations, they nevertheless strive toward the one and the same end of earthly peace.

Hence, even the heavenly city uses the earthly peace on its journey, and it is concerned about and desires the orderly arrangement of human wills concerning the things pertaining to mortal human nature, insofar as it is agreeable to sound piety and religion. It directs the earthly peace to the heavenly peace, which is so truly peace that it must be held and said that the only peace, at least of rational creatures, is the most ordered and most harmonious society enjoying God and each other in God. When that peace comes, there will not be mortal life, but a whole and certain life; not the ensouled body weighing down the soul in its corruption (Wis 9:15), but a spiritual body with no wants and with every part subordinated to the will. While it journeys, the heavenly city possesses this peace in faith, and out of this faith it lives justly when it directs to the attainment of that peace whatever good actions it performs toward God, and also those performed toward the neighbor, since the life of this city is certainly social.

Chapter 19

The style of dress or manner of living in which anyone follows the faith that leads to God does not matter to the heavenly city, so long as these are not in contradiction with the divine precepts. Thus, even philosophers, when they become Christians, are not required to change their style of dress or eating customs, which do not impede religion, though they are required to change their false teachings. Accordingly, that city does not care at all about the distinction that Varro made concerning the Cynics,[18] so long as nothing is done basely or intemperately.

18. The Cynics were a school of philosophers who adopted a distinctively shabby style of dress.

With respect to those three kinds of life, the leisurely, the active, and the combination of the two, although every one, through sound faith, can lead his life according to any one of them and attain the everlasting reward, what one holds through the love of truth and what one expends through the duty of charity are nevertheless important. Thus, no one ought to be so leisurely that he does not, in his leisure, consider the advantage of his neighbor; neither should anyone be so active that he does not consider the contemplation of God to be necessary.

In leisure, one ought not delight in slothful idleness, but in either the investigation or discovery of truth, so that everyone advances in it and does not withhold his discoveries from others. In action, no one ought to love honor or power in this life, because all is vanity under the sun (Eccl 1:2–3). Rather, the work itself that is done through the same honor or power should be loved, if it is done rightly and profitably. That is to say, it should be loved if it advances the well-being of the subjects, which is according to God, as we have argued earlier.

Because of this the apostle said, "He who desires the episcopacy desires a good work" (1 Tm 3:1). He wanted to explain that the name "episcopacy" is the name of a work not of an honor. Indeed, the word is Greek, and it comes from the fact that he who is set over others "superintends" them; that is, he exercises care for them. Indeed, the Greek word *skopos* means intention; therefore, for *episkopein* we can say, if we want, "superintend." Consequently, he who desires to be over others rather than to benefit others should understand that he is not a bishop.

Thus, no one is prohibited from zealousness for knowledge of the truth, because the life of learned leisure pertains to what is praiseworthy. On the other hand, to desire high position, without which a people cannot be ruled, is indecent, even if the position is held and administered in a decent manner. Because of this, charity for truth seeks holy leisure, while the requirements of charity accept just activity. If this latter burden is not imposed, one is free to grasp for and to contemplate truth. If, however, the burden is imposed, accepting it is on account of the requirements of charity. Even in this instance, however, delight in the truth is not abandoned completely, otherwise that sweetness might be lost and these requirements crush us.

Chapter 21

It is at this place that I will explain, as briefly and clearly as I can, what in the second book of this work I promised that I would demonstrate; namely, that, according to the definition that Scipio uses in the *Republic* of Cicero, there never was a Roman republic.[19] He succinctly defines a "republic" as "the affair of a people." If this definition is true, there never was a Roman republic, because Rome never was the affair of a people, which is Scipio's definition of a republic.

The reason for this is that he defined "a people" as "a fellowship of a multitude united through a consensus concerning right and a sharing of advantage." What he calls "a consensus concerning right" he explains in the dialogue by making it clear that it is not possible for a republic to be managed without justice. Therefore, where there is no true justice, there can be no right. What is done by right is indeed done justly; what is done unjustly, however, cannot be done by right. The iniquitous institutions of human beings must not be said or thought to exist by right, because even those institutions say that right flows from the fountain of justice, and that what is customarily said by those who do not understand right correctly— i.e. that right is the advantage of the strongest—is false.[20]

Accordingly, where there is no true justice, there can be no fellowship of men united through a consensus concerning right, and therefore there can be no people according to the definition of Scipio or Cicero. Moreover, if there is no people, neither can there be an affair of a people, but only of some sort of a multitude which is not worthy of the name of "a people." Consequently, if a republic is "the affair of a people," and there is no people which is not "united by means of a consensus concerning right," and there is no right where there is no justice, without doubt it must be concluded that where there is no justice, there is no republic.

Furthermore, justice is that virtue which distributes to everyone his due. What sort of justice is it, then, that takes a man away from the true God and subjects him to unclean demons? Is *this* to distribute to each his due? Or, is he who takes the ground purchased by someone and gives it to another who has no right to it unjust, but he who takes himself away from the dominion of the God who made him and enslaves himself to malicious spirits just?

Certainly, the cause of justice against injustice is argued very energetically and forcefully in that very same book, *The Republic*. Earlier, the case of injustice against justice was considered and it was said that the republic could not stand firm or be managed except through injustice. It was set down as the most powerful part of the argument that it was unjust for men

19. See II. 21.

20. In Book I of Plato's *Republic*, Thrasymachus defines justice as "the advantage of the strongest."

to serve other men as their masters, but that unless the imperial city to whom the great republic belongs follows such injustice it is not able to rule its provinces. The response from the side of justice was that this rule over the inhabitants of the provinces is just because servitude is advantageous for such men and is done for their benefit when it is done correctly—that is, when the license for wrongdoing is taken away from the wicked. Also, it was argued that they will be in a better condition as a result of having been subdued, because they were in a worse condition before being subdued.

In order to strengthen this reasoning, a famous example was stated as though it was borrowed from nature: "Why, then, does God rule man, the soul rule the body, the reason rule lust and the rest of the corrupt parts of the soul?"[21] Plainly, this example teaches well that servitude is advantageous to some and that serving God is indeed advantageous to all. In serving God, the soul correctly rules the body, and the reason in the soul subordinated to the Lord God correctly rules lust and the rest of the corrupt parts of the soul. Thus, when a man does not serve God, what in him can be reckoned to belong to justice? Indeed, when not serving God, the soul can in no way justly rule the body, or human reason the vices. Furthermore, if there is not any justice in such a man, without doubt neither is there any in a fellowship of human beings which consists of such men. Therefore, this is not that "consensus concerning right" which makes a multitude of human beings a "people," whose affair is called a "republic."

What shall I say concerning that "advantage," the sharing of which also unites a fellowship of men so that it is named "a people," as stipulated by the definition? If you carefully direct your attention, you will see that there is no advantage to any who live impiously, as do all who do not serve God but serve the demons who, the more impious they are, the more they want to receive sacrifice as gods, even though they are the most unclean spirits of all. Yet, what we have said about the consensus concerning right I think is sufficient to make it apparent that, according to this definition, there is no people which might be said to be a republic in which there is no justice.

If our enemies say that the Romans have not served unclean spirits but good and holy gods in their republic, must what we have already said sufficiently, indeed more than sufficiently, be repeated yet again? Who, except the excessively stupid or the shamelessly contentious, having arrived at this point after reading the earlier books of this work, finds it possible to doubt but that the Romans have up to this point served evil and impure demons? Nevertheless, in order to say no more about the sort of

21. *Republic* III. 25.

gods they are worshipping with sacrifices, I instead cite what is written in the law of the true God: "Anyone sacrificing to the gods, except only to the Lord, will be eradicated" (Ex 22:20). Thus, he who admonishes with such a threat did not want either good gods or evil ones to receive sacrifice.

Chapter 23

. . . We ourselves—his city—are the best and most radiant sacrifice. We celebrate this mystery through our offerings, which are known to the faithful, as we have argued in the preceding books.[22] Indeed, through the Hebrew prophets the divine oracles thundered that the offering of sacrificial victims by the Jews, a foreshadowing of the future, would cease, and that peoples from the rising of the sun to its setting would offer one sacrifice, as we see happening now.[23] From these oracles we have taken as much as seemed sufficient and have already sprinkled them throughout this work.

Thus, justice exists when the one and supreme God rules his obedient city according to his grace, so that it does not sacrifice to any whatsoever except Him alone. As a result, in everyone belonging to that same city and obeying God, the soul faithfully commands the body, and reason the corrupt parts of the soul, in accord with the lawful order. Consequently, just like a single just man, a fellowship and a people of just men lives by faith, which works through love, by which man loves God as God ought to be loved, and his neighbor as himself. Where that justice does not exist, truly there is no "fellowship of men united through a consensus concerning right and a sharing of advantage." If this justice does not exist, then a people does not exist, if this is the true definition of a people. Therefore, neither does a republic exist, for there is no affair of a people where there is no people.

Chapter 24

If, however, a people is not defined in that way, but in another—if, for example, it is said that a people is "a fellowship of a multitude of rational beings united through sharing in an agreement about what it loves"—then truly, in order to see the character of a people, what it loves must be considered. If it is not a fellowship of a multitude of beasts, but of rational creatures, and is united through sharing in an agreement about what it

---

22. Augustine treats this especially in X. 6, which is not included in this volume.

23. Augustine may have in mind Malachi 1:11.

loves, then, no matter what it loves, it is not unreasonable to call it "a people." It is a better people if it agrees in loving better things; a worse one if it agrees in loving worse things. According to this definition, the Roman people is a people, and its affair is without doubt a republic. However, history gives witness to what that people loved originally and subsequently, and by what morals it arrived at the bloodiest revolutions and then at social and civil wars, utterly shattering and annihilating concord itself, which is, in a certain sense, the well-being of a people. Of this we have said much in the preceding books. . . .

Book XX

Introduction

In Book XX, Augustine takes up the question of the last judgment. Most of Book XX is devoted to an analysis of the scriptural passages that refer to that end time, especially Chapter 20 of the Book of Revelation and Chapter 25 of Matthew's Gospel. In the first of these texts, the author reports having seen a vision in which Satan is chained up for a thousand years and then released for a brief period of time. As the selections from Chapters 9 and 11 make clear, Augustine argues that these thousand years should be understood as referring to the time period, however long it will be, between the first coming of Christ and his returning to judge the world at the end of history. Corresponding to the two comings of Christ are two resurrections, the second of which occurs at the last judgment as described by Matthew in the story of the separation of the sheep and the goats. The two comings of Christ and two resurrections are paralleled by two ways of speaking about the church. During the period prior to the last judgment, the church is not free from the tribulations of Satan and must militate against him. Only after the period that follows this one will the church reign triumphant with Christ. These passages are crucial insofar as they shed light on Augustine's understanding of the church's relationship to the political realities in the midst of which it currently finds itself.

Chapter 1

Since, God willing, I am about to speak of the day of the last judgment of God and to defend that truth against the impious and the unbelieving, I ought first to set down the divine testimony for that teaching, just as though laying the foundation of a building. Those who do not want to believe such testimony strive to oppose it with petty little human wranglings that are false and fallacious. Either they maintain that the testimony cited from the sacred writings means something else, or they simply deny that it was said by God, for I do not think that any mortal who understands these passages and believes them to have been written by the supreme and true God through holy souls, as indeed they were written, would resist and refuse them. I think this is true whether he expressly admits his agreement, or whether he is ashamed or afraid to admit it because of some vice, or even if, by an obstinacy bordering on insanity, he struggles most contentiously to defend what he knows or believes to be false against what he knows or believes to be true.

In confessing and professing, the whole church of the true God holds that Christ will come from heaven to judge the living and the dead. This we call divine judgment's "last day," which is to say, "the end time," for it is uncertain as to how many days this judgment might extend. No one, however negligently he reads them, does not know that it is the custom of the Sacred Scriptures to use "day" for a period of time. For that reason, when we speak of the "day" of the judgment of God, we add "last" or "final," for even now he judges, and from the beginning of the human race he has judged, sending the first human beings, those perpetrators of an enormous sin, out of paradise and exiling them from the tree of life. Without doubt he also judged when he did not spare the sinful angels (2 Pt 2:4) whose prince, having overthrown himself through envy, in envy overthrew mankind. Nor is it without God's sublime and just judgment that both in the lofty heavens and on the earth, the lives of both demons and humans are most miserable, completely full of errors and hardships. Yet, even if no one had sinned, God would not maintain the whole of rational creation, clinging most firmly to its own Lord in eternal happiness, without good and right judgment.

Not only does he judge the race of demons and the race of humans as groups, so that they are miserable as a result of the merits of the first members of their races, but he even judges the personal deeds of individuals which they perform through the choice of the will. Moreover, since even the demons pray that they might not be tormented (Mt 8:29), it is certainly not unjust that he refrains from punishing them, nor is it unjust that each is tormented for his own wickedness. Human beings also suffer punishments through divine agency for their own misdeeds—often visibly, always invisibly, either in this life or after death. Even though no human being acts rightly unless assisted by divine help, no demon or human being acts wrongly unless allowed to do so by the same divine and most just judgment. As the apostle says, "There is no iniquity with God" (Rom 9:14); and also, as he says elsewhere, "His judgments are inscrutable and his ways unsearchable" (Rom 11:33).

In this book, therefore, insofar as God grants it to me, I will argue not about the first judgments of God, nor about these intervening judgments, but about the final judgment, when Christ will come from heaven to judge the living and the dead. Truly, that day is especially now called the "day of judgment," for then there will be no place for ignorant complaining about why this unjust person is happy and why that just person is unhappy. Then will appear the true and full happiness belonging only to the good and the deserved and unmitigated unhappiness belonging only to the evil.

Chapter 2

Now, however, we learn to bear with equanimity the evils which even the good suffer and not to esteem highly the goods which even the evil obtain. In this way, especially with respect to those cases in which divine justice is not clear, divine teaching is salutary, for we do not know by which judgment of God it is that this good person is poor and that bad person is rich. One person is joyful whom we think ought to be tormented with grief because of his own moral decadence, while another is sad whose praiseworthy life convinces us that he ought to be joyful. An innocent person leaves a court of law not only unavenged but even condemned, either defeated by the iniquity of the judge or crushed by false testimony, while his guilty adversary, on the other hand, swaggers out not only unpunished, but with his claims vindicated. Here an impious person enjoys good health while there a pious person feebly wastes away. Thieving youths enjoy excellent health while infants who could not offend anyone even with a word are afflicted with the hostile cruelty of diseases. Someone useful to human affairs is torn away by a premature death, while another whom it would seem ought not to have even been born lives, and not just the normal span, but the longest of lifetimes. Someone abounding in crimes is elevated with honors while the shadows of obscurity bury another who is beyond reproach.

Who could gather all of the other cases of this kind? Who could count them all? If they were uniform in their incongruity, so that in this life, in which, as the holy psalm so eloquently expresses it, "man is like emptiness and his days pass away like a shadow" (Ps 144:4), only evil people obtain transitory and earthly goods and only good people suffer the same kind of evils, then such a situation could be referred to the judgment of God, which is just and even kind. Then we might reason that those who will not attain the eternal goods that bring happiness are, through temporal goods, either deluded due to their own wickedness or consoled due to the mercy of God, and that those who will not suffer eternal torments are, through temporal evils, either afflicted due to any of their own sins whatsoever, no matter how small, or goaded into fulfilling the virtues. As the situation is now, however, not only are some good people among evils and some evil people among goods, which seems unjust, but also evils for the most part befall evil people and goods for the most part come to good people. Consequently, the judgments of God become even more inscrutable and his ways even more unsearchable (Rom 11:33).[1]

To be sure, then, we do not know by what judgment God—in whom there is supreme power, supreme wisdom, and supreme justice; and no weakness, no rashness, and no iniquity—does these things or allows them to be done. Nevertheless, it is salutary for us to learn not to esteem highly those things, whether goods or evils, that we see to be common to both good and evil people, but to seek the good things that belong only to good people and to flee especially the evils which belong only to evil people. When we come to that judgment of God, the time of which is properly named "the day of judgment" and sometimes "the day of the Lord," it will be clear that all of God's judgments are perfectly just, not only those that will be made at that time, but also those that have been made from the beginning and those that will yet be made. At that time it will also be manifest by what just judgment of God it happens that so many, indeed almost all, just judgments of God are hidden from the perception and comprehension of mortals. Nevertheless, it is not hidden from the faith of the pious that what is hidden is just.

Chapter 9

. . . While the devil is bound for a thousand years, the saints reign with Christ for the same thousand years, which without doubt are to be understood in the same way, that is, as dating from the time of Christ's first coming. . . .

In one sense the "kingdom of heaven" must be understood to include both he who breaks what he teaches and he who does what he teaches, though the former is least in it and the latter great. In another sense, the "kingdom of heaven" is said to be that into which only he who performs what he teaches enters.[2] Thus, where both kinds of people are present, it is

1. See also I. 8 and V. 24.
2. Augustine's point is that Matthew 5:19 speaks of those who break the least of the commandments as being present in the kingdom of heaven, even though they

the church as it now is; where only one kind will be present, it is the church as it will exist then, when evil will not be within it. Therefore, even now the church is the kingdom of Christ and the kingdom of heaven.

Hence, Christ's saints reign with him even now, although indeed in another way than they will reign then. The tares, however, do not reign with him, even if they grow with the wheat in the church (Mt 13:30), for he reigns with Christ who does what the apostle says: "If you have risen with Christ, consider the things that are above, where Christ is seated at the right hand of God; seek the things that are above, not those which are on the earth" (Col 3:1–2). He also says that the communion of such people is in heaven (Phil 3:20). Finally, those who reign with him are those who are in his kingdom in such a way that they themselves also are his kingdom. In what way, though, are those others the kingdom of Christ who, not to mention anything else, even though they are in it until all stumbling blocks are collected from his kingdom at the end of the world (Mt 13:41), seek their own things there, not those of Jesus Christ?

Therefore, in the passage quoted above (Rev 20:1–6), the book of the Apocalypse speaks of this militant kingdom in which there is still conflict with the enemy and sometimes there is resistance from warring vices and at other times they fall back and are ruled. Such conflict will last until this militant kingdom reaches that most peaceful kingdom where it will be ruled without the foe. That passage of the Apocalypse thus also speaks of the first resurrection, which exists even now. Indeed, after having said that the devil is to be bound for a thousand years and afterwards freed for a brief period of time, the book then gives a summary of what the church will do in those thousand years, or what will be done within it, when it says, "And I saw thrones, and those sitting upon them, and judgment was given" (Rev 20:4). It must not be thought that this is said of the last judgment, but of the thrones of the rulers, and the rulers themselves, through whom the church is now governed. There seems no better way to construe the words "judgment being given" than what is said in the Gospel: "What you bind on earth will be bound in heaven also, and what you free on earth will be freed in heaven also" (Mt 18:18). Concerning such judging the apostle says, "What have I to do with judging those who are outside? Do you not judge those who are inside?" (1 Cor 5:12).

---

will be the least there, while Matthew 5:20 suggests that those who break the commandments will not be in the kingdom of heaven at all. Augustine's solution is that the first passage must speak of the kingdom of heaven, the church, as it now is, while the second speaks of the church after the last judgment, when there will be no wicked in the kingdom of heaven.

When the Apocalypse says, "And the souls of those slain on account of their witness to Jesus and on account of the Word of God," it should be understood as referring to what is said afterwards: "They will reign with Jesus for a thousand years" (Rev 20:4). That is to say, the souls of the martyrs will reign with him for a thousand years before their bodies will be returned to them. The souls of the pious dead are not separated from the church, which even now is the kingdom of Christ. Otherwise, no commemoration of them would be made at the altar of God in the communion of the body of Christ. Nor would it be of any advantage to someone in danger to run to Christ's baptism in order that his earthly life not be ended without it. Nor would it be of any advantage to run to reconcilation, if perhaps through penance or a bad conscience anyone was separated from the body of Christ. Why are these things done, unless because the faithful, even after they die, are members of his body?

Therefore, while those thousand years run down, their souls already reign with him, though not yet reunited with their own bodies. Thus, in another place in that same book it is read, "Blessed are the dead who die in the Lord; from this time forward, says the spirit, may they rest from their own labors, for their works follow them" (Rev 14:13). First, then, the church reigns with Christ among the living and the dead, as it does even now. As the apostle says, "Christ died so that he might rule both the living and the dead" (Rom 14:9). The Apocalypse mentioned only the souls of the martyrs because those who struggled for the truth clear up to death especially reign in death. From this part, however, we understand the whole, namely that the other dead also belong to the church, which is the kingdom of Christ. . . .

John says, "The rest of them did not come to life" (Rev 20:5), for "it is now the hour when the dead hear the voice of the son of God, and those who hear it will live" (Jn 5:25); therefore, the rest of them will not come to life. The passage that comes next—"until the thousand years are finished" (Rev 20:5)—must be understood as saying that they did not come to life when they should have, namely, by passing over from death to life. Therefore, when the day of the resurrection of the body comes, they will come out of their tombs not to life but to judgment, namely, to condemnation, which is called "the second death." Whoever has not lived until the thousand years are finished, that is, whoever has not heard the voice of the Son of God during the whole time to which the first resurrection pertains and has not passed over from death to life, will surely, in the second resurrection, which is the resurrection of the flesh, pass over with his flesh into the second death.

John continues by saying, "This resurrection is first; happy and holy is he who has a part in this first resurrection" (Rev 20:5–6); that is, happy and holy is he who participates in it. He is indeed a participant in it who not only comes back to life from the death of sin, but also remains in that life. "Over these," John says, "the second death has no power" (Rev 20:6). Therefore, the second death does have power over the rest, of whom it was said above, "The rest of them did not come to life until the thousand years were finished" (Rev 20:5). In that whole intervening time that is called a thousand years, however long any of them lived in the body, he did not return to life from the death in which his impiety held him, so that, by returning to life in this way, he might participate in the first resurrection and the second death not have power over him.

Chapter 11

"When the thousand years are finished," the Apocalypse says, "Satan will be freed from his prison, and he will go out to seduce the nations which are in the four corners of the earth, Gog and Magog, and he will draw those nations, which are as numerous as the sands of the sea, into war" (Rev 20:7–8). He will seduce them, then, in order to draw them into this war. Even earlier, through many and various evils, he was seducing them in whatever ways he could. Yet, "he will go out" means "he will break out from the hiding places of hatred into open persecution." This, with the final judgment imminent, will be the final persecution suffered by the holy church throughout the whole world, that is, by the entire city of Christ. It will be perpetrated by the entire city of the devil when each city will be at its greatest strength upon the earth.

Surely those peoples which he calls Gog and Magog are not to be taken as though they were some barbarian peoples in some part of the world, whether the Getae and Massagetae,[3] as some suspect on account of the first letters of these names, or some other foreign peoples also outside of Roman jurisdiction. Instead, it is indicated that they are throughout the whole world when the author speaks of "the nations which are in the four corners of the earth" and then remarks that they are "Gog and Magog." I find the meaning of the name "Gog" to be "the covering" and the meaning of the name "Magog" to be "from the covering," or, as it were, the house and he who proceeds from the house. They are, therefore, the peoples in which, as

---

3. The Getae were a Thracian tribe on the Danube; the Massagetae a Scythian people to the east of the Caspian.

we understood earlier, the devil was locked up, just as in a pit. The devil himself is in some way coming out and going forward from them, so that they are "the covering," he himself "from the covering." If, however, we refer both names to the peoples, not one to the peoples and the other to the devil, then they are also "the covering," for the ancient enemy is now locked up in them and somehow covered up, and they are also "from the covering" when they will erupt from concealed to open hatred.[4]

When the Apocalypse says, "And they went up over the breadth of the earth and they encircled the camp of the holy ones and the beloved city" (Rev 20:9), it certainly does not mean that they have come or will come to one place, as if to some one place that will in the future be the camp of the holy ones and the beloved city, for this city is nothing other than the church of Christ extending throughout the whole world. Therefore, wherever the church will be then—and it will be among all the peoples, for that is the meaning of the words "the breadth of the earth"—there will be the camp of the holy ones, there will be God's beloved city, there, surrounded by all her enemies, will be the church, encircled by the savagery of their persecution, for her enemies, too, will be there with the church among all the peoples. That is to say, the church will be squeezed, hard pressed, besieged in the straits of tribulations. It will not, however, desert its military duty, which is named by the word "camp."

Chapter 30

There are many other testimonies concerning the final judgment of God in the divine scriptures, and if I were to collect them all the list would be extraordinarily long. Therefore, let it suffice that I have proved that both the new and the old sacred writings predict it.[5] However, that the future judgment will be through Christ—that is, that Christ will come from

---

4. Contemporary scholars do not accept the meanings of the terms "Gog" and "Magog" that are given here. Augustine seems to have borrowed them from Jerome's *Commentary on Ezekiel* XI. 38. What should not be overlooked is that, like Jerome but unlike some other Christians, Augustine refuses to identify the names with any particular people or country. Ambrose, for example, had identified Gog with the Goths. See his *On the Faith, to Gratian* II. 16. This chapter should be compared with Augustine's criticism of Orosius in XVIII. 52. In both instances, Augustine is much less willing than some other Christians to assert that the millennium is at hand.

5. In sections of Book XX not included here, Augustine analyzes passages that speak of the last judgment found in Isaiah, Daniel, and Malachi.

heaven to judge—is not as clearly expressed in the Old Testament as in the new, for when in the Old Testament the Lord God says of himself that he will come, or when it is said of the Lord God that he will come, it does not necessarily follow that the texts are to be understood as speaking of Christ, since the Lord God is the Father and also the Son and the Holy Spirit. . . .

When we read in the prophetic writings that God will come to conduct the final judgment, even though no further distinction is recorded, the passages ought to be understood as referring to Christ simply because of the term "judgment." Even though the Father will judge, he will judge through the coming of the Son of Man, for the Father himself, through the revelation of his own presence, "does not judge anyone, but has given all judgment to the Son" (Jn 5:22), who will be revealed as a man who will judge, just as it was as a man that he was judged.

Who else is there of whom God speaks in the same way through Isaiah under the names of Jacob and Israel, of whose seed he took a body? It is written thus:

> Jacob is my servant; I will lift him up. Israel is my chosen one, my soul will take him to myself. I have given my Spirit to him, so that he might bring forth judgment to the peoples. He will not cry out, nor will he cease, nor will his voice be heard outside. A bruised reed he will not crush and a smoldering wick he will not extinguish, but in truth he will bring forth judgment. He will shine and will not be broken until he establishes judgment on the earth, and in his name the peoples will hope (Is 42:1–4).

In Hebrew, the passage does not have "Jacob" and "Israel." However, the Septuagint translators, wanting to point out how to interpret the words "my servant"—for that was said on account of the form of the servant in which the Most High showed himself to be the most humble—put down the name of the particular human beings in order to signify the family in which that form of the servant was taken up.[6] The Holy Spirit was given to him and, according to the Gospel witness, was indicated by the appearance of a dove (Mt 3:16; Jn 1:32). He brought forth judgment to the peoples, for he announced the future judgment that had been hidden from them. In his

6. As Augustine indicates, the Hebrew text of Isaiah does not identify the prophet spoken of here as Jacob or Israel. The Septuagint is a Greek translation of the Hebrew scriptures thought to have been begun in the third century B.C. This translation was held in great authority by Augustine and the Christian church generally during its first centuries. In the Septuagint, the servant is identified, as Augustine says, as Jacob or Israel. See also XVII. 7.

gentleness, he did not cry out, yet he did not cease proclaiming the truth. His voice was not and is not heard outside when he is not obeyed by those who are outside, cut off from his body. The Jews themselves, his own persecutors, who have been compared to the bruised reed that has lost its uprightness and the smoldering wick that has lost its light, he did not crush or extinguish. He spared them, for he had not yet come to judge them but to be judged by them. Surely he did bring forth judgment in truth by announcing to them a time when they would have to be punished if they persisted in their malice. His face shone on the mount (Mt 17:1–2) and his reputation shone on earth. He was not broken or crushed, because neither in himself nor in his church did he yield to his persecutors so that he would cease to be. Thus, what his enemies have said or are saying about him— "When will he die and his name pass away" (Ps 41:5)—has not happened nor will it happen, "until he establishes judgment on the earth." Behold! The hidden thing which we were seeking has been discovered. This is the final judgment, which he will establish on the earth when he himself comes from heaven.

We already see fulfilled in him what has been put down in the last part of the prophecy: "And in his name the peoples will hope." As a consequence of this hope of the peoples, which cannot be denied, may the final judgment also be believed, although it is impudently denied. Indeed, who would have hoped for what even those who are as yet unwilling to believe in Christ already see with us? Unable to deny it, they gnash their teeth and waste away. Who, I say, would have hoped that the peoples would soon be hoping in the name of Christ when he was arrested, bound, beaten, ridiculed, and crucified, when even the disciples themselves had lost the hope which they had already begun to have in him? What scarcely a single thief on a cross hoped for then, the peoples spread far and wide hope for now, and so that they may not die eternally, they are marked with that very cross on which he died.

Therefore, no one denies or doubts that the final judgment will be through Jesus Christ in such a manner as is announced by those holy writings except one who, through some strange sort of incredible animosity or blindness, does not believe those same writings which have already demonstrated their own truth to the whole world. We have learned, then, that these things will come about in or with that judgment: Elijah the Tishbite will come, the Jews will have faith,[7] the Antichrist will persecute, Christ

---

7. In a chapter not included here (Ch. 29), Augustine suggests, on the basis of the final verses of the book of Malachi, that quite probably Elijah will return just prior to the last judgment and convert the Jews to Christ.

will judge, the dead will be resurrected, the good and the evil will be separated, and the world will be burned and renovated.[8] That all these things will come must be believed. In what ways and in what order they will come, however, the experience of the events themselves will then teach with more completeness than human intelligence can attain now. Nevertheless, I think they will come about according to the order in which I have related them.

Two books pertaining to this work are left to me in order to complete, with the help of God, what was promised. One of them will treat the punishment of the wicked; the other the happiness of the just. In them, insofar as God grants it, the human arguments opposed to the divine predictions and promises will especially be refuted. The wretched, thinking themselves wise, are seen to gnaw on those arguments and thus scorn as false and ridiculous the foods of the healthy faith. Those who are wise according to God, on the other hand, hold that the strongest argument for all things which seem incredible to human beings and yet are contained in the Holy Scriptures, whose truth has already been declared in many ways, is the truthful omnipotence of God. They hold as certain that the truthful omnipotence of God could in no way lie to them in the Scriptures and that he can accomplish what, to the unbeliever, is impossible.

8. Augustine discusses the burning and rejuvenation of the world in some of the omitted chapters. As a scriptural basis for this view he cites passages such as 2 Pt 3:12 and Rev 21:1.

Book XXI

Introduction

Book XXI deals with the punishment of the damned. In its opening pages, Augustine notes that the idea of the eternal punishment of the body seems unbelievable to some. The incredulous want examples of how a physical body could suffer in this way, and in the selection from Chapter 4 Augustine tries to provide a few of them. He is aware, however, that eternal bodily suffering is contrary to the present nature of the human body and takes up that problem in the selection from Chapter 8. He also considers the view of the Platonists and Virgil, who held that wrongdoing is indeed punished after death, that the goal of such punishment is purification, and hence that such punishment is not eternal. A similar view had been offered by some Christian theologians, who thought that the devil's own punishment would come to an end at some point. In the selections from Chapters 23 and 24, Augustine explains why the church, basing itself on the Scriptures, rejects this opinion. Finally, in Chapter 27, he criticizes those who would attempt to purchase their escape from punishment in the afterlife through almsgiving rather than through spiritual regeneration.

Chapter 2

What can I cite that would convince the unbelievers that it is possible for ensouled and living human bodies not only not to be dissolved by death, but also to continue on in the torments of eternal fire? They do not want us simply to ascribe this to the power of the Almighty, but demand to be persuaded by some example. . . .

Chapter 4

Those who have investigated the natures of animals most inquisitively have recorded that the salamander lives in fire;[1] certain famous mountains of Sicily continually boil with flames and are not burned up, and have been this way for a very long time, from ancient times until now.[2] If these things are so, they are sufficient witnesses that not everything that burns is consumed. The case of the soul shows that not everything that is able to suffer is also able to die. Why, then, is it still demanded from us to produce examples of things by which we might teach that it is not unbelievable that the bodies of human beings punished with an eternal penalty do not lose their souls by fire, and that without damage they burn, and that without destruction they suffer?

The substance of the flesh will then have that quality bestowed on it by him who bestows on so many things the diverse wonders which we see and do not wonder at because they are so numerous. Who except God, the creator of all, has given to the dead flesh of the peacock the quality of not spoiling? Although that might seem incredible when heard, it happened in Carthage that this bird, cooked, was served to me, and I ordered that a suitable amount of meat be sliced off and kept. After a span of days long enough to cause any other cooked meat to spoil, it was brought out and set before me and produced no offensive smell. It was saved in the same way for more than thirty days and was found to be the same. After a year it was still in the same state, except that some of the flesh was drier and more shriveled. Who gave to chaff the cooling power of preserving buried snow or the warming power of ripening green fruit? . . .

Chapter 8

The unbelievers, however, might respond that they do not believe what we say about human bodies that will burn forever but never die, since we know that the nature of human bodies has been constituted much differently. Consequently, they might say that the reason which is given about those wonders of nature cannot be given in this case; hence, it cannot be said, "This force is natural, that is the nature of this thing," for we know that this is not the nature of human flesh.

For this, we possess a response from the holy writings: before the fall, human flesh was constituted differently, that is, so that it could never suffer death; after the fall, however, it is otherwise. Its changed qualities be-

---

1. Apparently this was not an uncommon view among naturalists in Augustine's time. Aristotle reports the view in *History of Animals* V. 19, 552b, but does not adopt it.

2. Presumably Mt. Aetna is meant.

come known in the hardships of this mortality, for it is not able to possess life forever. Likewise, it will be constituted differently in the resurrection of the dead than it is known to us now.

They do not, however, believe those writings in which one reads about the qualities of the life man lived in paradise and about how foreign to the necessity of death he was. Certainly, if they did believe we would not be arguing with them so painstakingly about the future penalty of the damned. Therefore, something must be brought forward from the writings of the most learned among them by which it might become clear that anything can become different from what the study of its nature had first shown it to be.[3] . . .

Therefore, let the unbelievers not fashion a conceptual fog for themselves from the notion of natures, as though something whose nature was known through their own human experience could not be made into something else by God. Indeed, even those very things which, in the natural course of events, are known by all, are not less wonderful than the things changed by God, and they would be stupendous to all those considering them if human beings were accustomed to wonder at wonders rather than at rarities.

Who, upon reflecting, considering the countless multitude of human beings and the great similarity in their physical characteristics, does not see that it is a vast wonder that each individual has a unique appearance? Who does not see that unless there were a likeness among themselves the human species would not be distinguished from the other animals, and yet, unless there were a dissimilarity among themselves, the individuals would not be distinguished from the other human beings? Thus, those we profess to be similar, we also find to be dissimilar. Furthermore, the consideration of dissimilarity is even more wondrous because a common nature seems more properly to demand similarity. Nevertheless, since those things which are rare are wondrous, much more is it wondered at when we discover two people so similar that we always or frequently err in distinguishing them. . . .

They have something else that even in our time could be pointed out. I think it ought to be sufficient to warn them that, even though they have directed their attention to something in some principle of nature and have made themselves very familiar with it, they ought not from that time forward dictate it to God, as though he could not alter and change it into something very different from what they have known. . . . The land of

---

3. Augustine goes on, in a passage not included here, to cite as such an example a celestial portent reported by Varro.

Sodom was not a horror, but now it is. Through a remarkable mutation, the one who founded natures turned its nature into something repugnantly different, and this change that occurred after such a long time continues for such a long time.[4]

Thus, as it was not impossible for God to establish what he willed, so it is not impossible for him to change the natures of what he has established into whatever he might will. From that ability a prolific multitude of those miracles called signs, revelations, portents, and prophecies grow up thick as a forest. If I wanted to bring these to mind and list them all, would there ever be an end to this work? The word "sign" comes from the verb for showing, for something is shown to be happening by signs; the word "revelation" comes from the verb for revealing; "portent" comes from the verb for portending, that is, for revealing beforehand; and "prophecy" from the words for saying beforehand, that is, for announcing the future.

One wishes that the interpreters of those miracles might realize how mistaken they are about them; or how they even do foretell the truth through them—but by the prompting of spirits whose concern is to entangle the minds of human beings worthy of such punishment in the nets of noxious curiosity; or how they chance upon something true simply by predicting so many things. These miracles happen as if they were contrary to nature and they are said to happen "contrary to nature." The apostle spoke according to the custom of human beings by saying that a wild olive grafted to an olive tree and partaking of the fatness of the olive is contrary to nature (Rom 11:17–24). Nevertheless, to us, these miracles called "signs," "revelations," "portents," and "prophecies," ought to show, reveal, portend, and prophecy that God will do what he has foretold he will do concerning the bodies of human beings. He will not be hindered by any obstacle, nor limited by any law of nature.

Moreover, how he has foretold what he will do has been explained sufficiently, I think, in the preceding book. Indeed, not everything pertaining to that topic from the old and the new Sacred Scriptures was collected there, but what I judged to have been sufficient for this work.

Chapter 16

The mercy of God flowing into the "vessels of mercy which he has prepared for glory" (Rom 9:23) is truly great. Consider this: during infancy, the first stage of human life, one submits to the flesh without any resis-

---

4. The story of the transformation of Sodom is found in Genesis 19 and Wisdom 10:6–9. It is also recorded by many other ancient writers.

tance. During the second stage, called childhood, reason has not yet taken up the fight against one's own vices and lies under the sway of the delights of almost every vice. Although the power to speak is present then and the child thus seems to have passed on from infancy, it is not yet fit to be commanded due to the weakness of its mind. Still, if an infant or a child has received the sacraments of the mediator and his life ends during those years, since he has been brought over from the power of darkness to the kingdom of Christ, not only is eternal punishment not prepared for him, but indeed after death he does not suffer any purifying torments. After death, spiritual regeneration alone suffices so that what the generation of the flesh has united to death might not be an obstacle.

When, however, a person comes to the stage which comprehends teaching and he is able to submit to the rule of law, then he must take up the war against the vices and he must wage it vigorously so that he is not led to damnable sins. If those vices are not yet strengthened through habitually winning, then they are more easily conquered and yield. If, though, they are habituated to conquering and ruling, then only through arduous toil are they overcome. That does not happen truly and sincerely except through a delight in true justice; this stems from belief in Christ. . . .

Therefore, whoever desires to escape everlasting punishment must not only be baptized, but also justified in Christ, and in this way he truly passes over from the devil to Christ. He should not imagine, however, that there will be any future purifying punishments except prior to that last, terrifying judgment. Nevertheless, by no means is it also necessary to deny that that future eternal fire will be proportioned according to the degree of deserved evil, so that it could be lighter for some and heavier for others. Either the force and heat of the fire itself may vary according to the punishment deserved by each, or the fire may burn equally but the distress be felt unequally.

Chapter 23

First, it is necessary to ask and to understand why the church has not been able to endure the human argument promising purification or forgiveness to the devil even after the greatest and lengthiest punishments.[5] It has not been due to spite that so many holy people, trained in both the old and the new Sacred Scriptures, have not granted cleansing and the happiness of the

5. The most notable proponent of this view was Origen (c. 185–c. 254), a famous Christian scholar and theologian. Some of Origen's views were condemned at a council in Alexandria in A.D. 400.

kingdom of heaven to angels of various and sundry qualities and quantities after punishments of various and sundry qualities and quantities. Rather, they saw that they could not void or weaken the divine pronouncement which the Lord predicted that he himself will bring forth and state at the judgment: "Depart from me, you cursed, into the eternal fire which has been prepared for the devil and his angels" (Mt 25:41). (In this way, he certainly shows that the devil and his angels will burn in eternal fire.) Also, it has been written in the Apocalypse, "The devil, who was deceiving them, was sent into a pool of fire and sulphur, where both the beast and the false prophet are also; and he will be tortured day and night for ever and ever" (Rev 20:10). In the first passage the word "eternal" was used; in the second "for ever and ever." With these words, divine scripture customarily signifies nothing other than what does not have a temporal end.

Surely, no other reason more just and more clear can be found why the truest piety holds as fixed and immobile that the devil and his angels will have no return to the justice and life of the saints than because Scripture, which misleads no one, says that God has not pardoned them but has, in the meantime, condemned them in advance. Having been pushed back into the prisons of murky hell for safe keeping, they will be handed over to the last judgment for punishing. Then eternal fire will receive them, and there they will be tortured for ever and ever. . . .

What sort of thinking is it, then, to suppose that eternal punishment is a fire lasting a long time and yet to believe that eternal life is without end, when Christ has said, including both in the very same place, in one and the same sentence, "Thus, these will go into eternal punishment, but the just into eternal life" (Mt 25:46)? If both are eternal, then certainly both ought to be understood either as long-lasting, but with an end, or as everlasting, and without an end. The terms are equal and related to each other: in the one place "eternal punishment" and in the other "eternal life." To say, however, in this one and the same statement, "Eternal life will be without end; eternal punishment will have an end," is absurd in the extreme. Therefore, because the eternal life of the saints will be without end, the eternal punishment for those who suffer it will undoubtedly also not have an end.

Chapter 24

This line of reasoning is also successful against those who, pleading their own case as though they were offering a greater mercy, attempt to oppose the words of God. They say that it is clear that those words are true, not because human beings will suffer the things which God has said they will, but because they deserve to suffer them. They say that God will give these human beings to the prayers of the saints; and then the more the saints pray for their enemies surely the holier the saints become; and then, being completely without sin, their prayer is more efficacious and more worthy of being heard by God. . . .

The reason why the church does not now pray for the wicked angels whom it knows to be its own enemies is the very same reason why the church, even though it will then be perfectly holy, will not pray at the last judgment for the human beings who are to be tormented by eternal fire. That is why the church prays for those who are its enemies among the human race now, for now is the time for fruitful repentence. For what does the church most especially pray on their behalf, except that, as the apostle says, "God might grant them repentence and that they might return to their senses from the traps of the devil, by whom they are held captive, according to his will" (2 Tm 2:25–6)?

If, therefore, the church were certain, so that it actually knew who those people are who, although still stationed in this life, are nevertheless predestined to go into the eternal fire with the devil, then it would not pray for them any more than for the devil himself. Because, however, the church is certain about no one, it prays for all its enemies, at least for all the human ones who are stationed in this body. Yet the church's prayer on behalf of everyone is not heard in every case. It is heard only on behalf of those who, even though they oppose the church, are nevertheless predestined, so that the church's prayer might be heard on their behalf and they might become sons of the church. If, however, some possess an impenitent heart all the way up to death and are not converted from enemies into sons, does the church still pray for them, that is, for the spirits of such people who are deceased? Why does the church not do so, except because a person who did not go over to Christ when he was in the body is now reckoned to be on the side of the devil? . . .

From the gentiles and the Jews, God will condemn none—not none at all—but none of those whom he predestined, for those whom he predestined he also called, justified, and glorified (Rom 8:30).

Chapter 27

It remains to respond to those who say that only people who have neglected to perform works of mercy by giving alms in proportion to their own sins will burn in the eternal fire. They say this because of what the apostle

James says: "Judgment is without mercy for anyone who did not show mercy" (Jas 2:13). They say that therefore he who performed works of mercy by giving alms, even though he has not corrected his abandoned ways but has lived abominably and worthlessly in the midst of his very own almsgiving, will be judged with mercy, so that either he will not be condemned at all or he will be freed from final damnation after a period of time. . . .

They do well to remind people to give alms in proportion to their sins, for if they said that alms of any sort are able to procure divine mercy for everyday sins and for great ones and for a habit of whatever sort of heinousness, so that remission would follow such things daily, they would themselves see that they are saying something absurd and ridiculous. Thus, they would be forced to admit that an exceedingly wealthy man would be able to make up for murders, adulteries, and any sort of wicked deeds by paying out an alms of ten pennies a day.

If that is most absurd and insane, but it is indeed asked what alms of mercy are proportionate for sins—for even the forerunner of Christ said of such alms, "Produce, then, fruits suitable for penance" (Mt 3:8; Lk 3:8)— then without doubt those who knife their own lives to death by perpetrating crimes daily will not be found to give such alms. In taking from others they seize a great deal more than they give, and by bestowing a puny portion of it on the poor they think that they nourish Christ. Believing that they have purchased, or rather are purchasing daily, a licence from him to commit evil, they instead, without concern, commit deeds that bring damnation. . . .

It must be admitted that those who are received by the righteous into the eternal tabernacles[6] are not endowed with such habits that their own life would be sufficient to rescue them without the support of the saints. Hence, for them, mercy especially triumphs over judgment (Jas 2:13). Nevertheless, it must not be thought that therefore any exceedingly wicked person, in no way having changed his life into a good or even a more tolerable one, is received into the eternal tabernacles because he has gratified the saints with the mammon of iniquity, that is, with wealth or riches that were wrongly acquired. Even if they were properly acquired, they were still not true riches, but what iniquity thinks are riches. Iniquity does not know what the true riches are, which those who receive others into the eternal tabernacles possessed in abundance.

6. Augustine is referring to the story of the dishonest steward who apparently used the "mammon of inequity" to insure that he would be welcomed into the eternal tabernacles, i.e. heaven. See Lk 16:9.

Consequently, there is a certain middle way of life. It is not so evil that, for those who live it, lavishness in giving alms is of no use for acquiring the kingdom of heaven. Through alms, the needs of the just are met and they become friends who might accept them into the eternal tabernacles. Nor is this way of life so good that it suffices by itself to attain such great happiness unless it obtains mercy through the merits of those whom they have made friends. . . .

Yet what that way of life is, and what those sins are which impede arriving at the kingdom of God but receive indulgence through the merits of the saints who are friends, is exceedingly difficult to discover and most dangerous to define. Certainly, up until the present time, I have not been able to arrive at a solution to these questions, although I have been busy investigating them. Perhaps this is because they are hidden in order that the enthusiasm to progress toward guarding against all sins not grow fat and lazy. . . .

This liberation, which occurs either by means of one's own prayers or by the intercession of the saints, brings it about that someone might not be lost to the eternal fire, not that someone already lost might be rescued from there after a certain period of time. To be sure, some think that what the scriptures say about the good ground bringing forth abundant fruit, some thirty, some sixty, some one hundredfold (Mt 13:8), must be understood as meaning that, according to the diversity of their own merits, some saints will free thirty human beings, some sixty, and some one hundred. Yet even those people usually suppose that this will happen on the day of judgment, not after the judgment.

Someone, upon observing people promising themselves, in a twisted way, immunity on account of this opinion, since it would seem that all would be able to attain liberation from the eternal fire in this way, is said to have responded most elegantly, "It is better to live well so that everyone might be found to be among those who will intercede for the liberation of others. Otherwise, the intercessors might be so few that each of them quickly reaches his own limit—either thirty or sixty or one hundred—with many remaining who could not then be rescued from their own punishment by the intercession of others. Among those unrescued might be found all who, by the vainest audacity, promised themselves the hope of the fruits of others."

This suffices for my response to those who do not reject the authority of the sacred writings which we have in common, but by misunderstanding them think that what will happen is what they themselves want to happen rather than what those Scriptures say. Thus, this response having been given as promised, I conclude this book.

Book XXII

Introduction

In the final book of his work, Augustine attempts to describe, to the extent possible, the city of God as it will be in its heavenly glory. In Chapter 6, he returns to the considerations on Rome with which he began The City of God, *but now Christ, the founder of the heavenly city, is shown to be infinitely superior to Romulus, the founder of Rome, and the security enjoyed in heaven is contrasted with the false security of the earthly city. The next section of the book deals with the miracles that confirm the superiority of the city of God. A particularly vivid account of one such miracle has been included (Ch. 8). Augustine goes on to examine the criticisms of the doctrine of the bodily resurrection of the saints that had been raised by Platonists and others. His response to two such issues are included in our selections. The first is whether aborted fetuses will participate in the resurrection of the body (Ch. 12–13); the second concerns the presence of the female body in heaven (Ch. 17). Augustine goes on to suggest that it is inappropriate for the Platonists to criticize the doctrine of the resurrection of the body since a combination of the views of Plato and Porphyry would yield a similar teaching (Ch. 27). Finally, in the last chapters of the work, Augustine does his best to explain what life in heaven will be like, considering how the saints will see God and what sort of society they will enjoy there.*

Chapter 1

. . . It is God who made the world in the beginning, full of all good things, both visible and intelligible. In it he established nothing better than the spirits to whom he gave an intelligence and furnished with the capacity to contemplate God himself. He also bound them together in the single society which we call the holy and heavenly city. In that city, God himself is the reality by which they might be sustained and made happy—their common food and life, as it were. He assigned free choice to the intellectual nature in such a way that, if it willed, it might abandon God—its own happiness, to be sure—with uninterrupted misery being the result. He knew beforehand that certain angels would abandon such a great good through pride—a pride by which they would will to be able to attain a happy life on their own. Nevertheless, he did not take away this power of free choice from them, but judged it to be better and more efficacious to bring good out of evil than to refuse to allow evils to exist.

Indeed, evils would not exist at all unless such a changeable nature, which was good and was established by the supreme God and unchangeable good who makes all things good, made evils for itself by sinning. The testimony of this sin even demonstrates that this nature was made good, for unless this nature were itself a great good—though clearly not equal to the one who fashioned it—then its abandonment of God, as of its own light, could not have been evil for it. Consider the example of blindness, which is a similar defect. Blindness is a defect of the eye which indicates that the eye was created for the purpose of seeing light. Thus, through that very defect, the part of the body capable of receiving light is shown to be more excellent than the rest of the parts of the body. The excellence of the eye is, then, the only reason why its being without light is a defect. In the same way, the nature which at one time enjoyed God illustrates the superiority of its own foundation even by the very defect by which it is miserable because it does not enjoy God.

He made the voluntary fall of the angels liable to the most just penalty of eternal unhappiness, and to those who endured in the supreme good he gave the reward of endurance itself, so that they might be certain of their own enduring in it without end. He also made man righteous, with the same free choice—an earthly animal, to be sure, but one worthy of heaven if he would cling to the author of his own being. In the same way, a misery appropriate to a nature of this sort would follow if man deserted God. As in the case of the angels, God knew beforehand that, even though man would sin through abandoning him by violating his law, he would not take away man's power of free choice, for at the same time God foresaw the good that he himself would make from the evil of man. Through his own grace, he is gathering from the offspring of mortals properly and justly condemned a people so numerous that they might replace and restore that portion of the angels that fell. Thus, that beloved and heavenly city is not being cheated of the number of its own citizens; indeed, perhaps it will rejoice in an even more abundant population.

Chapter 6

Let us reconsider what Cicero finds remarkable about the reputed deification of Romulus:

> What is quite remarkable about Romulus is that the other human beings who are said to have become gods lived in ages when human beings were less learned, so that reason was more inclined to fabrication since the ignorant were easily induced into believing. We realize, however, that the age of Romulus was less than six hundred years ago, when writing and teaching were already firmly established, the primitive ignorance of the uncultivated life of man having been eliminated.[1] . . .

Now, Marcus Tullius Cicero was one of the most learned of human beings, and he was the most eloquent of all, and he said that the belief in the divinity of Romulus was wondrous because it arose in learned times which did not accept false fables. Yet who except Rome—and a small, toddling Rome at that—believed Romulus to be a god? Later on, it was necessary that what they had received from their elders be preserved, so that the city, having suckled this superstition in its mother's milk, as it were, might grow up to be such a great empire that from its position of pre-eminence, as from the highest ground in a particular region, it might inundate the other peoples which it dominated with this opinion. Thus, these peoples did not truly believe that Romulus was a god but nevertheless said so in order not to offend the city to whom they were enslaved by calling its founder something other than he was called by the Romans, who believed the superstition not through a love of error, but through an error of love.

On the other hand, although Christ is the founder of a heavenly and everlasting city, it did not believe him to be God because it was founded by him, but instead it deserves to be founded because it believes. Rome, already built and dedicated, worshipped its own founder in a temple just as though he were a god; Jerusalem, however, laid its own founder, Christ, who is God, in the foundation of its faith so that it might be able to be built and to be dedicated. Loving its founder, the former city believed him to be god; believing its founder to be God, the latter city loved him. Just as the former city first loved, and even willingly believed a falsehood about what it loved to be good, so the latter city first believed, in order that, with correct faith, it might not heedlessly love what is false but what is true.

1. *Republic* II, 10. On Cicero, see the note on II. 21. On Romulus, see the note on I. 34.

Leaving aside the many great miracles which persuasively showed Christ to be God, divine prophecies most worthy of belief preceeded him. These prophecies, which our forbearers believed would be fulfilled, are now shown to have been already fulfilled in him. Concerning Romulus, however, one hears and reads what happened, and that he founded Rome and reigned there, but not what was prophesied earlier. The writings about Romulus hold that it was believed that he was received among the gods; they do not teach that it happened.[2] Certainly there are no wondrous signs which show that it truly occurred. The female wolf (*lupa*) that nursed Romulus and Remus would surely seem to be conspicuous as a great portent, yet how and to what extent does it demonstrate that Romulus was a god? Even assuming that the *lupa* was not a harlot but a beast—for *lupa* can mean either[3]—it is still the case that, though she nursed them both, Romulus's brother is not held to be a god. . . .

I know that Cicero argues—in *The Republic*'s third book, if I am not mistaken—that the best city does not go to war except for the sake of keeping faith or for the sake of securing safety. What he means when he says "for the sake of securing safety," or how he wants "safety" to be understood, he shows in another passage:

> Private individuals often flee from those punishments which are felt by even the dullest—want, exile, bondage, flogging—when a swift death is offered to them. Death, however, which would seem to free individuals from punishment, is itself punishment for cities. A city ought to be so constituted that it would be everlasting. Therefore, the annihilation of a republic is not natural, as is the annihilation of a human being, for whom death is not only necessary, but very often even welcome. When a city, however, is destroyed, wiped out, and extinguished, it is as if—to compare small things to large ones—this entire world perished and dissolved.[4]

(Cicero stated this last sentence as he did because he thinks, like the Platonists, that the world will never perish.)

Thus, it is clear that Cicero wanted a city to go to war for the sake of securing the safety by which it might, as he says, "forever" endure in this world, even though its individual inhabitants are always dying and being born. The city is like the shade of the olive, laurel, or other such

2. See Livy I. 16.

3. In Latin, the word *lupa* can refer either to a female wolf or to a harlot. See Livy I. 4, 7.

4. *Republic* III. 23.

trees, which is perennial even though the individual leaves fall and grow
back.

Certainly, as he says, death, which often frees individuals from punishment, is not always a punishment for individual human beings, but it is for
the whole city. Accordingly, it is appropriate to ask whether the Saguntines
acted rightly when they chose to destroy their entire city rather than break
faith with the Roman republic.[5] They are praised by all the citizens of the
earthly republic for their action, but I do not see how they were able to obey
Cicero's position. It says that war must not be waged except for the sake of
keeping faith or for the sake of securing safety, but it does not say how one
must choose if, in a single moment of peril, the two conflict so that one
cannot be preserved without the loss of the other. Surely, if the Saguntines
had chosen safety, they would have had to have abandoned faith with
Rome; if they kept faith, certainly safety had to be lost, which is what
happened.

The safety of the city of God, however, is the sort that is able to be kept,
or rather acquired, along with faith and through faith. Indeed, no one can
come to that city by losing faith. This thought produced many great martyrs who possessed the most steadfast and enduring hearts. Romulus did
not have, nor could he have had, a single one of such martyrs when the
belief that he was a god arose.

Chapter 8

"Why," the enemies of the city of God ask, "do those miracles which you
claim to have happened not happen now?" I could, indeed, say that they
were necessary before the world believed in order that the world might
believe. With the whole world believing, any non-believer still asking for
wonders in order to believe is himself a great wonder. Our enemies, however, say this in order to believe that those earlier miracles did not happen
either. Why, then, is it sung everywhere with such great faith that Christ,
in the flesh, was was taken up into heaven? Why, in learned times which
rejected every impossibility, did the world, without any miracles, so very

---

5. The Spanish city Saguntum was besieged by Hannibal in 218 B.C. at the beginning of the Second Punic War. Instead of breaking faith with Rome and surrendering, the Saguntines held out despite tremendous suffering. It is said that they even
resorted to cannibalism and mass suicide. The city was finally destroyed by
Hannibal. Augustine recounts the story in III. 20, which is not included in this
collection.

miraculously believe unbelievable events? Will the critics reply that these things were believable and were therefore believed? If so, why do they themselves not believe? Briefly stated, the dilemma is this: either some unbelievable things, which nevertheless occurred and were seen, produced faith in another unbelievable, unseen thing; or else assuredly one thing, so believable that it needed no miracles in order to persuade people, refutes their excessive disbelief.

I might state this dilemma, but only in order to refute the excessively vain, for we cannot deny that many miracles have been performed which testify to that one, grand, salutary miracle by which Christ ascended into heaven with the flesh in which he was resurrected. Both the miracles that were performed and the faith on account of which they were performed were all recorded in the same truthful books. These miracles became known so that they might produce faith; through the faith which they produced they become even more known. Indeed they are read among the peoples so that they might be believed; they would not be read among the peoples unless they were believed.

Even today miracles are being performed in his name, either through his sacraments or else through the prayers or relics of his saints.[6] They do not, however, shine with the same clarity so that they should be published with a glory as great as that of the earlier ones. Certainly the canon of the sacred writings, which had to be limited, caused those miracles described in it to be recited everywhere and to become fixed in the memory of all peoples, while these present miracles are scarcely known by all the inhabitants of the city or locality where they are performed. Generally, even there only a very few know of them and the rest do not, especially if the city is large. Also, when they are reported to others elsewhere, their authority is not such that they are believed without difficulty or doubt, even though they are proclaimed to Christian believers by believers.

The miracle which took place at Milan when I was there, when a blind person received sight, was able to reach the attention of a multitude. This was because the city is large, because the emperor was there at the time, and because the event was witnessed by an immense number of people who were rushing to the place where bodies of the martyrs Protasius and Gervasius had been found. Although they were hidden and entirely unknown, they were revealed in a dream to the bishop, Ambrose, and discov-

---

6. Augustine was hesitant to believe in reports of contemporary miracles earlier in his life, but he had clearly changed his mind by the time this was written. See the remarks of G. Bardy in *Bibliothèque Augustinienne*, vol. 37, 825–31.

ered.[7] There the blind man saw daylight and the old darkness was pushed away.

In Carthage, however, who except for a very few knew about the healing of Innocent, the ex-advocate of the deputy prefecture. I was there and viewed it with my own eyes. My brother Alypius[8] and I had come from overseas. We were not yet priests, but we were already serving God. Innocent, a most religious man, with his entire household, received us and we were staying with him at the time. He was being treated by doctors for numerous and entangled fistulas in his rectum. The doctors had already operated and were now employing other treatments of the art of medicine. He had suffered lengthy and severe pains in that operation. Yet one of the many abscesses had escaped the attention of the doctors. It was so concealed that they had not even touched it, though they ought to have opened it with the knife.

Eventually, all the fistulas which they had opened and treated were healed. Only the one remained, on which they labored with no effect. Innocent grew suspicious of the delays and was terrified that he might be operated on again.

Another doctor, his household physician, who had not even been allowed to watch how the first operation was performed, had predicted that a second one would be needed. Angered, Innocent had thrown him out of the house, and he barely took him back. Finally Innocent blurted out, "Are you about to cut on me again? Are the words of the man whom you did not want to be present about to come true?" They ridiculed the inexperienced doctor and soothed the man's fears with encouraging words and promises. Many more days passed, but nothing they did helped. Still, the doctors stood by their promises to bring that abscess to an end not with the knife but with medicines. They also called in another doctor, Ammonius, who was quite well thought of in that profession. He was still alive then, though very old. After examining the area he promised Innocent just what the other doctors, basing themselves on their own diligent training, had promised. The authority of Ammonius put his mind at ease, and Innocent, just as if he were already healed, wittily and hilariously ridiculed the domestic physician who had predicted another operation in the future.

---

7. Augustine also relates this event, which occurred in A.D. 386, in *Confessions* IX. 7. 16.

8. Alypius and Augustine originally became friends as boys in Thagaste, and they would remain such throughout their lives. Alypius later became bishop of Thagaste.

Why drag out the story? After many days had passed, wasted in futility, the doctors, exhausted and embarrassed, admitted to him that he could be healed only by the knife. Innocent was terrified; he grew white with fear and was tremendously distraught. When he had collected himself enough to speak, he ordered the doctors to go away and not return.

Worn out from weeping and constrained by necessity, he could think of nothing to do except to call in a certain Alexandrian who had a great reputation as a surgeon to perform the operation that, in his anger, he did not want the others to perform. The Alexandrian surgeon came and examined the scars of the labors of the first surgeons with the eye of an expert. He then fulfilled the duty of a good man and persuaded Innocent that those who had labored so much on him, and whose work he admired upon inspection, should instead have the benefit of completing his cure. He added that it was true that he could not be healed except through operating. The Alexandrian said that it was repugnant to his character to seize, by completing the small part that remained, the honor of such a great deed from people whose labor, which he observed and admired in the scars, was so extremely skillful and painstakingly diligent. The original surgeons were restored to Innocent's favor and it was agreed that, with the Alexandrian surgeon standing by, they themselves would open the abscess with the knife. All now agreed that it could not be cured in any other way. The matter was put off until the following day. After the surgeons left, such a great wailing arose in the house from the tremendous grief of its master that it was like the lamenting at a funeral. We could hardly restrain it.

Holy men were visiting Innocent every day: Saturninus, of blessed memory, who was then the bishop of Uzalis; the priest Gulosus; and deacons from the church at Carthage. Among them, and the only one of the group still living, was Aurelius, who is now bishop and whom I must name with the reverence he is due. When calling to mind the wondrous work of God, we have spoken of this event often, and I have found that he has remembered very well what I am recounting. When they visited Innocent in the evening, as was their custom, he begged them with pathetic tears to do him the honor of being present at his funeral in the morning rather than at his suffering. Such great fear of his earlier suffering invaded him that he did not doubt but that he would die at the hands of the doctors. They consoled him and urged him to believe in God and to bear his will courageously. Then we went in to prayer. When, according to custom, we knelt and bowed to the ground, he cast himself down as if he had been thrown down by someone propelling him with great force, and he began to pray. Who could explain with words how he prayed—the feeling, the emotion, the river of tears, the groaning and gasping that were shaking every part of his body and almost cutting off his breath? Whether the others were still praying or whether their attention was distracted by Innocent I do not know. I, however, was not able to pray at all. I said only this briefly in my heart: "Lord, what prayers do you hear of your own, if you do not hear these?" It seemed to me he could do nothing more, except to die praying. We got up, received the bishop's blessing, and parted company. Innocent begged them to be present in the morning; they urged him to be calm.

The day he had feared dawned. The servants of God were present as they had promised to be. The doctors arrived. All the preparations which the hour demanded were made. The terrifying metal instruments were brought out. Everyone was silent with suspense. While those having the greatest influence with Innocent were consoling his failing spirits, his limbs were arranged on the couch for the hands of the surgeon. The knots of the bandages were untied. The area was unwrapped. The doctor examined it and, knife in hand, looked for the abscess to be cut. He searched for it with his eyes, probed for it with his fingers, and finally hunted for it in every way—but he found only a completely healed scar. A description of the rejoicing and praise and thanksgiving to the merciful and omnipotent God that now poured forth from the mouths of all in tears of joy should not be attempted by my words. Let it be imagined rather than described. . . .

Even now, then, many miracles occur. The same God who performed the ones we read about still performs them through those whom he wills and in the way he wills. The recent ones, however, are not known so widely as the earlier. They are not pounded, like gravel, into the memory by repeated reading so that they will not pass out of mind. Even where care is taken, as it is now beginning to be among ourselves, to read to the people accounts of those who receive such benefits, those who are present hear it just once, and most of the people are not present. Consequently, those who were present do not keep in mind what they heard after a few days, and scarcely anyone is found who passes on what he heard to someone who was not present. . . .

Chapter 12

Our opponents the Platonists are accustomed to the most detailed questioning, and in such questioning they ridicule our belief in the resurrection of the flesh. They ask whether an aborted fetus will rise again, and because the Lord said, "Amen, I say to you, not a hair of your head will perish" (Lk 21:18), they ask whether all will have in the future the same height and strength or different bodily sizes. If the sizes of the bodies will be the same, how will aborted fetuses, if they, too, will rise again, acquire what they did not have in their body mass before? Or, if they will not rise again because they were not born but aborted, they ask the same question about little children: when they die in childhood, how will they gain the body size that we see they now lack? . . .

Chapter 13

I do not dare affirm or deny that aborted fetuses, who would have been alive in the womb where they died, will be resurrected. Nevertheless, if they are not excluded from the number of the dead, I do not see how the resurrection of the dead would not extend to them as well. Either not all of the dead will rise again and there will be some human souls that once had human bodies—although within the wombs of their mothers—that will remain forever without bodies, or else at the resurrection all human souls will receive their own bodies, which they had wherever they lived and which they left wherever they died—in which case I do not see how I can say that the resurrection of the dead will not extend even to those who died in the wombs of their mothers. Whichever of these views one holds concerning fetuses, if they rise again, whatever we say about infants already born must also be understood as applying to them.[9]

Chapter 17

Because the Scriptures say, "until we all reach the perfect man, the standard of the full maturity of Christ" (Eph 4:13) and "conforming to the image of the Son of God" (Rom 8:29), some believe that women will not arise as female. They say instead that all will arise as males, since God made only the man from the clay, and the woman from the man.[10] It seems to me, however, that those who do not doubt that there will be both sexes at the resurrection are wiser.

9. What Augustine suggests about infants and children is that, in the resurrection of the body, they will acquire a body such as they would have had in the prime of their life. However, he adds that there is no reason to be adamant about this, since even if their resurrected body is still like that of a child, there will be no weakness in it. See XXII. 16, which is not included in this volume.

10. Jerome attributes this view to Origen but denies holding it himself. *Apology against Rufinus* I. 28.

Then there will be no lust, which is now the cause of disorder, for before they had sinned, the man and the woman were naked, but they were not disordered. Thus, defects will be taken away from those resurrected bodies but nature will be maintained. The female gender, though, is not a defect, but a nature. It will then indeed be exempt from copulation and giving birth, but the female body parts will still exist. They will not be accommodated to the old use, but to a new beauty. This new beauty will rouse the one who sees it to feel—not lust, which will not then exist—but praise for the wisdom and mercy of God, for he both made what did not exist and liberated from corruption what he had made. . . .

Thus, the woman is a creature of God just like the man. Unity is commended by her being made from the man. Moreover, Christ and the church are prefigured by the manner in which she was made, as has been said. Consequently, he who established the two sexes will re-establish them.

Finally, Jesus was himself asked by the Sadducees, who denied the resurrection, whose wife a woman will be whom seven brothers married in succession, each one wanting to raise up offspring to his deceased brother, as the law had commanded. "You err," he said, "not knowing the Scriptures or the power of God" (Mt 22:29). Although it was a point at which he might have said, "the woman you ask about will herself be a man, not a woman," he did not say it, but instead said, "in the resurrection they will not marry or take wives, but are like the angels of God in heaven" (Mt 22:30). Thus, they are equals of the angels in immortality and happiness; they are not equals in the flesh, just as they are not equals in the resurrection, which the angels do not need because they cannot die.

Therefore, the Lord said that there will be no marriage in the resurrection, not that there will be no women, and he said this in a situation where he might have solved the question being considered more easily by simply denying that there will be a womanly sex in the resurrection, if he had foreseen that females will not exist there. Indeed, he even affirmed that there will be women there by saying "they will not marry (*nubere*)," a term which pertains to women, "nor take wives," which pertains to men. Thus, those who are accustomed to marrying or taking wives here will be present there, but there they will not do those things.

Chapter 27

Plato and Porphyry each said certain things, and if they had been able to communicate them to each other, they might perhaps have become Christians. Plato said that souls are not able to exist in eternity without bodies, for he said that after quite a long period of time the souls of even the wise return to bodies.[11] Porphyry, however, said that a fully purified soul, when it has returned to the Father, will never return to the evils of the world.[12] Accordingly, suppose that Plato had given to Porphyry the truth that he had seen—that even the fully purified souls of the just and the wise will return to human bodies—and that Porphyry had likewise given to Plato the truth which he had seen—that no holy souls will return to the miseries of corruptible bodies. Each would not then have had only a single truth, but both would have had both truths. I think that they would have seen that it follows both that souls return to their bodies and also that they receive the sort of bodies in which they might live happily and immortally. The reason is that, according to Plato, even holy souls will return to human bodies; and according to Porphyry, holy souls will not return to the evils of this world.

Hence, let Porphyry say with Plato, "Holy souls will return to bodies," and let Plato say with Porphyry, "Holy souls will not return to evils," and they will both agree that holy souls return to bodies in which no evils are suffered. Such bodies will be nothing other than the sort of bodies which God promises—happy souls living in eternity with their own eternal flesh. As far as I can tell, they would both readily concede to us that those who profess that the souls of the saints will return to immortal bodies would also allow that they return to their own bodies, the bodies in which they endured the evils of this world and in which they worshipped God in piety and fidelity so that they might be freed from those evils.[13]

Chapter 29

Let us now consider, to the extent that the Lord deigns to assist us, what the saints will do in their immortal and spiritual bodies, with their flesh living not carnally but spiritually. In truth, though, I do not know what that activity—or rather that rest and leisure—will be, for I have not ever seen it through my bodily senses. If I say that I have seen it mentally, by means of my understanding, then what is our understanding compared to that excellence? As the apostle says, "There is the peace of God which surpassses all understanding" (Phil 4:7). What understanding does he

11. *Republic* X. 618b–619e; *Phaedrus*, 249a.
12. On Porphyry, see the note on X. 14.
13. This chapter should be compared with XII. 27.

mean, except ours, or perhaps even that of the holy angels? Indeed, he does not mean God's understanding. If, then, the saints will live in the peace of God, surely they will live in that peace which surpasses all understanding. That it surpasses our understanding, there is no doubt. If, however, it surpasses even that of the angels, so that it would seem that he who said "all understanding" did not leave out them, then we ought to take this passage to mean that neither we nor any angel are able to know the peace of God by which God himself is peaceful, as God knows it. Thus, this peace surpasses every understanding—with the exception, surely, of his own.

Yet, because we have been made partakers of his peace according to our own capacity, we know that highest peace within ourselves and among ourselves and with him, to the highest extent of which we are capable. In the same way, the holy angels know it according to their own capacity. The capacity of human beings, however, is now far below that of the angels, no matter what mental progress human beings might make. Indeed, one must consider how great that man was who said, "We know in part and we prophecy in part, until that which is perfect arrives" and "Now we see reflections obscurely, but then we will see face to face" (1 Cor 13:9,12). The holy angels, who are also called "our angels," see that way already.

They are called "our" angels because, torn away from the power of darkness, given the pledge of the Spirit, and carried over to the kingdom of Christ, we have already begun to belong to those angels with whom we will live together in the holy and supremely sweet city of God itself, about which I have already written so many books. In this way, then, the angels of God are our angels, just as the Christ of God is our Christ. They belong to God because they did not abandon him; they belong to us because they have begun to have us as fellow citizens. Moreover, the Lord Jesus said, "See to it that you do not despise one of these little ones, for I say to you, their angels in heaven always see the face of my father who is in heaven" (Mt 18:10). Therefore, as they see, so will we see; but we do not see in that way yet. It is on account of this that the apostle says what I cited just a moment ago: "Now we see reflections obscurely, but then we will see face to face." That vision is preserved for us as the reward of faith; the apostle John says of it, "When he appears, we will be like him, for we will see him as he is" (1 Jn 3:2). The "face" of God must be understood as his manifestation, not as the part of a body such as we have and call by that name.

Consequently, when I am asked what the saints will do in that spiritual body, I do not say that I already see, but I say what I believe, according to what I read in the psalm: "I believed, and hence I have spoken" (Ps 116:10). Thus I say that they will see God in the body itself, but whether they will see God through the body itself, as we now see the sun, the moon, the stars, the sea, and the earth and the things that are in it through the body, is no small question. It is difficult to assert that the saints will then have such bodies that they will not be able to close and open their eyes whenever they want; yet it is more difficult to assert that anyone there who closes his eyes will not see God. . . .

The question is whether the saints will see God through the eyes of the body when they have them open. If, in the spiritual body, the eyes—which are, of course, also spiritual—will be able to see only as much as these eyes which we have now, then without doubt they will not be able to see God. Consequently, such eyes will be of a very different power than the ones we have now if that immaterial nature which is not contained in space but is completely present everywhere will be seen through them. While we say that God is both in heaven and in earth—in fact, he himself says through the prophet, "I fill heaven and earth" (Jer 23:24)—we are not about to say that God has one part in heaven and another part on earth; rather, he is entirely in heaven and entirely on earth, not at alternating periods of time but both at the same time, as no material nature can be. Hence, the power of those eyes will be greatly enhanced, not so that they might see more keenly than certain snakes or eagles are thought to see (for however great their keenness of perceiving, animals also see nothing other than material things), but so that they might also see immaterial things. . . .

If we could be completely certain about the reasoning of the philosophers when they argue that intelligible things are seen by the gaze of the mind and sensible things—that is, bodily things—by the sense of the body in such a way that the mind is not able to look upon intelligible things through the body nor bodily things through itself, then indeed it would be certain that God could in no way be seen through the eyes of even a spiritual body. Both true reason and prophetic authority ridicule that line of reasoning, however. Indeed, who is so averse to the truth that he dares to say that God does not know material things? Does God therefore have a body with eyes, through which he is able to learn about material things? . . .

Therefore, as it is agreed that material things are seen by spirit, what if the power of the spiritual body will be such that spirit might also be seen by the body? After all, "God is spirit" (Jn 4:24). Moreover, everyone knows his own life—the life by which he now lives in the body and the life which makes his earthly limbs grow and makes them alive—not through material eyes but through an inner sense. Yet everyone sees the lives of others through the body, even though the lives of others are invisible. On what basis do we distinguish living bodies from non-living ones, unless we see bodies and, at the same time, the lives which we would not be able to see except through the body? With material eyes, however, we do not see lives without bodies.

Accordingly, it could happen, and it is quite believable, that we will then see the worldly bodies belonging to the new heaven and the new earth in such a way that, through the bodies which we will wear and which we will observe, we will see, with the most transparent clarity, wherever we turn our eyes, God—present everywhere, governing the whole universe, material things included. It will not be as it is now, when the invisible realities of God are observed through understanding the things which have been made, observed through an obscure reflection and in part (Rom 1:20; 1 Cor 13:12). Now the faith by which we believe is more important in us than the material things we perceive through the material eyes.

The human beings among whom we live are living and show the motions of life, so that when looking at them we do not believe but see that they are alive. Even though we are not able to see that they are alive without their bodies, we nevertheless observe the life in them through their bodies, without the slightest doubt. In the same way, wherever we will turn those spiritual eyes of our bodies, we will also behold through our bodies the immaterial God ruling over all things.

Therefore, either God will be seen through those eyes in such a way that they will have some capacity similar to the mind through which even immaterial nature will be perceived—though this is either difficult or impossible to demonstrate through any examples or testimonies of divine Scripture—or else, what is easier to understand, God will be so known and so visible to us that he will be seen in spirit by each of us in each of us, seen by everyone in everyone else, seen in himself, seen in the new heaven and the new earth and in every creature which will then exist, seen even in every body through bodies, wherever the eyes of the spiritual body will direct their penetrating view. Even our thoughts will be open to each other, for the words of the apostle will then be fulfilled. After he had said, "Do not judge before the time," he then added, "until the Lord comes, both bringing to light things hidden in darkness and making the thoughts of the heart manifest; then each person will have his praise from God" (1 Cor 4:5).

Chapter 30

How great will be that happiness where there will be no evil, where no good will be concealed, where there will be leisure for the praises of God, who will be all in all! I do not know what else would be done where there will be no inactivity due to any idleness nor any labor due to any need. I am also advised about this by the sacred song, when I read or hear, "Happy are those who dwell in your house; they will praise you forever" (Ps 84:4).

Because there will be no necessity then, but a full, certain, secure, and everlasting happiness, every limb and organ of the incorruptible body, which we now see assigned to the various tasks of necessity, will be proficient in the praising of God. All those numbers of the harmony of the body, concerning which I have spoken already, which are now hidden, will not be hidden then, but arranged through the whole body, both inside and out. With the other great and marvelous things that will be seen there, they will inflame rational minds through a delight in rational beauty into praising such a great artificer. I do not presume to define rashly what the movements of such bodies will be there, for I am not able to unravel that question. Nevertheless, both their movement and posture, like their appearance itself, will be fitting, whatever they will be, for only what is fitting will exist there. Certainly, wherever the spirit will want to be, the body will be there immediately, and the spirit will not want anything that could not be fitting for the spirit or the body.

True glory will be there; no one will be praised through error or flattery. True honor, which will be denied to no one worthy, will be offered to no one unworthy. No one unworthy, however, will even seek it, for only the worthy will be permitted to be there. True peace will be there, for no one will suffer opposition, either from himself or from another. The reward of virtue will be God himself, who gave the virtue and promised himself as its reward, for there could be nothing better or greater. Indeed, what else did he mean when he said through the prophet, "I will be their God, and they will be my people" (Lv 26:12) except "I will be what satisfies them; I will be everything that is properly desired by human beings—life and health and nourishment and abundance and glory and honor and peace and all good things"? The saying of the apostle, "so that God may be all in all" (1 Cor 15:28), is correctly understood in this way also. He himself, who will be seen without end, loved without surfeit, and praised without fatigue, will be the end of our desires. This gift, this affection, this activity, will surely be common to all just as eternal life itself is common to all.

Who is fit to ponder, much less to declare, what degrees of honor and glory according to merit there will be? That there will be such degrees is not to be doubted. That happy city will see this great good in itself also: no inferior will envy any superior, just as now the rest of the angels do not envy the archangels. No one will want what he has not received, although he will be tied by a supremely peaceful bond of concord to the one who has received it, just as in the body the finger does not want to be the eye, though the peaceful joining of the whole body contains both of these. In this way, therefore, anyone who has a lesser gift than another will also have this gift: he will not want more. . . .

The free will of that city will be one in all and indivisible in each. Freed from every evil and filled with every good, it will enjoy the delight of eternal gladness without ceasing. Having forgotten all sins and all punishments, it will not therefore forget its own liberation and so be ungrateful to its own liberator. Insofar, then, as they pertain to rational knowledge, that city remembers its own past evils completely; insofar as they pertain to sense experience, it forgets them completely.

The most expert physician knows almost all the diseases of the body as they are known by that art. Not having suffered the diseases himself, however, he does not generally know them as they are felt by the body. Thus, there are two ways of knowing evils: in one way, evils are not concealed from the power of the mind; in another, they cling to sensory experience. Indeed, in one way, every vice is known through the teaching of wisdom; in another way, they are known through the dissolute life of foolishness. Accordingly, there are also two ways of forgetting evils. One who has studied and learned them forgets them in one way; one who has experienced and suffered them forgets them in another. The first forgets if he neglects the study of evils; the second if he is rid of misery.

It is according to this second manner of forgetting that the saints will not remember past evils. They will be rid of all evils in such a way that every sensation of them will be thoroughly deleted. Nevertheless, not only their own past evils, but even the everlasting miseries of the condemned, will not be concealed from their power of knowing, which will be great in them. Otherwise, if they will not know that they themselves were wretched, how, as the psalm says, "will they sing of the mercies of the Lord forever" (Ps 89:2)? Surely there will be nothing more delightful for that city than this song to the glory of the grace of Christ, by whose blood we have been freed.

There will these words be accomplished: "Rest, and see that I am God" (Ps 46:11). . . . This Sabbath will be more apparent if the number of the ages is enumerated just like the number of the days of creation, as if the days of creation correspond to those periods of time which have been expressed by the Scriptures, for one discovers that there are seven such ages. The first age, corresponding to the first day, extends from Adam up until the flood; the second age, extending from there up until Abraham, is not equal in time to the first, but in the number of generations—indeed, they are each found to have had ten. From that point there follow, as the evangelist Matthew divides them, three ages until the coming of Christ.[14] Each of those three extend fourteen generations: from Abraham until David is the first; from David until the exile in Babylon is the second; and from the exile until the birth of Christ in the flesh is the third. Thus, five ages have been completed.

The sixth is occurring now. It should not be estimated by any set number of generations, since the scripture says, "It is not for you to know the time, which the Father, in his own power, has established" (Acts 1:7). After this age God will rest, as on the seventh day, when he will cause the seventh day—and we will be that day—to rest in God himself. To discuss thoroughly each of these ages in turn at the present time would be tedious. Nevertheless, this seventh age will be our Sabbath. Its end will not be at sunset, but will be the Lord's day—an eternal eighth day sanctified by the resurrection of Christ, which prefigures the eternal rest, not only of the spirit but also of the body. There we will rest and see, see and love, love and praise. Behold what will be in the end without end! For what else will our end be, except to reach the kingdom in which there is no end?

I think that I have, with the help of the Lord, fulfilled my obligation of writing this enormous work. May those for whom it is too little or too much pardon me. May those for whom it is just sufficient give solemn thanks, not to me, but to God with me.

14. See Mt 1:17.

The Compatibility of
Christianity and Politics

Introduction

Although The City of God *is surely Augustine's most complete statement concerning the political implications of Christianity, he also considered the topic in other writings, including two important letters written not long before* The City of God *was begun.*

The occasion of the first of these (Letter 91) was a pagan riot that broke out in 408 in the town of Calama, which was not far from Hippo. During these disturbances, the pagans attacked some Christian clerics and Christian property. Afterwards, an elderly pagan named Nectarius wrote to Augustine, asking that he intervene in the case in order to mitigate the impending punishment of the citizens of Calama.[1] In responding to Nectarius, who claimed to be inspired by patriotic zeal, Augustine argues that, even from a purely political point of view, Christianity is superior to paganism.

The second letter (Letter 138) is a response to Marcellinus,[2] who had written to Augustine asking for help in answering some objections raised against the Christian faith by a group of influential pagans with whom he was in frequent contact.[3] One of their charges was that Christianity was incompatible with good political rule. In responding, Augustine is forced to show that some of the most famous commandments of the Sermon on the Mount are not inimical to politics. This letter was written in 412; Augustine would begin The City of God *in 413, and some of its themes are already hinted at in this letter.*

---

1. This letter survives as #90 in Augustine's correspondence.
2. On Marcellinus, see the note on *City of God* I, preface.
3. This letter survives as #136 in Augustine's correspondence.

From Letter 91, to Nectarius

I do not find it odd but praiseworthy that your heart burns with love for your country even as your limbs grow colder with age. I also admit, not unwillingly but wholeheartedly, that you not only call to mind but also demonstrate through your life and morals that there is no boundary or limit to the good of caring for our country. We would thus like to have such a citizen as you for that higher country in whose holy love, according to our little measure, we struggle and toil among those for whom we care, helping them to reach that country. Were you a citizen there, you would think that there is no boundary or limit to caring for the small portion of that city making its journey on this earth. Paying in advance the duties owed to a better city, the result would be that much greater for you. You would be about to find endless joy in the eternal peace of that city, having set for yourself, in your labors in this life, no limit to caring for it.

Until that happens, however—and it is not beyond hope that you will be able to attain, or are even now thinking most prudently about attaining, that fatherland to which the father who begot you in this life has preceeded you—until that happens, I say, forgive us if, for the sake of that country that we desire never to leave, we sadden your country, which you desire to leave flowering in full bloom. If we were to discuss those flowers with your Prudence, there is no reason to think that it would be difficult to persuade you, or even that it would not easily occur to you on your own, how a city ought to flower and bloom. The most famous poet of your literature memorialized some flowers of Italy, but we have not experienced in your country "the men that made that land flower" so much as "the arms that made it glow"—indeed, not arms that made it glow but flames that made it burn.[4] If such a great crime were to go unpunished, without an appropriate correction of the depraved, do you think that you would be leaving your country in full bloom? O flowers, producing not fruit but thorns! Consider whether you would prefer that your country bloom with piety or impunity, with correct morals or bold outrages. Consider these things and see whether you surpass us in love of your country, whether your desire for it to bloom is greater or truer than ours.

Reflect a little on those books of the *Republic*,[5] whence you drank in that

---

4. Augustine refers sarcastically to a passage in Virgil's *Aeneid* (VII. 643–44) in which the poet speaks of "the men that made Italy flower" and "the arms that made it glow." Some Christian buildings were burned in the pagan riot that occasioned the exchange of letters between Nectarius and Augustine.

5. Cicero's *Republic* rather than Plato's is meant.

disposition of a most devoted citizen, that "there is no boundary or limit to the good of caring for our country." Reflect, I ask you, and notice how much frugality and continence are praised there, and also fidelity to the marriage bond, and chaste, honorable, and upright morals. When a city abounds in such things, it must truly be said to bloom. These morals, however, are taught and learned in the churches growing throughout the world, which are, as it were, the holy schools of the peoples. This is especially the case with piety, through which the true and truthful God is worshipped. He not only commands the undertaking but also grants the completion of all those things through which the human mind is prepared and made fit for dwelling in the divine society of the eternal and heavenly city. Therefore, he has foretold that the images of the many false gods would be overthrown and he has decreed that they be overthrown. Indeed, nothing renders human beings more contrary to society because of a life of depravity than the imitation of such gods as are described and extolled in their literature.

Furthermore, consider those most learned men who investigated and even described in private discussions the qualities the republic or earthly city ought to have more than they established or fashioned such qualities through their public actions.[6] For models to be imitated in the instruction of the character of the young, they proposed human beings whom they deemed to be admirable and praiseworthy rather than the gods. Indeed, there is the case of the youth in Terence.[7] By staring at a painting on a wall portraying the adultery of the king of the gods, he was inflamed to the lust that gripped him by the example of such an authority. In no way would he have wavered through desire or become immersed in deed in that disgraceful action if he had chosen to imitate Cato rather than Jove.[8] Yet how could he do that when he was compelled to adore Jove rather than Cato in the temples? Perhaps we ought not bring forth from comedy these passages that convict the debauchery of the impious and their sacrilegious superstition. Yet read or call to mind that in those same books it is prudently argued that the words and actions of comedies can in no way be accepted if

6. Augustine is referring to the discussion in Cicero's *Republic*.

7. *The Eunuch* 584–91. The youth described there is inflamed to lust by a painting of Jove's visitation of Danae. Augustine also discusses this passage from the comic poet Terence in *Confessions* I. 16. 26.

8. Cato the Censor (232–147 B.C.) was a model of austere Roman virtue. He is not to be confused with Cato of Utica, who committed suicide rather than submit to the rule of Caesar.

they are not consonant with the morals of those accepting them.[9] Thus, it is established by the authority of the most eminent men, outstanding in the republic when they were discussing the republic, that the most decadent human beings are made worse by imitating the gods—not true gods, to be sure, but false and fictitious ones. . . .

From Letter 138, to Marcellinus

. . . You added that they say that the preaching and teaching of Christ are not at all suitable for the morals of a republic. They have in mind the precept that we should not return evil for evil to anyone, but turn the other cheek to anyone who strikes us, give our tunic to anyone who takes our coat, and walk a double journey with anyone who would force us to go with him (Mt 5:39–41). They assert that all of these things are contrary to the morals of a republic. "Who," they say, "would permit something to be taken from him by an enemy, or not want to return evil to the pillagers of a Roman province according to the right of war?" Perhaps I would refute more strenuously these and other such statements of the critics, or of those saying such things not to criticize but to inquire, if these debates were not held with men who are liberally educated. As it is, why is it necessary to drag out the discussion? Let us rather ask, How is it that those who "chose to overlook wrongs received rather than punish them" were able to govern and enlarge the republic that they changed from being small and poor to being great and wealthy?[10] How could Cicero, praising the morals of Caesar, who was surely the administrator of the republic, say that he was wont to forget nothing except wrongs done to him?[11] In saying this Cicero was either praising or flattering him greatly. If it was praise, he knew that Caesar was such a person; if it was flattery, he was pointing out that the ruler of a city ought to be the sort of person that he was falsely commending Caesar to be. Yet what is not returning evil for evil except abhorring the lust for vengeance? What is choosing to overlook wrongs received rather than punish them except forgetting wrongs?

When such things are read in the works of their authors, they are praised and applauded. Statements such as "choosing to overlook rather than punish wrongs received" are viewed as proclaiming and describing behavior

---

9. Augustine would seem to refer to Cicero's *Republic* (IV. 10), although that part of the work exists today only in fragments.

10. Sallust, *Catiline* 9. 5.

11. *Pro Ligario* 12. 35.

that would be worthy to raise up a city that would rule over many peoples. But when it is read that divine authority commands that "evil must not be returned for evil," when this salutary advice is preached from the pulpit to congregations of people, to the public, as it were, to schools of both sexes and of all ages and ranks, religion is accused of being inimical to the republic.[12] If this advice were listened to in the manner it deserves to be, it would found, consecrate, strengthen, and enlarge the republic much better than did Romulus, Numa, Brutus, and the rest of those famous men of the Roman race.[13]

What is a republic except the affair of a people?[14] Surely a common affair is an affair of the city. And what is a city except a multitude of human beings joined in a certain bond of concord?[15] One reads in their books, "A diverse and restless multitude soon became a city by means of concord."[16] What precepts of concord were ever decreed to be proclaimed in their temples? Indeed, in their misery they were forced to ask how they could worship their gods without offending any of them since they were fighting amongst themselves. If they wanted to imitate the discord of the gods, the city would totter and fall through breaking the bond of concord. This began to happen later through the civil wars, as little by little morals paled and were corrupted.

But who, even from another religion, is so deaf as to be unaware of the great many precepts of concord that are read in the churches of Christ—not precepts sought in human disputations but precepts written by divine authority? Even those precepts which they prefer to criticize rather than learn about pertain to concord: to turn the other cheek to one who strikes, to give our cloak also to one who wants to take our coat, to walk a double journey with one who forces us to walk a single one. Surely these things are done so that evil is overcome by good, or rather that the evil in an evil man is overcome by good and the man is freed from an evil that is not external and foreign but inner and personal, an evil that devastates him more grievously and dangerously than the inhumanity of any external enemies.

12. Augustine puns on the word "republic" in this sentence: religion preaches sound advice to the "public" but is accused of harming the "re-public."

13. On Romulus, see the note on I. 34. On Numa, see the note on III. 9. Brutus led the revolution against the tyranny of the Tarquins; that revolt led to republican rule in Rome.

14. See the note on II. 21.

15. See Cicero's *Republic* I. 25.

16. Sallust, *Catiline* 6. 2.

Therefore, he who conquers evil with good patiently foregoes temporal conveniences in order to teach how such things, the excessive love of which made the evil man evil, are scorned for the sake of faith and justice. In this way, the wrongdoer might learn from the very person whom he wronged what sort of things they are for the sake of which he did wrong. Repenting, he is overcome not by ferocious violence but by the benevolence of forebearance, and is thus brought to concord, which is more beneficial to the city than anything else. The right time for this to be done is when it seems that it will be profitable for him for whose sake it is done, so that correction and concord will be achieved in him. This must at least be done in the mind, even if another result would occur should the man needing this medicine for correction and reconciliation—for curing and healing, as it were—not want to be corrected or reconciled.

Otherwise, if we pay careful attention to the words and suppose that we must observe the precepts in their specific details, then it is not required to turn the right cheek if the left is struck, since the Scripture says, "If anyone has struck your right cheek, turn to him your left" (Mt 5:39). The left cheek, however, is more likely to be struck, for it is easier to strike a blow with the right hand. But this passage is usually understood as if it were written, "If anyone has attacked your better possessions, give to him your lesser; otherwise, in your zeal for vengeance rather than forbearance you might scorn eternal goods for the sake of temporal ones, whereas temporal goods should be scorned for the sake of eternal ones, just as the left for the right."

This was always the intention of the holy martyrs. A final, just vengeance is demanded when there is no longer any occasion for correction, namely, at the last and supreme judgment. Now, however, we must above all else be careful so that patience, which is more valuable than everything that an enemy can take from us against our will, is not itself lost to the desire for vengeance. Indeed, another evangelist records the same idea without mentioning the right cheek, but calls it only "the other cheek" (Lk 6:29). The idea is understood somewhat more distinctly in the first version, while the latter simply recommends the same patience as the former.[17] Thus, a just and pious man ought to be prepared to endure patiently the malice of those whom he seeks to make good, so that the number of the

---

17. By specifying the right and left cheeks, which stand for eternal and temporal goods, the version of the command given in Mt 5:39 is more precise than the version given in Luke, which recommends the same patience but does not distinguish between left and right cheeks.

good grows, rather than add himself, through like malice, to the number of the wicked.

Finally, these precepts refer to a disposition of the heart, which is within oneself, rather than to a deed, which is manifest, so that patience and benevolence are to be held in the hidden places of the soul, and openly performed when it seems that they will be profitable for those for whom we must bear good will. This is plainly shown by the fact that Christ the Lord himself, the unique exemplar of patience, responded when he was struck in the face by saying, "If I have spoken evil, give evidence of the evil; but if I have spoken well, why do you hit me?" (Jn 18:23). Thus, if we study the words, he certainly did not fulfill his own precept, for he did not turn the other cheek to the one who had struck him, but rather forbade the one who had done this to increase his wrongdoing. Nevertheless, he had come prepared not only to be struck on the face but also to be crucified for the sake of those at whose hands he was suffering these things. As he hung on the cross, he prayed for them saying, "Father, forgive them, because they do not know what they are doing" (Lk 23:34).

Nor does the apostle Paul seem to have fulfilled the precept of his Lord and Master when, having been struck on the face also, he said to the chief priest: "God will strike you, you whited wall; you sit to judge me according to the law and against the law you command me to be struck" (Acts 23:3–5). And when the bystander said to him, "Are you reviling the chief priest?" he chose to warn them through ridicule, so that those who were wise might understand that the whited wall—that is, the hypocrisy of the Jewish priesthood—had already been destroyed at the coming of Christ. Hence, he said, "I did not know, brother, that he is the chief priest, for it is written, 'do not speak evil of the chief of your people,'" although doubtless he who had grown up among that people and was educated there in the law could not have been unaware that he was the chief priest, nor could he in any way have deceived those to whom he was so well-known into thinking that he was unaware.[18]

Therefore, these precepts of patience are always to be retained in readiness in the heart, and benevolence, which prohibits returning evil for evil, must always be abundant in the will. However, with respect to those who, contrary to their own will, need to be set straight, many things must be

18. Augustine's argument is that Paul himself did not observe the precept about turning the cheek in this particular instance, but rather indicated ironically that the authority of the Jewish priesthood had already been replaced by the authority of Christ.

done with a certain benevolent harshness. Their welfare rather than their wishes must be considered, and this has been praised most lavishly in their writings about the ruler of a city. In correcting a son however severely, paternal love is surely never lost sight of. What is not wanted and what is painful is nevertheless done to one who appears to require healing through pain, even against his will. Accordingly, if this earthly republic kept the Christian precepts, wars themselves would not be waged without benevolence, so that, for the sake of the peaceful union of piety and justice, the welfare of the conquered would be more readily considered. He whose license for wrongdoing is wrested away is usefully conquered, for nothing is less prosperous than the prosperity of sinners, which nourishes punishable impunity and strengthens the evil will, which is, as it were, an enemy within.[19]

The twisted and depraved hearts of mortals nevertheless think that human affairs are prosperous when the splendor of buildings is attended to and the collapse of souls is not, when massive theatres are built up and the foundations of the virtues are undermined, when the insanity of extravagance is glorified and the works of mercy ridiculed, when actors grow dissolute on the affluence of the rich and the poor barely have the necessities of life; when God, who cries out against this public evil through public declarations of his teachings, is blasphemed by impious peoples and such gods are demanded as those in whose honor the theatrical disgraces of body and soul are celebrated.

If God permits these things to abound, then his anger is more severe. If he leaves them unpunished, then his punishment is more terrible. When he overturns the support of the vices, however, and renders copious lusts impoverished, his affliction is merciful, for even in mercy, if it were possible, would wars be waged by the good, so that by taming unbridled desires they would destroy these vices which ought to have been rooted out and subdued by just rule.

Indeed, if Christian teaching condemned all wars, then the advice given in the Gospel to the soldiers asking for salvation would have been to throw down their arms and quit the military completely. What they were told, however, was, "Terrorize no one, accuse no one falsely, and be content with your pay" (Lk 3:14). With these words he commands them to be content with their own pay; he certainly does not prohibit them from serving as soldiers.[20] Hence, let those who say that the teaching of Christ is

19. On correcting sinners, see the section on "The Use of Persecution."
20. See the selection from *Against Faustus the Manichaean* in the section on "War."

contrary to the republic give us an army of the sort of soldiers that the teaching of Christ commands. Let them give us such provincial subjects, such husbands, wives, parents, children, masters, servants, kings, judges, and finally such payers and collectors of public taxes of the sort commanded by Christian teaching, and then let them dare to say that this teaching is contrary to the republic; indeed, let them even hesitate to confess that it is, if observed, a great benefit for the republic.

Yet what am I to respond to those who say that many evils have befallen the Roman empire through Christian emperors? This sweeping accusation is fraudulent, for if I were to recount certain things about past emperors, I could cite similar evils, or perhaps even more grievous ones, about emperors who were not Christians. They might then understand that these failings were not the fault of the teaching but of the men, or that the failings were not the fault of the emperors but of those without whom emperors are unable to do anything.

Their own writings speak clearly enough about the time when the Roman republic began to decline.[21] Long before the name of Christ shown forth upon the earth it was said, "O city for sale and already about to perish, if it finds a buyer!"[22] Also, in his book on *The War with Catiline*, which certainly preceded the coming of Christ, the same most illustrious historian does not fail to mention the times when "first the army of the Roman people became accustomed to making love and drinking, to marveling at statues, fancy paintings, and embossed vases, to seizing them privately and publicly, to plundering shrines, to polluting everything sacred and profane."[23] Thus, when the avarice and greed of corrupted and abandoned morals were sparing neither human beings nor even those they thought to be gods, then the laudible dignity and welfare of the republic began to decline. It would take too long to relate the subsequent advance of the worst vices and how much evil the prospering of that iniquity brought to human affairs. Let them hear their own satirist speaking the truth with his babbling:

> Once humble fortune kept the Latin women chaste.
> Toil and brief sleep, working Tuscan fleeces,
> hands hardened and chapped, Hannibal just outside the city,
> and husbands standing guard at the Colline rampart,

---

21. This paragraph anticipates the arguments of Book II of *The City of God*.
22. Sallust, *The War with Jugurtha* 35. 10.
23. Sallust, *Catiline* 11. 6.

did not permit their little dwellings to be touched by vice.
Now we suffer the evils of a long peace.
Luxury, more savage than arms, bore down upon us,
avenging the world that was conquered.
No accusation or deed of lust is lacking
since Roman poverty perished.[24]

How then can you expect me to magnify the great number of evils that
iniquity, encouraged by the rise of prosperity, ushered in, when indeed
even the more prudent among the pagans who directed their attention
toward these matters realized that losing Roman poverty needed to be
grieved more than losing Roman wealth? Integrity of morals was preserved
through poverty, but through wealth a horrible wickedness, worse than
any enemy, breached not the walls but the mind of the city.

Thanks be to the Lord our God who sent us extraordinary help against
these evils. What if we were without the cross of Christ most prominently
and firmly fixed in such a great rock of authority, making us steady as we
cling firmly to it, so that we are not swept away and sucked into the enormous whirlpool of this world by those advising and propelling us toward
evil? Where would the river of this dreadful wickedness not carry us? Who
would not be covered over? Into what depths would it not have plunged
us?

In this filthy confluence of the worst morals and of the old depraved
teaching, it was especially fitting for heavenly authority to arrive and to
succor, persuading us to voluntary poverty, continence, benevolence, justice, concord, true piety, and the other bright and powerful virtues of life.
It was fitting not only for the sake of living this life most properly, nor only
for the sake of a most harmonious unity in the earthly city, but also for the
sake of attaining everlasting well-being and the heavenly and divine republic whose peoples are everlasting.

Faith, hope, and charity make us citizens in that republic. As long as we
journey far from it, we endure—if we are not able to correct—those who
want the republic that the first Romans founded and enlarged by means of
their virtues to stand firm by permitting vices to go unpunished. Even if
they did not have that true piety toward the true God that could lead them
into the eternal city through a salvific religion, those first Romans preserved a certain sort of uprightness that could suffice for founding, enlarg-
ing, and preserving the earthly city. God thus showed in the most wealthy

24. Juvenal, *Satire* VI. 287–95.

and illustrious Roman empire how great the power of civil virtues without true religion is, so that it might be understood that when true religion is added human beings are made citizens of another city, a city whose king is truth, whose law is charity, whose boundary is eternity.[25] . . .

25. This paragraph should be compared with V.15–16.

Law and Self-Defense

Introduction

From the time of his conversion to Christianity in 386 to his ordination as Bishop of Hippo in 395, Augustine wrote several dialogues. He casts one of these, On Free Choice, *as a discussion between himself and his friend Evodius. In the course of the dialogue, Evodius argues that it is wrong to defend oneself against violent attack because in so doing one would necessarily be loving temporal goods or goods pertaining to the body rather than the eternal goods of the soul. Such disordered love or lust is the essence of wrongdoing. In the course of explaining why he holds this view, Evodius makes a distinction between the human law, which is used to govern human cities and condones such self-defense, and the eternal law of God, which governs the world and presumably punishes it.*

The extent to which the opinions articulated by Evodius are shared by Augustine is not completely unambiguous. Nevertheless, the argument about self-defense and the distinction between temporal and divine law would become crucial in subsequent debates concerning law in the West, especially the debates concerning natural law.

On Free Choice I. 5.11–6.15.

AUGUSTINE: It seems to me that it should first be discussed whether either an attacking enemy or a plotting assassin may be killed in defense of one's life, liberty, or chastity without any lust[1] being involved.

EVODIUS: How can I declare that those who fight in defense of such things

---

1. The Latin word *libido*, which is translated here and elsewhere as "lust," refers in Augustine's works not only to illicit sexual desire but to any disordered love which prefers lower or temporal goods to divine or eternal ones. It has already been established in the dialogue that these lower goods are goods that can be lost against one's will, while higher goods cannot be lost except voluntarily. See XIV. 15.

213

as these, which can be lost against their will, are free from lust? Or if such things cannot be lost against their will, why is it necessary to go so far as to kill a human being in defense of them?

AUGUSTINE: Then the law is not just which allows a traveler to kill a robber in order to avoid being killed by him. Nor is the law just which allows any man or woman, if able, to slay a violent rapist before the rape is committed. Also, a soldier is commanded by law to kill the enemy; if he refrains from such killing he is punished by his commander. What shall we dare say: that these laws are unjust, or rather that they are not laws? For it seems to me that an unjust law is not a law.

EVODIUS: I notice that the law is sufficiently protected against an accusation of this kind. The law gives license to lesser wrongdoings among the people it governs so that the greater ones might not be committed. The death of an unjust aggressor is a lesser evil than that of a man who is only defending himself. It is much more horrible that a human being should be violated against his will than that a violent attacker should be killed by his intended victim.

Moreover, in killing an enemy the soldier acts as an agent of the law. That is why he can easily fulfill his duty without lust. And the law itself, which was enacted for the protection of the people, cannot be accused of lust, since the legislator, assuming that he enacted it at God's command, that is, in accordance with the mandates of eternal justice, was able to do so without any lust at all. And even if the law was decreed with a measure of lust, it does not follow that it must be obeyed out of lust, for a good law can be enacted by a bad man. For the sake of argument, suppose that a man who has become a tyrant accepts a bribe from another man who, in his own interest, wants him to pass a law prohibiting the taking of any woman by force, even with a view to marriage. The law will not be evil simply for its having been enacted by an unjust and corrupt man. One can, therefore, obey without lust the law that, for the protection of the citizens, commands the use of violence to repel the violent attack of an enemy. The same can be said for all agents who are subject by law to some higher authority.

Still, I fail to see how these people are blameless because the law is blameless, for the law does not oblige them to kill but only leaves it in their power to do so. Hence, they are free not to kill anyone for the sake of things that can be lost against their will and thus should not be loved. Concerning life, some people may perhaps wonder whether it is not in some way removed from the soul when the body dies. If, however, life can be removed from the soul, then it should be despised; if it cannot, then there is nothing to fear. Concerning chastity, though, who would doubt but that it is located in the soul itself, seeing that it is a virtue? Hence, it cannot be wrenched away from someone by a violent rapist.[2] Whatever he who was killed was about to wrench away was such that it was not in our control, and so I do not understand how we can call it our own. Consequently, I do not blame the law that permits such attackers to be killed, but I do not see how I might defend those who kill them.

AUGUSTINE: Much less can I see why you seek a defense for people whom no law holds to be guilty.

EVODIUS: No law, perhaps, among the ones that are manifest and read by human beings. I do not know whether or not, if divine providence administers all things, they might be held guilty by some stronger and most secret law. Before that law, how are those people free from sin who are defiled by human killing for the sake of things that ought to be despised? Therefore, it seems to me that the law written to govern a people is right to permit these things, and also that divine providence rightly punishes them. The human law deals with crimes that need to be punished if peace is to be maintained among ignorant human beings and does so to the extent that those matters can be regulated by man. The other sins have other suitable penalties, from which, it seems to me, only Wisdom can free us.

AUGUSTINE: I laud and approve this distinction of yours. Although it is sketchy and less than perfect, it is nevertheless bold and it aims at higher things. It seems to you that the law enacted for the governance of cities makes many concessions and leaves many things unpunished that are nevertheless punished by divine providence, and rightly so. Just because it does not achieve everything, what it does achieve should not be condemned.

Yet, if it is agreeable to you, we should consider more carefully how far wrongdoings should be avenged by the law that restrains peoples in this life. Next we should consider the remaining wrongdoings, which are punished more inevitably and in secret by divine providence.

EVODIUS: I agree—if one could somehow reach the limits of so great a topic, for I think it is infinite.

AUGUSTINE: Indeed! Yet pull yourself together and, relying on piety, walk in the paths of reason. No path is so steep and difficult that it cannot, with the help of God, become perfectly smooth and easy. Let us, then, depend-

---

2. Concerning Augustine's position that a rapist cannot take one's chastity, see also I. 16 and 18.

ing on God and begging for his help, pursue the inquiry that we have charted.

First, tell me whether or not the written law is helpful to human beings living in this life.

EVODIUS: Clearly it is, for peoples and cities are made up of such human beings.

AUGUSTINE: What about human beings themselves and peoples? Do they belong to the class of things that cannot perish or be changed, but are altogether eternal? Or are they changeable and subject to time?

EVODIUS: Who would doubt that they are clearly changeable and subject to time?

AUGUSTINE: Therefore, if a people is moderate and serious and a most diligent guardian of the common utility, and if everyone in it thinks less of the private good than the public good, is it not right to enact a law permitting this people to choose for itself the magistrates through whom its affairs—that is, its republic—are to be administered.[3]

EVODIUS: Absolutely right.

AUGUSTINE: Now, imagine that same people, having become depraved little by little, so that it prefers the private to the public good, sells its votes, is corrupted by those who covet honors, and turns the regime over to shameful and villainous people. Is it not also right that, if some good and most capable man is to be found, he might remove from the people the power to bestow honors and hand it over to a few good men, or even one?

EVODIUS: That is also right.

AUGUSTINE: Therefore, although these two laws would appear to be opposed to each other, one of them assigning the power to bestow honors to the people and the other removing it, and although the second law was enacted in such a way that both of them could in no way exist in the same city at the same time, are we to say that one of them is unjust and ought never to have been produced at all?

EVODIUS: In no way.

AUGUSTINE: Therefore, if it is agreeable to you, let us call that law "temporal" which, although it is just, can nevertheless justly be changed in the course of time.

EVODIUS: Let us call it so.

---

3. On the meaning of the word "republic," see the note on II. 21.

AUGUSTINE: What about the law called the "supreme reason," which must always be observed and in virtue of which the wicked deserve misery and the good a life of happiness, and in virtue of which, moreover, the law that we agreed to call "temporal" is rightly enacted and rightly changed? Can that law of supreme reason seem to any intelligent being to be other than incommutable and eternal? Can it ever be unjust that the wicked be miserable and the good happy? Or that a moderate and venerable people choose their own magistrates, but a dissolute and iniquitous people be deprived of this privilege?

EVODIUS: I see that this is an eternal and unchangeable law.

AUGUSTINE: I think that you also see that there is nothing just and lawful in that temporal law that human beings have not derived from this eternal law. If it is just that a people at one time bestowed honors and equally just that at another time it did not, this temporal vicissitude, as may be expected from the fact that it is just, was derived from the eternal law, in virtue of which a just and venerable people always bestows offices, but a frivolous one does not. Or does it seem otherwise to you?

EVODIUS: I agree.

AUGUSTINE: To explain briefly and to the best of my ability this notion of an eternal law that is impressed upon us: it is that by which it is just that all things be most perfectly ordered. If you think differently, say so.

EVODIUS: I have no objection, since you speak the truth.

AUGUSTINE: Since, therefore, this is the one law from which all the temporal laws enacted for the governance of human beings are made to vary, can that one law itself be made to vary in any way?

EVODIUS: I understand that it cannot be made to vary at all. No force, no accident, no deterioration of things could ever bring it about that it is not just that all things be most perfectly ordered.

War

Introduction

Of all the political topics that Augustine treated, he is perhaps most famous for his discussions of war. Included here are two important selections in which the problem is considered.[1] The first is taken from a letter that Augustine sent to Boniface, the governor of the Roman province of Africa, in 418. Boniface is at least interested in Christianity, but his duties involved, among other things, leading troops into battle. Augustine's advice to him is relatively straightforward and striking in its simplicity.

More complicated is the second selection, which is bound up with the issue of Manichaeism. Manichaeism was a religious movement that originated in Persia in the third century A.D. By the time Augustine was a young man it had spread throughout the Roman empire. The movement, which was essentially dualistic, saw creation as a battleground between light and darkness, spirit and matter, God and Satan. According to Manichaeism, human salvation consisted in freeing the spark of light imprisoned in the human body. One of the means to be used in this struggle to overcome the powers of darkness was asceticism.

Early in his life, Augustine himself was attracted to Manichaeism and followed it for nine years. After his conversion to Christianity, he was drawn into controversy with Manichaeism and wrote several treatises against it. The longest of these is a work against a Manichaean named Faustus. The argument centered on the problem of evil. As a monotheist, Augustine thought it possible to reconcile the presence of evil in the world with divine providence as long as one understood that God did not actually will evil but permitted it for the sake of a greater good. Faustus, for his part, was unable to square God's goodness with the existence of evil in the world. In order to solve this problem, he was ultimately

---

1. See also Letter 138 in the section on "The Compatibility of Christianity and Politics," the selection from *On Free Choice* in the section on "Law and Self-Defense," and *The City of God* IV. 15; XVIII. 2; XIX. 7, 12, and 13.

forced to postulate the existence of two separate and independent gods, one good and one evil.

As part of his attack on the Christian faith, Faustus criticized the Old Testament for advocating ideas and actions that are incompatible with divine providence. Among the passages from the Old Testament that bothered Faustus most were those describing the wars waged by Moses. In order to meet Faustus's criticisms, Augustine was forced to explain how the wars waged by Moses, and indeed war generally, could be understood as being in accord with divine providence.

From Letter 189, to Boniface

. . . Do not think that it is impossible for anyone serving in the military to please God. Among those who did so was the holy David, to whom the Lord gave such great testimony. Among them also were many just men of that time. Among them also was the centurion who said to the Lord, "I am not worthy that you should enter under my roof, but only say the word and my servant will be healed; for I, too, am a man under authority and have soldiers under me: I say to one, 'go,' and he goes, and to another, 'come,' and he comes, and to my servant, 'do this,' and he does it." And the Lord said about him, "Amen, I say to you, I have not found such faith in Israel" (Mt 8:8–10). Among them also was Cornelius,[2] to whom was sent the angel who said, "Cornelius, your alms have been accepted and your prayers heard" (Acts 10:4). When the angel advised him to send for the blessed apostle Peter and hear from him what he ought to do, he sent a religious soldier to bring the apostle to him. Among them also were those soldiers who came to John to be baptized. John was the holy precursor of the Lord and friend of the bridegroom. The Lord himself said of him, "There has arisen no one born of woman greater than John the Baptist" (Mt 11:11). When they asked him what they should do, he replied to them, "Terrorize no one, accuse no one falsely, and be content with your pay" (Lk 3:14). He surely did not prohibit them from serving in the military when he commanded them to be content with their pay.

Those who serve God with the highest discipline of chastity, renouncing all worldly actions, indeed have a greater place before God. "Yet everyone," as the apostle says, "has his own proper gift from God, one after this manner, another after that" (1 Cor 7:7). Some, then, fight for you against

---

2. Cornelius was also a centurion. This story to which Augustine refers is found in Acts 10.

invisible enemies by praying; you toil for them against visible barbarians by fighting.[3] Would that there were one faith in all, for there would be both less toiling and the devil with his angels would be more easily overcome! Yet, because it is necessary in this world that the citizens of the kingdom of heaven are troubled by temptations among the erring and impious in order that they might be tried and tested as gold in the furnace (Wis 3:6), we should not want to live with only the holy and the just before the time in order that we might deserve to receive that life in its own time.

Therefore, when you are arming for battle, think first that even your bodily strength is a gift of God. In this way, you will not think of using the gift of God against God. When fidelity is promised it must be kept, even to an enemy against whom war is being waged. How much more must it be kept with a friend for whom the war is fought! The will should be concerned with peace and necessity with war, so that God might liberate us from necessity and preserve us in peace. Peace is not sought in order to provoke war, but war is waged in order to attain peace. Be a peacemaker, then, even by fighting, so that through your victory you might bring those whom you defeat to the advantages of peace. "Blessed are the peacemakers," says the Lord, "for they will be called children of God" (Mt 5:9). If human peace is so sweet for attaining the temporal well-being of mortals, how much more sweet is divine peace for attaining the eternal well-being of the angels! Let necessity slay the warring foe, not your will. As violence is returned to one who rebels and resists, so should mercy be to one who has been conquered or captured, especially when there is no fear of a disturbance of peace. . . .

Against Faustus the Manichaean XXII. 73–79.

The eternal law, which commands maintaining the natural order and forbids disturbing it, places some human actions in a middle position, so that when human beings take it upon themselves to do these actions, their audacity is rightly blamed, but when they do them in carrying out a command, their obedience is justly praised. In considering the natural order, one must consider what is done, by whom it is done, and under whose command it is done. If Abraham had sacrificed his son of his own accord,[4]

3. Some years after this letter was written Boniface formed a political alliance with the barbarian Vandals, whom he invited into Africa in 429. He later fought against them, but by then their position was too strong, and Africa was overrun. Augustine died while his city was being beseiged by the Vandals.

4. The reference is to the famous story in Genesis 22.

what would he have shown himself to be except horrible and insane? As God was commanding him, however, did it not prove him to be faithful and devoted? The truth itself shouts this out so clearly that Faustus is in awe at its voice; seeking tooth and nail for something to say against this same Abraham, he does not have the audacity to blame him for this action. Or perhaps this famous deed did not occur to him, though it is so well-known that, without reading about it or searching for it, it comes to mind simply because it is sung by so many tongues and painted in so many places that it strikes the ears and eyes of even the deliberately unaware!

If killing one's own son of one's own accord is detestable, but doing so while subject to God's command is found to be not only not culpable but truly praiseworthy, why then, Faustus, do you blame Moses because he despoiled the Egyptians?[5] If the so-called "human wickedness" of the agent vexes you, you should be in awe of the divine authority of the one giving the command. Or are you prepared to censure even God himself for willing that such things be done? Then "Get behind me, Satan, for you do not understand which things are of God, and which are of men" (Mt 16:23). How I wish that as you, like Peter, have deserved to hear this rebuke, so you might afterwards proclaim that which you now blame in God because of your weak understanding, just as Peter afterwards announced to the Gentiles as a glorious proclamation what had at first displeased him when the Lord willed it to happen.

Therefore, if even human stubbornness and a deformed and twisted will understand that, with regard to right actions, it is of great importance whether an act is committed through human desire and rashness or whether it is in compliance with the command of God—who knows what, when, and to whom he grants permission or gives orders, and what is suitable for someone to do or suffer—then no one will wonder or be aghast at the wars waged under Moses.[6] The reason for this is that, as Moses was following divine commands, he was not savage but obedient, and God, in ordering such things, was not savage but was deservedly repaying those who had earned them and was striking with awe those who deserved it.

What is it about war that is to be blamed? Is it that those who will die someday are killed so that those who will conquer might dominate in peace? This is the complaint of the timid, not of the religious. The desire for harming, the cruelty of revenge, the restless and implacable mind, the savageness of revolting, the lust for dominating, and similar things—these are

5. See Ex 11:1–3; 12:35–6.
6. See Ex 17:8–16.

what are justly blamed in wars. Often, so that such things might also be justly punished, certain wars that must be waged against the violence of those resisting are commanded by God or some other legitimate ruler and are undertaken by the good.

Because wars are found in the order of human affairs, that very order justly constrains men either to command or to obey with respect to such affairs. If this were not true, John, when asked by the soldiers who came to be baptized "What should we do?" would have answered, "Throw away your weapons, give up the army, never strike or harm or subdue anyone." However, because he knew that, even though they might do such things in performing military service, they are not murderers but ministers of the law, and not avengers of their own injuries but defenders of public well-being, he answered, "Terrorize no one, accuse no one falsely, and be content with your pay" (Lk 3:14). Because the Manichaeans customarily and openly speak evil of John, let them listen to the Lord Jesus Christ himself commanding that the money which John tells the soldiers to be content with be returned to Caesar: "Return to Caesar the things that are Caesar's, and to God the things that are God's" (Mt 22:21). After all, the purpose of handing over tribute money is so that the soldiers necessary on account of war might be paid. Also, there is the case of the centurion who said, "I am a man under authority and have soldiers under me: I say to one, 'go,' and he goes, and to another, 'come,' and he comes, and to my servant, 'do this,' and he does it" (Mt 8:9). Christ praised his faith; he did not order him to desert.

At this point, however, it would be tedious, and unnecessary, to enter into a discussion about just and unjust wars, for it makes a great difference by which causes and under which authorities men undertake the wars that must be waged. The natural order, which is suited to the peace of mortal things, requires that the authority and deliberation for undertaking war be under the control of a leader, and also that, in the executing of military commands, soldiers serve peace and the common well-being. Moreover, it is wrong to doubt that a war which must be waged, undertaken under the authority of God, whether in order to constrain, crush, or subjugate the pride of mortals, is undertaken rightly, since even a war which is waged out of human desire can do no harm to the incorruptible God or to his saints. Insofar as the patience of the saints is tried and their souls humbled, and they suffer fatherly correction, they are benefited rather than harmed. No one can have any power over them except what has been given to him from above (see Jn 19:11); for, "There is no power except from God" (Rom 13:1), who either commands or permits it.

Therefore, a just man, if he should happen to serve as a soldier under a human king who is sacrilegious, could rightly wage war at the king's command, maintaining the order of civic peace, for what he is commanded to do is not contrary to the sure precepts of God, or else it is not sure whether it is or not. In this latter case, perhaps the iniquity of giving the orders will make the king guilty while the rank of a servant in the civil order will show the soldier to be innocent. Since all this is true about a just man serving a sacrilegious human king, how much more innocently may the man who wages war at God's command be occupied in the administration of wars? After all, everyone who serves God knows that he can never command what is evil.

If anyone supposes that God could not have commanded anyone to wage war because in later times the Lord Jesus Christ said, "I say to you, do not resist evil, but if anyone should strike you on the right cheek, offer him the left as well" (Mt 5:39), he should understand that this does not refer to a disposition of the body but of the heart.[7] There is the sacred resting place of virtue, and such were the hearts of our fathers, the just men of ancient times.

Order, however, required a planned succession of events and a distinction of ages, so that first it would become apparent that even earthly goods—including human kingdoms and victories over enemies, for the sake of which the city of the impious, greatly diffused throughout the world, worships idols and demons—belong to nothing other than the power and choice of the one true God. For the same reason, the Old Testament concealed in earthly promises the secret of the kingdom of heaven, which was to be opened at the opportune time, and made it, in a way, rather opaque and shadowy. When the fullness of time arrived so that the New Testament, which was veiled and prefigured in the Old, might be revealed, it was then demonstrated through clear testimony that there is another life for the sake of which this life is to be scorned and another kingdom for the sake of which the adversity of all earthly kingdoms is to be patiently endured.

For this reason, the name "martyr," which means "one who testifies," is given to those who, according to the will of God, give this testimony by their confessions, sufferings, and deaths. The number of those who testify is so great that if Christ, who called to Saul from heaven, changed him

---

7. Augustine explains this teaching more completely in Letter 138, which may be found in the section on "The Compatibility of Religion and Politics." See also *The Lord's Sermon on the Mount* I. 19–20, which is not included in this volume.

from a wolf to a sheep, and sent him into the midst of wolves, willed to bring all these who testify into one army and to sustain them in battle as he did the Hebrew fathers, what peoples could resist? What kingdom would not submit? Nevertheless, so that the most radiant testimony might be given to the truth, which now had to teach that God is to be served not for the sake of temporal happiness in this life but for the sake of eternal happiness hereafter, that which is commonly called unhappiness had to be borne and endured.

Therefore, in the fullness of time, the Son of God, made from a woman, and made under the law so that he might redeem those who were under the law, and made out of the seed of David according to the flesh, sends his disciples as sheep into the midst of wolves and admonishes them not to fear those who can kill the body but cannot kill the soul. He also promises that the completeness of the body will be restored, even to the recovery of each hair. He orders that Peter's sword be replaced in its sheath and restores the enemy's ear that had been cut off to its previous condition. He says that he could order legions of angels to destroy his enemies, but that he must drink the cup which the Father's will had given him. Setting the precedent, he drinks the cup; he hands it on to his followers, revealing by his precept and confirming by his example the virtue of patience: "Therefore God raised him from the dead and gave him the name which is above every name, so that at the name of Jesus every knee might bend in the heavens, on the earth, and under the earth, and every tongue confess that Jesus is Lord, in the glory of God the Father" (Phil 2:9–11).

The patriarchs and prophets, therefore, reigned in this world in order to point out that God gives and takes away such kingdoms; the apostles and martyrs did not reign here, to make it clear that the kingdom of heaven is to be preferred. The former waged regal wars to show that such victories are due to the will of God; the latter, not resisting, were killed so that they might teach that dying for faith in the truth is a preferable victory. The prophets, however, knew even in those times to die for the truth; the Lord himself refers to this, saying "From the blood of Abel to the blood of Zacharia" (Mt 23:35).

Later, what was prophesied in the psalm under the figure of Solomon (whose name means "the peaceful one") about Christ the Lord (for he himself is our peace) began to be fulfilled: "All the kings of the earth will worship him and all peoples serve him" (Ps 72:11). Christian emperors, full of piety and reliant upon Christ, have gained most glorious victories over sacrilegious enemies who had placed their hope in the rites of idols and demons. From the most straightforward and well-known examples, some of which have now been preserved in writing, it is known that although the soothsayings of the demons deceived their followers, the predictions of the saints strengthened theirs.

If, however, these vain people find it remarkable that God taught one thing then to those who gave out the Old Testament, when the grace of the New was veiled, but another to the proclaimers of the New Testament, when the obscurity of the Old was unveiled, let them notice Christ the Lord himself changing what he had said and saying something else. Christ says, "When I sent you without bag, or wallet, or shoes, did you lack anything?" And they said, "Nothing." Then he said to them, "Now let anyone who has a bag take it, and also a wallet; and let anyone who lacks a sword sell his coat and buy one" (Lk 22:35–36). Surely, if vain people should find such contrasting passages, one in the Old and the other in the New Testament, they would holler that it proves they are opposed to one another. So how will they respond now, when the same person says, "In the past I sent you without bag, or wallet, or shoes, and you lacked nothing; now, however, let anyone who has a bag take it and also a wallet, and let anyone who has a tunic sell it and buy a sword"? Do they not understand how there is no inconsistency in the one giving instructions here, but that the precepts or advice or permissions must be changed according to the planned succession of differing times? If they say that he spoke of taking a bag and a wallet and buying a sword on account of some hidden meaning, why do they not admit that the same, one God earlier commanded the prophets to wage war and later prohibited the apostles from doing so on account of some hidden meaning?

Not only are the words of the Lord contained in the passage which we have quoted from the Gospel, but the deeds of the obedient disciples also conformed to them. At first they went without bag or wallet and lacked nothing, as is clear from the Lord's question and their response. Later, when he gave them the command about buying a sword, they said, "Here are two swords," and the Lord replied, "It is enough" (Lk 22:38). Thus, we find Peter with a weapon when he cut off the attacker's ear, and his audacity in acting on his own accord was stopped because, even though he had been told to take a sword, he had not been told to use it. The will of the Lord—why he had ordered arms to be borne by those whom he did not want to use arms—was certainly hidden. Nevertheless, it belonged to him to give orders according to his plan and for them to fulfill his orders without shrinking from them.

It is, therefore, malicious to blame Moses for waging war since he ought to be blamed less if he were to wage war on his own accord than if he were not to do so when God commanded it. Moreover, to dare to blame God himself because he commanded such things, or not to believe that a just and good God was able to command such things, is the mark of a human being, to put it mildly, unable to consider that for divine providence, extending in time through all things high and low, what arises is not a novelty and what dies does not vanish, but all things, individually, in their own order of natures or merits, either give way or succeed or abide. Furthermore, a correct human will is joined to divine law and inordinate human desire is checked by the order of divine law, so that a good man wills nothing other than what is commanded and a wicked man can do nothing more than what is permitted, and he can do that only in such a way that he cannot accomplish without punishment what he wills unjustly.

In all things which human weakness abhors or fears, then, only iniquity is justly condemned; the others are either derived from the attributes of natures or earned through wrongdoing. Moreover, a man becomes iniquitous when he loves things for their own sake which should be embraced only for the sake of something else and desires for the sake of something else those things which should be loved in themselves. In this way, he disrupts in himself, to the greatest extent possible, the natural order which the eternal law commands to be maintained. A man is just when he does not desire to use things except for the sake of what has been divinely established and, in particular, enjoys God for God's own sake, and enjoys himself and his friend in God for the sake of the very same God. Whoever loves the love of God in a friend, loves the friend for the sake of God.

Furthermore, if iniquity or justice do not pertain to the will, then they are not in our power; moreover, if they are not in our power, then no reward or punishment would be just, and no one thinks that except the foolish. Yet the ignorance whereby a man does not know what he ought to will and the weakness whereby he cannot do everything he does will, come from the hidden order of punishments and from the inscrutable judgments of God, in whom there is no iniquity (Rom 9:14). Indeed, it was recorded for us in the faithful word of God that Adam sinned; and that in Adam all die, and that "through him sin entered the world and through sin death" (Rom 5:12), was written truly. That in this punishment "the body is corrupted and weighs down the soul, and its earthly dwelling pulls down the mind thinking about many things" (Wis 9:15) is most true and well-known to us; and that from this just punishment nothing liberates except merciful grace, is certain. Thus, the apostle, groaning, exclaims, "I am an unhappy man! Who will free me from the body of this death? The grace of God through Jesus Christ our Lord" (Rom 7:24–25).

Still, whatever the distribution of God's judgments and mercies might be, why one man is thus and another is otherwise happens through causes which are hidden, but nevertheless just. Even so, we are not ignorant that all these things happen according to the judgment or mercy of God, although the measures, numbers, and weights by which God, the creator of everything which exists naturally, arranges all things lies concealed. God is not the author of sin; nevertheless, he is the governor even of it. Thus, sins, which would not be sins if they were not against nature, are judged and governed and given the places and conditions they deserve, in order that they might not be permitted to disrupt and disfigure the nature of the universe.

Because this is so; and because of this mystery about the judgments of God and the actions of human wills, in which some are corrupted and others practice moderation through the same prosperity, and some are unmade and others make progress through the same adversity; and because all human and mortal life on earth is a testing, who knows which human beings will benefit and which will be hindered by reigning or serving or living leisurely or dying in peace, or giving orders or fighting or conquering or being killed in war? Although this is so, it is nevertheless also established that such things are a benefit only if they come through divine kindness and an obstacle only if they come through divine judgment.

What then? Should we leap into rash blaming of not only human beings but God? Those who gave out the Old Testament (who were at the same time announcing in advance the New) served by killing sinners, while those who gave out the New Testament (who were at the same time explaining the Old) served by being killed by sinners. Nevertheless, both served the one God, who was teaching through diverse but complementary times that temporal goods are to be sought from him and scorned for his sake, and that temporal afflictions can be ordered by him and ought to be endured for his sake.

What, then, was cruel about what Moses ordered or did when, ardently loving in holiness the people entrusted to him and desiring them to serve the one true God, he acted as he did after he learned that they had fallen into making and worshipping an idol and had prostituted their shameless minds to demons? Moses punished by the sword only a few of them, while God himself, whom they had offended, willed, in his lofty and secret judgment, all those deserving it to be struck down (Ex 32:9–10). What Moses did both frightened the people for their well-being in the present and confirmed their discipline for the future. Who does not recognize in Moses' words that he did what he did with no cruelty but in great love, for he prayed for their sins, saying, "If you will forgive their sin, forgive it, and if not, delete me from your book" (Ex 32:32)?

Anyone of prudence, piously comparing Moses' killing and his prayer, sees most clearly how great is the harm to the soul of fornicating through likenesses of demons,[8] since Moses' violence is due to his love. So also the apostle not cruelly but lovingly handed over a man to Satan for the destruction of the flesh in order that the spirit might be saved in the day of the Lord Jesus (1 Cor 5:5). He also handed over others so that they might learn not to blaspheme (1 Tm 1:20).

The Manichaeans read apocryphal books written by unknown hack writers of fables under the name of the apostles.[9] These writings would have deserved the approval of the holy church at the time of their writing if the holy and learned men then living and able to judge such things had considered their contents true. In these books the Manichaeans read that the apostle Thomas, while travelling and completely unknown, was at a certain wedding feast. When slapped by a servant, he had cursed the man, inflicting a lasting, savage punishment on him, for when the servant went out to the well in order to serve water to the guests, a lion rushed up and killed him. The hand with which he had struck the apostle's head a light blow was torn from his body, fulfilling the word of that same apostle, who had hoped and prayed for that. A dog carried the hand to the table at which the apostle himself was reclining. What could seem more cruel than this? Yet, unless I am mistaken, it is also written in that book that because Thomas sought a pardon for the man in the world to come, the man received the compensation of a greater benefit.

Thus, the apostle was commended by this frightening deed to the people who did not know him as being dear to God; he also looked to the eternal well-being of the servant after his life here was brought to an end. Whether the narrative is true or fictitious is not of present interest, for certainly the Manichaeans, by whom those scriptures which the ecclesias-

8. With the phrase "fornicating through likenesses of demons," Augustine refers to the worshipping of idols.

9. Not only did the Manichaeans reject many of the Scriptures accepted by the Christians (such as the Old Testament), but they also accepted certain scriptures which the Christians rejected. Among the latter group was the Gospel of Thomas, to which Augustine refers. Augustine's point is that if even the books accepted only by the Manichaeans contain an example of punishment that can be reconciled with the injunction to turn the other cheek, then they should not attack Moses, since his punishing of the Israelites can also be so reconciled.

tical canon rejected are accepted as true and genuine, are compelled to acknowledge that this story displays the virtue of patience, which the Lord teaches, saying, "If anyone strikes you on the right cheek, offer him your left also" (Mt 5:39). This virtue can exist in the disposition of the heart, even if it is not exhibited in the acts of the body and the expression of words, since the apostle, when slapped, did not turn the other side to the man striking him or advise him to strike again, but instead prayed to God to pardon the insulting man in the world to come but not to leave the insult unpunished in the present one. Clearly, Thomas inwardly held a feeling of love and outwardly sought an example of correction.

Whether this story is true or fictitious, why are the Manichaeans unwilling to believe that with such a disposition of soul the servant of God, Moses, cut down with the sword the makers and worshippers of the idol when his own words suffice to show that he prayed for a pardon for their sin in such a manner that, unless his request was to be granted, he wanted to be removed from God's book? What similarity is there between a stranger being slapped by the palm of the hand and God liberating the Israelites from the servitude of Egypt, transporting them through the divided sea, covering over their pursuing enemies with the waves, and then being abandoned and scorned for an idol? If we compare the punishments, what similarity is there between being killed with a sword and being slaughtered and mutilated by wild beasts? After all, in applying the public law judges sentence those guilty of a greater crime to be killed by beasts rather than to be slain by the sword.

The Use of Persecution

Introduction

During the early years of the fourth century, the Christian church in North Africa and elsewhere was persecuted by Roman authorities. Some of the Christians bravely accepted death in the glory of martyrdom rather than betray the Christian cause; others avoided the ultimate penalty by surrendering their copies of the Sacred Scriptures into the hands of government officials. By the time the persecution ended, the church in North Africa was bitterly divided. Those who had or were thought to have cooperated with the persecutors were shunned as traditores *or "traitors" by rigorists who held that any concessions made to the authorities during the time of persecution constituted an utter betrayal of Christ.*

The tensions in the African church grew into open schism after the more rigorous group refused to acknowledge the authority of Caecilian, who had been consecrated bishop of Carthage by a man whom the rigorists claimed to be a traditor. *The opposition to Caecilian, whose legitimacy was affirmed by more than one ecclesiastical inquiry, came to be led by a certain Donatus, and his followers soon became known as Donatists. Some of the Donatists turned to violence and were labeled* circumcelliones *by their Catholic opponents for their encircling attacks. In 405 an imperial edict came down against the Donatists, imposing on them such penalties as confiscation of church property and the loss of certain civic rights. The imperial policy became harsher after 411, when an important commission at Carthage ruled definitively against them. Despite being condemned as heretical, the Donatist movement managed to survive until North Africa was conquered by Islamic warriors.*

Augustine inherited the problem of the Donatist schism upon becoming the Catholic bishop of Hippo. During his episcopate, imperial policy against the Donatists became more aggressive and the problem developed into a crisis that would trouble Augustine until the end of his life. His response to that crisis was varied: he reached out to the Donatists to call them back to unity; he wrote

theological treatises against them; he opposed the imperial policy of persecuting
them, then acquiesced in it and provided a justification for it, and then again
pleaded for mercy.

The selections included here represent Augustine's varied responses to the
question concerning the use of force with respect to religion. In the first passage,
taken from the relatively early work, On True Religion, *Augustine suggests*
that the way of Christ, humbly tolerating insult rather than opposing it, prefers
persuasion to persecution. The second selection is taken from a letter written in
approximately 408 to Vincentius, the bishop of a group of Donatists known as
Rogatists because they were originally led by a bishop named Rogatus.
Vincentius was also formerly a fellow student of Augustine at Carthage. In this
letter Augustine says that he has recently been converted to the use of forceful
persecution against the Donatists and goes on to explain his change of heart. In
the third selection, a letter written in 411 to the imperial commissioner
Marcellinus, who was also a conscientious Catholic and a personal friend, Au-
gustine begs for leniency for a group of Donatists who had attacked two members
of the Catholic clergy.

From *On True Religion*, XVI.31

Christ did nothing by force, but did everything by persuading and warning. Indeed, the old slavery having been ended, the time of liberty dawned.[1]
Man was already being suitably and profitably persuaded that he had been
created with free choice. By performing miracles, Christ instilled faith in
the God that he was; by his suffering, he instilled faith in the humanity that
he was bearing. Hence, speaking to the crowds as God, he denied his own
mother when she was announced to him (Mt 12:46–50); yet, the Gospel
says that as a boy he was subordinate to his parents (Lk 2:51). In his teaching, God appeared; in his stages of growing up, a human being. Also, about
to change the water into wine, he said as God, "Go away from me, woman.
What do you want of me? My hour is not yet come" (Jn 2:4). However,
when the hour in which he would die as a human being had come, he
recognized his mother from the cross and commended her to the disciple
whom he loved more than the others (Jn 19:26–27).

To their ruin, the peoples, followers of pleasures, desired riches; he
wanted to be poor. They longed for honors and empires; he did not want to
become a king. They thought that the bodily generation of children was a

---

1. By "the old slavery," Augustine refers to the condition of mankind under the
Mosaic law; "the time of liberty" refers to the reign of the Gospel.

great good; he scorned such a union and such descendents. In their pride, they abhorred insults; he withstood every kind of insult. They judged injuries to be intolerable; what greater injury is there than to be condemned though just and innocent? They cursed bodily pain; he was flogged and tortured. They were afraid to die; he was punished with death. They thought that the cross was the most degrading kind of death; he was crucified. All the things which we, not living rightly, were desiring to have, he deemed of little account by abstaining from them. All the things which we, deviating from the zeal for truth, were desiring to avoid, he destroyed by enduring them. No sin can be committed unless that which he scorned is desired or that which he endured is evaded.

From Letter 93, to Vincentius

Section 1

. . . The Donatists are too active; it does not seem to me to be useless to repress and correct them through the authorities who have been ordained by God.[2] Already we rejoice at the correction of many, who so truly hold and defend the Catholic unity and are so glad to be liberated from their previous error that we marvel at them in great and joyful thanksgiving. Because of some incomprehensible force of custom, they would in no way have considered changing for the better unless, struck with terror, they had directed their thoughts to the consideration of truth. They feared that if they suffered temporal travails fruitlessly and endured them vainly,[3] not for the sake of justice but for the sake of perversity and human obstinacy, they would afterward, having despised his gentle warnings and paternal scourgings, find nothing in the presence of God except the deserved punishments of the impious.

Having become teachable by considering these things, they would find the church promised to all peoples not in the slanders and fables of human beings but in the divine books, and they would see with their own eyes the church restored. Then they would not doubt that the Christ, foretold in those books but not now seen, is above the heavens. . . .

2. Augustine refers to the imperial authorities who were at this time pursuing a policy of suppression against the Donatists.

3. Augustine is referring to the loss of certain civic privileges, including some property rights, suffered by the Donatists.

Section 2

. . . What about that other kind of most serious sickness—a sickness of those who are not agitated or daring, but, under the weight of a certain entrenched indolence, say to us, "Indeed, what you say is true; there is nothing which might be replied to it; but it is hard for us to abandon the tradition of our forebears"? Is it not healthy to shake them up by means of a code involving temporal annoyances, so that just as they might rise from a lethargic sleep, they might also wake up to the well-being of unity? . . .

Section 3

However, you might reply that these measures are not advantageous for some people. Should the practice of medicine be given up because the sickness of some is incurable? You consider only those who are so obdurate that they will not accept this discipline. Of such people the Scripture says, "I have scourged your children futilely; they did not accept discipline" (Jer 2:30). I think, however, that they were scourged because of love, not hatred.

You should also consider the many people about whose well-being we are rejoicing. If they were frightened and not taught, this would seem to be a sort of improper domination. Again, if they were taught and not frightened, they would remain obdurate because of entrenched custom and would move more sluggishly to set out upon the way of well-being.

Indeed, once reason was restored to them and the truth was revealed in the divine testimonies of Scripture, they answered us that they had desired to come over into the communion of the Catholic church but were terrified of the violent hostilities of wretched human beings.[4] To be sure, that violence ought to be despised, both for the sake of justice and for eternal life, but until they are made strong, we must not despair at the weakness of such people but be patient with them. We must not forget what the Lord himself said to Peter before he became strong: "You are not able to follow me now, but later on you will follow me" (Jn 13:36).

However, when salutary teaching is joined to useful fear, so that not only does the light of truth drive out the darkness of error, but the power of fear also breaks the evil chains of custom, then we rejoice, as I said, over

4. Augustine would seem to have in mind the reprisals of the Donatist community against those who broke ranks and came over to the Catholic side.

the many who bless and give thanks to God with us. For in fulfilling the promise that the kings of the earth would serve Christ (Dn 7:27), God has in that way cured the sick and healed the weak.[5]

Section 4

. . . Who is able to love us more than God? Yet, he not only teaches us continually in a pleasant manner but also frightens us continually for our own well-being. To the gentle bandages by which he consoles he also often adds the most stinging medicine of tribulation. He tries even the pious and religious patriarchs with famine (Gn 12:10; 26:1; 41:53–42:5; 43:1–2), prods a stubborn people with more severe penalties, and, so that the apostle's "strength might be perfect in weakness" (2 Cor 12:7–9), does not take away the thorn of the flesh from him, even though asked three times to do so. Let us love even our enemies, for that is just and God commands it "so that we might be children of our father, who is in heaven, who makes his sun rise upon the good and the evil and sends rain upon the just and the unjust" (Mt 5:44–45). However, even as we praise these gifts of his, let us also ponder his scourging of those whom he loves.

Section 5

You think that no one ought to be compelled to justice, although you read that the father of the house said to his servants, "Whomever you find, compel to come in" (Lk 14:23). . . . You also think that force should not be used to liberate a human being from disastrous errors, although you see through the most certain examples that God himself does this, and no one's love is more profitable for us than his. You also hear Christ saying, "No one comes to me unless the father draws him" (Jn 6:44), but that happens in the hearts of all who turn to him through fear of divine wrath. . . .

Section 8

If it were always praiseworthy to suffer persecution, it would have been sufficient for the Lord to say, "Blessed are they who suffer persecution" without adding "for the sake of justice" (Mt 5:10). Likewise, if it were

---

5. The promise concerning the "kings of the earth" is fulfilled in the conversion of the Roman emperors; this enables the Donatists to be brought back from their error.

always culpable to apply persecution, it would not be written in the sacred books, "Anyone slandering his neighbor in secret, him I will persecute" (Ps 101:5). Therefore, sometimes a person suffering persecution is unjust and a person employing persecution is just.

Clearly, the wicked have always persecuted the good and the good the wicked. The wicked persecute by harming through injustice; the good by advising through discipline. The former persecute without bounds; the latter temperately. The former are enslaved to desire; the latter to charity. One who slaughters does not consider how he hacks, but he who cures does consider how he dissects. The one persecutes what is healthy; the other what is rotting. The impious killed the prophets; the prophets also killed the impious (1 Kgs 18:4, 40). The Jews scourged Christ; Christ also scourged the Jews. The apostles were handed over to human power by human beings; the apostles also handed over human beings to the power of Satan (1 Tm 1:20). In all these matters, what else should be considered except this: who among them acted for the sake of truth and who for the sake of iniquity, who acted for the purpose of harming and who for correction?

Section 9

Do the critics say that no example is found in the Gospels or the apostolic writings of anything being requested from the kings of the earth on behalf of the church against the enemies of the church? Who denies that? The following prophecy, however, was not yet fulfilled: "And now, understand and learn, you kings who judge the earth; serve the Lord in fear" (Ps 2:10–11). What was already fulfilled, though, was what is stated a little earlier in that same psalm: "Why did the nations rage and the peoples practice folly? The kings rose up and the rulers assembled into one against the Lord and against his Christ" (Ps 2:1–2).[6]

Truly, if past events in the prophetic books prefigured future ones, both the age of the church under the apostles and the present age of the church were prefigured in that king named Nebuchadnezzar (Dn 3). What was prefigured when this king compelled the pious and just men to wor-

---

6. Augustine's argument is thus that the first verses of Psalm 2 refer to the period when the church was being persecuted, while the later verses refer to the present period, the one in which the church has temporal power. Since the Scriptures were written by the apostles in the earlier period, they do not show the church appealing to temporal political authorities. Now, however, the second age has come, and it is appropriate for the church to appeal to those authorities.

ship an image and, when they refused, sent them into the flames (Dn 3:1–23) was fulfilled in the age of the apostles and martyrs. What was prefigured in the same king a little later, when, having turned to honoring the true God, he decreed in his own kingdom that whoever blasphemed the God of Shadrach, Meshach, and Abdenego would be subject to appropriate penalties (Dn 3:95–6), is being fulfilled now. Therefore, the first age of that king signified the earlier ages of the unbelieving kings, in which the Christians suffered on account of the impious; but the later age of that king signified the later ages of the believing kings, in which the impious suffer on account of the Christians.

Section 10

With respect to those who wandered off because they were led astray by the wicked in the name of Christ, clearly severity is tempered and greater clemency is maintained in order that the sheep of Christ will not also wander off and have to be called back to the flock in another manner. This greater clemency is maintained in order that through the coercive means of exile and fines, they are warned to consider what and why they suffer, and in order that they might learn to prefer the Scriptures which they read to the rumors and malicious deceits of human beings. Who among us, or among you, does not praise the laws adopted by the emperors against the sacrifices of the pagans? Certainly a much more severe penalty was established for that; indeed, there is capital punishment for that impiety. However, the reason held for rebuking and coercing you is to warn you to depart from an error rather than to punish you for a crime.[7] . . .

Section 12

Concerning requesting or enforcing the commands of earthly powers against schismatics and heretics, those Donatists from whom you Rogatists have separated yourselves were indeed, as far as we have heard, most energetic both against you and against the Maximianists.[8] We can even prove

7. Augustine's point is that many of the Donatists have wandered off because they mistakenly thought they were following Christ, in whose name they were being misled by others. As a result, their penalty is milder than that of the pagans who simply reject Christ.

8. Both the Rogatists, among whom Vincentius is the bishop, and the Maximianists, were splinter groups who separated themselves from the main part of the Donatist movement. Both groups suffered reprisals for acting in this way.

this with reliable documents of their deeds. Moreover, before you were separated from them, when Julian was emperor,[9] they said in their own petition to him that "justice lay with him alone." They knew for certain that he was an apostate and saw him given over to idolatry. Thus, either they confess that idolatry is just or they are not able to deny that they are wicked liars for saying that justice lay with him alone when they realized that idolatry had a greater place with him. Perhaps you admit there was an error in their words, but what do you say about the act itself? If nothing that is just should be requested from the emperor, why was Julian asked for what was thought to be just?

Section 15

... Why is it not permissible for the Christian world to ignore what those who accused Caecilian could not prove?[10] Should those whom Christ has sown in his own field—that is, in this world—and has commanded to grow among the weeds until the harvest (Mt 13:24–30), not be counted as Christians because in this case in which they were not participants in the discussions, they preferred to believe the judges who were placing themselves in danger by judging, rather than the defeated litigants? Likewise, should all the thousands of the faithful among all peoples, a multitude which the Lord compared to the stars of the heavens and the sands of the sea and to whom he promised and delivered a blessing in the seed of Abraham (Gn 12:3; 15:5; 22:17–18), not be counted as Christians for the same reason?

Certainly a crime does not defile anyone who does not know of it. How could the faithful, dispersed throughout the whole world, have known about the crime of betrayal when the accusers, even if they knew about the crime, were nevertheless unable to demonstrate it? Surely this very ignorance demonstrates that they are innocent of this crime.[11] Are the innocent, then, to be falsely accused of a crime because they did not know whether the charge against another was true or false? What room is left for inno-

9. Julian the apostate was emperor from 361 to 363; he attempted to return the empire to paganism. Augustine's point is that the Donatists are behaving hypocritically when they complain about appeals from the Catholics to the imperial authorities, since they did the very same thing, and to a pagan emperor at that.

10. On Caecilian, see the introduction to this section.

11. The Donatists accused the Catholics of the crime of betraying Christ because they did not separate themselves from those who supposedly did betray the faith by handing over the Scriptures. Augustine's point is that Catholics cannot possibly be guilty of such a crime because they do not know whether it even occurred.

cence if it is criminal not to know the crimes of others? Furthermore, if, as I have said, this very ignorance demonstrates that the peoples of all the world are innocent of the crime, then how great a crime is it to be separated from the communion of these innocent people?

The deeds of the guilty that are not able to be demonstrated to the innocent or to be believed by them do not pollute anyone even when they are known, if they are endured for the sake of the fellowship of the innocent. The good must not be abandoned for the sake of the wicked, but the wicked must be endured for the sake of the good, just as the prophets endured those against whom they were saying such things. They did not leave the communion of the sacraments[12] of that people. In the same way, the Lord himself endured the guilty Judas all the way up to his deserved end and permitted him to take part in the sacred supper along with the innocent. The apostles also endured those who were preaching Christ out of envy (Phil 1:15,18), which is the vice of the devil himself, and Cyprian[13] endured the avarice of his colleagues, which, following the apostle (Eph 5:5; Col 3:5), he calls idolatry.[14]

Finally, whatever was done by those bishops then, even if perhaps it was known by some of them (I do not mean to treat them unfairly) is now not known by anyone. Why, therefore, is peace not loved by all? It would be easy for you to think along these lines, or perhaps you already do. At any rate, it is still better that you love earthly possessions, so that by fearing their loss you might consent to the truth which you know, than that you love that most vain glory of human beings which you think you will lose if you consent to the truth that you know.

Section 17

I have yielded to the evidence placed before me by my colleagues. My original position was that no one should be compelled into the unity of

12. The Donatists argued that since Caecilian was ordained by a sinful person, the sacraments administered by him and his clergy were also invalid. Thus, they denied the legitimacy of the Catholic sacraments, maintaining that the efficacy of a sacrament was dependent upon the holiness of the one who administered it. Augustine would maintain instead that the efficacy of a sacrament depends upon Christ, not upon the holiness of the priest or the lack thereof. Augustine's position became standard Christian teaching.

13. Cyprian: bishop of Carthage from about 248 until his martyrdom in 258. He was also a famous Christian theologian. Both the Catholics and the Donatists revered his work and considered his views to be authoritative.

14. Letter 55, 25 and 27.

Christ, but that we should act with words, fight with argumentation, and triumph with reason, so that we would not have those whom we knew to be professed heretics pretending to be Catholics. This opinion of mine was not conquered through words being spoken against it but through examples which demonstrate the contrary. First, the example of my own city was placed before me. Although it was totally on the Donatist side, it was turned to Catholic unity through fear of the imperial laws. Now we see that it so detests the destructiveness of your enmity that one might believe that it was never Donatist at all. So many other cities were recounted to me by name that, by means of these instances, I realized that what the Scripture says could also be interpreted correctly with respect to this matter: "Give an opportunity to the wise man, and he will become wiser" (Prv 9:9). . . .

How many thought the true church to be the Donatist party simply because security was making them too sluggish, squeamish, and lazy to acknowledge the Catholic truth! How many were barred from entering, having heard the rumors of the slanderers who were saying that we place I know not what upon the alter of God! How many, believing that the party to which a Christian belongs does not matter, thus remained in the party of the Donatists because they were born there and no one was compelling them to leave and pass over to the Catholics!

Section 18

. . . Some say, "We were frightened away from entering the Catholic faith by false rumors. We could not have known that they were false unless we entered, but we would not have entered unless we were compelled. Thanks be to the Lord, who took away our fear with this scourge. Through experience he taught us how vain and empty the lying rumor was that had been spread about his church. Because of this, we now believe the accusations made by the authors of this heresy to be false, since their followers have fabricated accusations so false and so poor." Others say, "Indeed, we were thinking that it did not matter where we held the faith of Christ, but thanks be to the Lord, who collected us from schism and showed us that it is appropriate for the one God to be worshipped in unity."

Section 19

Was I to oppose and contradict my colleagues by impeding these gains of the Lord, so that the sheep of Christ, straying off into your mountains and hills—that is, your swellings of pride—might not be collected into the fold of peace, where there is "one flock and one shepherd" (Jn 10:16)? . . .

Let the kings of the earth serve Christ, even by enacting laws for the sake of Christ. Your predecessors exposed Caecilian and his companions to the punishment of the kings of the earth by false accusations. May the lions be turned to crush the bones of the detractors. May Daniel himself, proved innocent and liberated from the den in which the detractors perish, not intercede for them (Dn 6:23–25), for "He who prepares a pit for his neighbor will himself most justly fall into it" (Prv 26:27).

Section 20

Rescue yourself, brother, while you live in this flesh, from the wrath which will come for the stubborn and the proud. When the fear inspired by temporal power attacks the truth, it is a glorious trial for the just and the strong, but a dangerous temptation for the weak. However, when it proclaims the truth, it is an advantageous warning for the prudent who are wandering astray, but a torment for the foolish. Yet, "there is no power except from God. He who resists power, resists the order of God, for rulers are not a source of fear for good conduct but for wicked. If you want to be without fear of power, do good and you will have praise from that power" (Rom 13:1–3). If, on the one hand, power, favoring the truth, corrects someone, he who was corrected receives praise from that power. If, on the other hand, power is hostile to the truth and rages against someone, he who is crowned victor[15] receives praise from that power. . . .

Section 23

. . . How can we believe that we have received from the divine writings the revealed Christ if we do not also accept from them the revealed church? It does not matter whatever handles and hooks anyone might weave together against the simplicity of the truth, whatever fog of subtle falsities anyone might spread about. Clearly, he who preaches a Christ who did not suffer and rise on the third day will be anathema, because we have accepted the truth of the Gospel: "It was necessary for Christ to suffer and rise from the dead on the third day" (Lk 24:46). In the same way, he who preaches a church other than the communion of all peoples will be anathema, because we have also accepted the truth which comes next in the Gospel: "And in his name penance and remission of sins must be preached to all peoples,

---

15. The expression "he who is crowned victor" is a reference to Christian martyrdom.

beginning with Jerusalem" (Lk 24:47). We ought also to hold firmly that "Whoever preached to you other than what you received, let him be anathema" (Gal 1:9).

Section 26

. . . The pagans can curse us more than the Jews,[16] on account of the laws which the Christian emperors enacted against the worship of idols.[17] Nevertheless, many of them were set straight and were turned to the true and living God, and are being turned daily. Clearly, however, if the Jews and the pagans thought the Christians to be so few as you are—you who assert that you are the only Christians—they would not bother to curse us, but would never stop laughing at us. Are you not afraid that the Jews might say to you, "Your Paul referred this scripture to your church: 'Rejoice, you who are sterile, who do not give birth; break forth and cry out, you who are not in labor; for the deserted woman has many more children than she who has a husband' (Gal 4:27; Is 54:1). In citing this passage, he indicated that the number of Christians would surpass the number of Jews. If, however, you are the church of Christ, why are you so few?" . . .

Section 28

. . . It is of the church that it is said, "As the lily among the thorns, so is my beloved among the daughters" (Sg 2:2), and the schismatics cannot be called thorns except by the wickedness of their morals nor daughters except by their common participation in the sacraments.[18] It is the church which says, "From the ends of the earth I have cried out to you, when my heart was troubled" (Ps 61:2). In another psalm, the church says, "Disgust

16. Vincentius thought that the use of imperial laws against the Donatists would scandalize the pagans and Jews and thus make them adamant against the Christian faith.

17. After the emperors came over to the Christian cause, paganism began to lose the civil privileges it had formerly enjoyed. It was not actually prohibited until the time of Theodosius. Attempts to close pagan shrines in Africa sometimes led to violence and riots.

18. It was Augustine's position that the sacraments of the Donatists were in fact valid and efficacious, since the efficacy of the sacrament depends not upon the personal holiness of the one who administers it but upon the power of Christ. As a result, Augustine insisted that if a Donatist came back to Catholicism, rebaptism was unnecessary.

242   *The Use of Persecution*

has held me back from sinners abandoning your law" and "I saw the foolish and I was distraught" (Ps 119:53,158).

It is the church which says to her spouse, "Tell me where you feed, where you rest at midday, so that I do not become as one hidden among the flocks of your companions" (Sg 1:7); that is, as it is said in another place, "Make known to me your right hand, and those taught by the heart in wisdom" (Ps 90:12). Shining with light and burning with charity, you rest among those so taught, just as at midday, so that I will not rush, as one hidden—that is, as one concealed and unknown—into the flock of your companions, that is, the flock of the heretics, but into your flock. The church calls them "companions" here, just as he calls the thorns "daughters." This is done because of their common participation in the sacraments, and about them it is said elsewhere: "You, my confidant, my guide, my intimate, who took sweet food together with me; in the house of the Lord we walked in agreement; let death come upon them and let them go down to hell alive" (Ps 55:13–15). This is just like what happened to Dathan and Abiron, the impious authors of schism (Nm 16:30–33).

Section 29

The response to the request to know where her spouse feeds and rests is immediately given to the church: "If you do not know yourself, O beautiful among women, go out and follow the footprints of the flocks and feed your kids in the tents of the shepherds" (Sg 1:8). That is the response of the sweetest spouse! He says, "if you do not know yourself" because surely "the city built upon a mountain cannot be hidden" (Mt 5:14), and therefore he says, 'you are not as one hidden, so that you run into the flocks of my companions.' I am "the mountain prepared upon the top of the mountains, to which all peoples will come" (Is 2:2). Therefore, "if you do not know yourself" means 'not in the words of the slanderers but in the testimonies of my books.' It means that because of you it is said, "Stretch out your cords and make your stakes strong; you will extend both on the right and the left; your seed will inherit peoples, and cities which were abandoned, you will inhabit" (Is 54:2–3). . . .

Section 30

It is said of the smallness of the church in comparison with the multitude of the wicked that "Narrow and tight is the way that leads to life, and there are few who walk on it" (Mt 7:14). On the other hand, it is said of the multitude of the church that "Your seed will be as the stars of the heavens and the sands of the sea" (Gn 22:17). Truly, the same faithful, who are holy and good, are both few in comparison with the many wicked and many considered in themselves, for "the children of the abandoned are many, more than of she who has a husband," (Is 54:1; Gal 4:27); and "many will come from the east and the west and they will rest with Abraham and Isaac and Jacob in the kingdom of heaven" (Mt 8:11); and God "produces for himself an abundant people, striving for good works" (Tt 2:14); and in the Apocalypse (Rev 7:9), many thousands, which "no one can number" are seen "from every tribe and tongue in white robes and palms" of victory. It is the church that is sometimes obscured and, as it were, clouded by a multitude of scandals, when "in the dark of the moon the sinners bend their bows in order to shoot arrows at the upright of heart" (Ps 11:2). Yet, even then the church shines forth in those who are strongest. If some distinction should be drawn among these divine words, perhaps it is not without reason that it was said of the seed of Abraham, "as the stars of the heavens and the sands on the coastline of the sea." By "the stars of the heavens" the very few, the very strong, and very brilliant might be understood, but by "the sands of the seashore" the great multitude of the weak and carnal. Sometimes, in a tranquil age, these sands appear to be at rest and free, but they are also sometimes overwhelmed and disturbed by waves of tribulations and temptations.

Section 34

Therefore, it is the church which swims with the wicked fishes in the net of the Lord (Mt 13:47). It is always separated from them in heart and in morals and it leaves them so that it might be shown to her husband "glorious, not having a blemish or a wrinkle" (Eph 5:27). It waits for the bodily separation on the seashore—that is, at the end of the world (Mt 13:48–50). While waiting, it corrects those whom it is able to correct and endures those whom it cannot correct. Nevertheless, it does not abandon the unity of the good on account of the iniquity of those whom it does not correct.

Section 46

"Why," you say, "do you seek us? Why do you receive us, whom you call heretics?" See how easily and briefly I reply: we seek you because you are lost, in order that we might rejoice over the found as we used to sorrow over the lost. We call you heretics, but that is prior to your being converted to the Catholic peace and stripping off the error in which you are entangled. When you come over to us, you surely abandon what you were, so that you do not come over to us as heretics.

"Then baptize me," you say. I would do so, if you had not been baptized already, or if you had been baptized not by Christ but only by Donatus or Rogatus.[19] The Christian sacraments do not make you a heretic, but your depraved dissension. The good that remains in you must not be denied on account of the evil that proceeds from you. However, you have that good that remains in you to your own detriment, if you do not have it from the source of the good that you have. . . .

Section 50

Hear, through me, the voice of the Lord's wheat in the field laboring among the chaff until the final winnowing on the Lord's threshing floor (Mt 3:12), which is the whole world—the voice through which "God called the earth, from the rising of the sun to the setting" (Ps 50:1), where even the children praise the Lord (Ps 113:1): anyone who uses this imperial law as an opportunity for persecuting you, not through love of your correction but through hatred for you as an enemy, displeases us.

Also, no earthly thing is able to be possessed rightly by anyone except by divine right, by which all things belong to the just, or by human right, which is in the power of the kings of the earth.[20] Therefore, you falsely call "yours" what you do not justly possess and what, according to the laws of the kings of the earth, you have been commanded to give up. In vain do you say, "We have labored in amassing these things," when you read in the Scriptures, "The just will eat the labors of the impious" (Prv 13:22). Nevertheless, anyone who uses this law, which the kings of the earth, serving Christ, have promulgated for the correction of your impiety, as an opportunity for covetously seeking your property, displeases us. Finally, anyone who holds the goods for the poor or the basilicas of the assemblies, which you have been holding in the name of the church but which are certainly owed only to that church which is the true church of Christ, and does so not through justice but through avarice, displeases us. Anyone who receives someone expelled by you for some shameful deed or crime in the same way as they receive those who have lived among you without crime, except for the error by which you are separated from us, displeases us.

19. On Rogatus, see the introduction to this section.
20. On Augustine's views concerning property, see the following section.

However, you cannot easily make such claims as these, and even if you could, we still endure some whom we are not able to correct or punish.[21] We do not leave the threshing floor of the Lord on account of the chaff (Mt 3:12), nor do we rip the nets of the Lord on account of the bad fish (Mt 13:47–48), nor do we abandon the flock of the Lord on account of the goats which will have to be separated at the end (Mt 25:32–33), nor do we move out of the house of the Lord on account of the vessels made basely (2 Tm 2:20).

Section 53

Do not think that anyone can pass over from error to truth or from any sort of sin, whether great or small, to correction, without penance. However, it is a shameless error to want to accuse the church, which all the divine testimonies prove to be the church of Christ, of treating those who deserted her but then returned through repenting differently from those who were not yet within her and then received her peace for the first time. The former are humbled more completely, the latter are received more leniently. She loves both and both are healed by her serving them in maternal charity. . . .

Letter 133, to Marcellinus

The bishop Augustine sends greetings in the Lord to his eminent and deservedly distinguished lord and very dear son, Marcellinus.[22]

I have learned that the Circumcelliones[23] and clerics of the Donatist party of Hippo, whom the administrators of public discipline have brought to judgment for their deeds, have been heard by your Nobility. I have also learned that most of them have confessed to committing the homicide of the Catholic presbyter Restitutus and the beating of another Catholic presbyter, Innocentius, and of ripping out his eye and cutting off his finger. Because of this, I have been overwhelmed with the greatest anxiety that

21. The Donatists, at least in the eyes of the Catholics, were excessively rigorous and even fanatical in their insistance that only the holiest of the holy could be included in the church, as the issue of the *traditores* demonstrates. They were unwilling to make any concessions to human weakness. Augustine's view is that the church ought to be more accommodating, tolerating wrongdoers in its midst even while attempting to improve them.

22. On Marcellinus, see the note on I, preface.

23. On the Circumcelliones, see the introduction to this section.

your Excellency might determine that these people should be punished by
the laws so severely that their punishment will match their deeds. Therefore, with this letter I beg of you—by your faith, which you have in Christ
through the mercy of Christ the Lord himself—by no means do this or
allow it to be done.

Although we are able to overlook the annihilation of those who might be
regarded as having been brought to trial not by our accusations but by the
indictment of those to whom the guardianship of public peace belongs, we
still do not want the sufferings of the servants of God to be avenged by
retaliatory punishments of an equal degree, as though the punishment and
the deed were interchangeable. We are not opposed to wicked human beings being denied the license to commit crimes, but we want that to be the
end of it, so that, alive and with their body parts unmutilated, they might
either be directed away from diseased disturbances to the calm of health by
the coercion of the laws or cut off from malicious deeds and turned to some
useful deed. This is indeed called "condemnation," but who does not understand that it should be termed a benefit rather than a punishment when
the audacity of savageness is not set free nor the remedy of repentence
taken away?

Fulfill, Christian judge, the duty of a pious father. Be angry at iniquity
in such a way that you remember to consider humanity, not cultivating the
lust for taking vengeance on the atrocities of sin, but applying your will to
healing the wounds of sin. Do not lose the fatherly concern which you
maintained in the inquiry itself, when you extracted the confession of such
wicked deeds not by stretching them on the rack, not by furrowing them
with talons, not by burning them with flames, but simply by beatings with
rods—the manner of punishment customarily used by school teachers,
parents themselves, and often even by bishops in their judgments.[24] Therefore, do not avenge harshly what you discovered leniently. It is more important to find out what happened than it is to punish it. Hence, even the
most gentle men consider a concealed deed carefully and urgently in order
that they might discover whom they might spare. Consequently, it is generally necessary that the investigation be conducted most rigorously, so
that when the wickedness is revealed, clemency might appear.

Truly, all good works love to be set in the light, not for the sake of
human glory, but, as the Lord says, "that they might see your good works

---

24. Torture was an accepted and even required practice in Roman law. Augustine
is praising Marcellinus for his gentleness is applying the practice to those accused
in this case.

and glorify your father, who is in heaven" (Mt 5:16). Thus, the apostle was not satisfied to warn us to practice clemency, but also to make it known: "Let your clemency be known to all human beings" (Phil 4:5). In another place he says, "showing clemency to all human beings" (Tt 3:2). Moreover, that most remarkable gentleness of the holy David, when he mercifully spared the enemy who had been handed over to him (1 Sam 24:2–7), would not be so outstanding if his power were not equally apparent. Therefore, let the power of avenging not make you callous since the necessity of examining did not drive out your gentleness. Having discovered the deed, do not now seek the executioner when you did not want to call in the torturer in the investigation.

Finally, you have been sent here for the sake of the church.[25] I declare this course of clemency to be advantageous for the Catholic church; or rather, so that I do not appear to exceed my authority, I declare that this is advantageous for the church attached to the diocese at Hippo Regius. If you do not hear a begging friend, hear the considerations of a bishop. Because I speak to a Christian, I have not spoken arrogantly, especially in such a case as this, in saying that it is appropriate for you to listen to the command of a bishop,[26] my eminently and deservedly distinguished lord and very dear son.

I realize that ecclesiastical cases are referred principally to your Excellency. However, because I believe that this concern belongs to that most distinguished and outstanding of men, the eminent proconsul, I have sent him a letter also. I beg you not to oppose it but to pass it on to him yourself, and to bring it to his attention if it is necessary. I implore you both not to judge our intercessions, suggestions, or anxieties to be insolent. Do not tarnish the sufferings of the Catholic servants of God, which ought to be useful for the spiritual building up of the weak, by reciprocating in kind against the enemies at whose hands they suffered. Instead, hold judicial severity in check. Most of all, because you are sons of the church, do not neglect to commend your faith and the clemency of your mother.

May the omnipotent God increase your Eminency with all good things, my eminent and deservedly distinguished lord and very dear son.

---

25. Marcellinus was sent by the imperial government to North Africa precisely to deal with the problems pertaining to the church there.

26. Marcellinus is an imperial commissioner in North Africa who takes commands from his superiors in the Roman government. Augustine apologizes for appearing to command someone not under his authority but says that he is justified in speaking so forcefully because he is a Christian bishop speaking to a Christian.

Property

Introduction

As bishop of Hippo, one of Augustine's first duties was to preach. Hundreds of these sermons have come down to us, giving us a glimpse of Augustine's preaching style and his pastoral concerns. Not least among these pastoral concerns was the issue of the Donatists.[1] During the course of the controversy, Roman authorities confiscated a certain amount of Donatist property and handed it over to the Catholics.

In the selection from an extemporaneous sermon on John 1:32–33 that follows, Augustine turns to the issue of estates or villas that have been taken away from the Donatists by the imperial government. He defends this confiscation of property by arguing that property rights do not have their foundation in rights established directly by God but in human rights conferred by temporal authorities. His argument would have enormous implications for subsequent Christian political theorists.[2]

From *Tractates on John* VI, 25–26.

. . . Look, there are the villas. By what right do you protect these villas? By divine or human right? Let them reply, "Divine right we have in the Scriptures; human right in the laws of the king." On what basis does anyone possess what he possesses? Is it not by human right? By divine right "The earth and its fullness belong to the Lord" (Ps 24:1). God made the poor and the rich from the one clay, and the one earth supports both the poor and the rich. Nevertheless, by human right one says, "This villa is mine; this

1. On the Donatists, see the introduction to the section on "The Use of Persecution."

2. Augustine's position can be contrasted with that of, for example, Locke. See his *Second Treatise on Government*, 5.

house is mine; this slave is mine."

Thus, by human right, by the right of emperors. Why? Because God has distributed these same human rights to the human race through the emperors and kings of the world. Is it your wish that we read the laws of the emperors and deal with the villas according to them? If you want to possess them by human right, let us read out the laws of the emperors. Let us see if they wanted anything to be possessed by heretics.

"Yet what is the emperor to me?" they ask.[3] You possess the land according to the right of the emperor. Conversely, take away the rights of the emperors, and who will dare to say, "That villa is mine," or "That slave is mine," or "This house is mine"? If, however, in order that these things might be held from human beings, the rights of kings have been accepted, do you want us to recite the laws, so that you might be joyful because you have even one garden and so that you might not attribute it to anything except the clemency of the dove[4] that you are permitted to remain even there? It is plainly read in the laws that the emperors have commanded that those outside the communion of the Catholic church, who usurp the name "Christian" for themselves, not wanting to worship the author of peace in peace, might not dare to possess anything in the name of the church.

Yet they say, "How does the emperor pertain to us?" I have already said, though, that the issue is dealt with by human right. The apostle, however, wanted kings to be served. He wanted kings to be honored, and he said, "Revere the king" (1 Pt 2:17). Do not say, "How does the king pertain to me?" How, therefore, do possessions pertain to you? Possessions are possessed through the rights of kings. You have said, "How does the king pertain to me?" Do not talk about your possessions, for you have renounced the very same human rights by which possessions are possessed. . . .

3. Rettig points out that Augustine is quoting Donatus's own response to imperial legates in 347. See *Tractates on the Gospel of John*, Vol. I (Washington: Catholic University of America Press, 1988), 152, n. 77.

4. Augustine uses the image of the dove to refer to the Catholic church. This sermon is based on the text of Jn 1:32–33, in which a dove is shown descending upon Christ.

The Status of Women

Introduction

No book of the Scriptures commanded more of Augustine's attention than Genesis. His contacts with Manichaeism, Neoplatonism, and Pelagianism forced him back again and again to contemplate the relationship between God and creation described in the first three chapters of the Bible's first book. The finest fruit of his extended study of the biblical account of creation and the fall was a work of twelve books which required fourteen years to write, a work entitled On the Literal Interpretation of Genesis.

In the course of that work, Augustine had occasion to treat the nature and status of women. Three such passages have been selected for inclusion in this volume. In the first, Augustine asserts that sex is a matter pertaining to the body, not the mind. Consequently, women, too, must be said to be made in the image of God, for they also have a rational soul. The saying of Paul, then, that "the woman is the glory of the man" (1 Cor 11:7), must be understood only as a metaphor for the division of the mind into two different parts, one concerning temporal and the other eternal matters. The other two passages include Augustine's reflections on why the woman is said to be the man's "helper" in Genesis 2:18. The woman is to be a helper in the task of procreation, since this is the reason for which the distinction of the sexes exists. He also explains in brief outline the threefold purpose of marriage.[1]

On the Literal Interpretation of Genesis III. 22.

Some[2] have conjectured that the inner human being was made at that time (Gn 1:27) and that the body of the human being was made afterwards, at

1. Also pertaining to the topic of this section are *City of God* XII. 24 and 28; XIV. 22; and XXII. 17.

2. Taylor suggests that Origen is one of the "some" to whom Augustine refers. See *The Literal Meaning of Genesis*, Vol. 1 (New York: Newman Press, 1982), 246, n. 70.

the point where the scripture says, "and God fashioned the human being out of the clay of the earth" (Gn 2:7). Thus, they surmise that when the Scripture says "he made man in his image" (Gn 1:27) it refers to the spirit, but when it says "he fashioned" it refers to the body. They have not noticed that he could not have made them male and female (Gn 1:27) except according to the body.[3]

Of course, it might be most subtly argued that the mind of the human being—that is, the rational life through which the human being was made according to the image of God—divides into a part directed toward the truth of eternal contemplation and a part directed toward the administration of temporal things, and that the mind was thus, in a sense, made male and female, with the one part considering and the other part obeying. Yet, in this distinction, the image of God is not spoken of correctly, unless the image is understood as only that part of the mind which clings to contemplating unchanging truth. The apostle Paul speaks according to this subtle metaphor when he says that only the man is the image and glory of God, but that "the woman is the glory of the man" (1 Cor 11:7).

Thus, although the external differences of sex belonging to the bodies of the two human beings might be understood as a metaphor for the internal mind in a single human being, nevertheless a woman, because she is a woman by means of her body, is also renewed in the spirit of her own mind in the recognition of God according to the image of the Creator, wherein there is no male or female. As women are not separated from this grace of renewal and this reformation of the image of God (even though their bodily sex might be a metaphor according to which the man alone is said to be the image and glory of God), so in the original condition of humanity, since the woman was a human being also, she certainly had her own mind, and a rational mind, according to which she, too, was made in the image of God.

However, on account of the unity of marriage, the Scripture says that "God made man in the image of God" (Gn 1:27). So that no one might think that only the spirit of man was made, even though man is made in the image of God only according to the spirit, after "he made man" the scripture adds "he made them male and female", in order that it would be understood that the body, too, had already been made.[4] . . .

3. Augustine's point is that those who say that the phrase "he made man in his image" in Gn 1:27 refers to the creation of the mind and the phrase "God fashioned the human being" in Gn 2:7 refers to the body are mistaken, for Gn 1:27 also says that "he made them male and female." Such a distinction of the sexes implies that the body had to have been made at that time.

4. In other words, the first part of Gn 1:27, "God made man in the image of

IX. 5.

If the woman was not made to be a helper for the man in generating children, for what help was she made (Gn 2:18)? Perhaps she would toil on the earth beside him. However, there was no labor in paradise, so that he might need help, and even if there was, a male would be a better helper. This could also be said about providing company, supposing that the man was perhaps weary of solitude. How much more agreeable it is for two friends to eat, drink, and talk together than for a man and a woman to dwell in common. Suppose it was necessary in order to live together for one to command and the other to obey, so that contrary wills would not disturb their peaceful cohabitation. An order for maintaining this would not have been lacking if one were created first and the other later, especially if the second were created from the first, as was the woman. Will anyone say that God, if he so willed it, could not have made a male from the rib of the man as he did the woman? Therefore, I do not find that the woman would be a helper for the man if the reason of bearing offspring is rejected.

IX. 7.

I do not see, then, how else the woman was made to be a helper for the man, if the reason of generating children is rejected, and I do not know at all why it would be rejected. Why does faithful and pious virginity have great merit and honor before God, unless because in this "time of refraining from embracing" (Eccl 3:5), when an enormous throng from all the peoples suffices to fill up the number of the saints, the lust for taking in vulgar pleasure does not claim for itself what is not now demanded by the necessity of producing sufficient offspring?[5]

Finally, the weakness of both sexes, inclining them toward the destruc-

---

God," is in the singular to indicate the unity of marriage, while the second part, "he made them male and female," is in the plural to indicate that the body was already made at that time.

5. Augustine's point here is this: to refrain from sexual pleasure, to live in the state of virginity, is meritorious in the era of the New Testament but was not viewed in the same way in the Old Testament. This is because in earlier times there was a greater necessity for the people of God to multiply. The shift in the merit of virginity from earlier times to the present would make no sense if the distinction of the sexes were not for the purpose of procreation. See Taylor's note on this passage in *The Literal Meaning of Genesis*, Vol. 2 (New York: Newman Press, 1982), 268, n. 33.

tion of depravity, is rightly removed by honorable marriage, so that what could have been a duty for the healthy is a remedy for the sick.[6] Simply because incontinence is evil, it is not the case that marriage—even a marriage uniting incontinent people—is not good. Indeed, this good of marriage is not blameworthy on account of the evil of incontinence, but on account of the good of marriage, the evil of incontinence is permitted (cf. 1 Cor 7:6). The good that marriage has, the good by which marriage is good, can never be a sin.

This good of marriage is threefold: fidelity, offspring, and sacrament.[7] By fidelity, it is meant that there will be no intercourse with anyone else outside the marriage bond; by offspring, that children are to be accepted lovingly, raised tenderly, and educated religiously; by sacrament, that the marriage is not to be severed, and that, if abandoned, one may not marry someone else in order to produce offspring. This is like a rule for marriage,[8] by which the fertility of nature is embellished or the depravity of incontinence is governed. . . .

6. Augustine's view is that prior to original sin the sexual passions would have been subject to the human will. As a result of that sin, the sexual passions are not so subject and human beings are prone to incontinence. Among other things, marriage is also good because it provides a remedy for this incontinence. See also XIV. 24.

7. Augustine had expressed his views on marriage more fully in an earlier work entitled *On the Good of Marriage*. He also discusses the threefold nature of that good in that work.

8. "A rule for marriage" as opposed, for instance, to "a rule for monks."

Lying

Introduction

Not least among the innovations which Augustine introduced into political thought is his condemnation of lying. Plato, for example, taught that political leaders might well find it necessary to tell "noble lies" or "lies in speeches" for the good of their followers.[1] The principle goal of Cicero's classical rhetoric was persuasion, which is not necessarily the same thing as telling the truth.[2] Christian morality, however, looked askance (to put it mildly) at the practice of lying. This was especially the case with respect to lying about God or the gods. The goal of eternal salvation, the highest of all goods, required correct knowledge about divine affairs; poetic fictions about the gods were no longer beneficial for human beings. In the passage which follows, written about 424, Augustine explains what lying is and why certain lies are more culpable than others.[3]

Enchiridion 6, 18–19.

At this point there arises a most difficult and intricate question, about which I finished a very large book when necessity pressed me for a response.[4] The question is whether it might ever pertain to the duty of a just human being to lie. Some go so far as to contend that it is sometimes a good and pious deed to commit perjury and to say something false about matters pertaining to the worship of God and about the very nature of God. It

---

1. Consider, for example, *Republic* 331c, 382a–d, 414c–415d, 459c–d.

2. See Ernest L. Fortin, "Augustine and the Problem of Christian Rhetoric," *Augustinian Studies* 5 (1974), 85–100.

3. This passage from the *Enchiridion* should be compared with *City of God* IV.27; VI.6; VI.10; and XVI.30.

4. Augustine completed the work entitled *On Lying* in 395. He also wrote a treatise entitled *Against Lying* in 420.

seems to me, however, that every lie is surely a sin, but that the state of mind with which someone lies and the matters about which someone lies are very important. Thus, he who willingly lies in order to benefit another does not sin in the same way as he who willingly lies in order to harm another, nor does he who sends a traveller on the wrong way by lying harm him as much as he who corrupts another's way of life with a deceiving lie.

Certainly no one who says what is false when he thinks it to be true will be judged a liar, for, with respect to his own mind, he does not deceive but is deceived. Thus, one who sometimes carelessly holds what is false, believing it to be true, should not be accused of lying but of being rash. On the other hand, he who says what is true when he thinks it to be false, is, with respect to his own mind, a liar. Insofar as the matter pertains to his mind, he does not say what is true because he does not say what he thinks— even though what he says might be found to be true. He who unknowingly speaks the truth through his mouth while consciously and willingly lying is in no way free from the charge of being a liar. Thus, considering not the things that are spoken about but only the intention of the speaker, he who unknowingly says what is false because he thinks it is true is better than he who carries about a mind that lies consciously but unknowingly says what is true. The former does not have one thing in his mind and another in his words; the latter, no matter what the case actually is with respect to the matter he speaks about, hides one thing in his heart and expresses another with his tongue, and that evil is the characteristic of lying.

In considering the things that are spoken about, however, the matter about which one lies or is deceived is very important. Although to be deceived would be less evil than to lie insofar as the will of a human being is concerned, it is more tolerable to lie about matters that are separate from religion than to be deceived about matters that need to be believed and known so that God can be worshipped. To illustrate this by means of examples, let us suppose that one person, while lying, announces that someone who is dead is alive, and that another person, while being deceived, believes that Christ, after a certain period of time, will die again. Is it not incomparably preferable to lie in the first way than to be deceived in the second? Is it not much less evil to lead someone into the first error than to be led by someone into the second?

Therefore, being deceived in certain things is accompanied by great evil; being deceived in certain other things is accompanied by small evil; in still other things it is accompanied by no evil; and in some things it is even accompanied by some good. It is a great evil for a human being to be deceived when he does not believe what leads to eternal life, or when he does believe what leads to eternal death. It is a small evil for a human being to be deceived when, mistaking falsity for truth, he incurs temporal harm, which the patience of the believer turns to good use, as happens when someone, thinking a person who is wicked to be good, suffers evil at his hands.

There is no accompanying evil, however, for a human being who is deceived when he believes a wicked person to be good but suffers nothing evil from him. Nor does this human being fall under the prophetic curse: "Woe to those who call evil good" (Is 5:20). This saying must not be understood as being about human beings, but about the things by which human beings are evil. Hence, he who calls adultery good is rightly accused by the voice of the prophet; however, he who calls a human being whom he thinks is chaste good, not knowing that he is an adulterer, is not deceived in his understanding of what is good and evil but in the concealed deeds of human conduct. He calls a human being good in whom he thinks there exists what he knows to be good. He says that adultery is evil and chastity good, but he says that the person is good, not knowing that he is not chaste but an adulterer.

Furthermore, if someone escapes a disaster through error—as I said earlier happened to me on the road—something good even comes to the person through the error.[5] However, when I say that for someone to be deceived in certain things is accompanied by no evil or even by some good, I do not say that the error itself is not an evil or that it is some good. Rather, I refer to the evil that does not occur and to the good that does occur through erring; that is, to what does or does not result from the error. In itself, the error is always an evil—a great evil if it concerns great things, a small one if it concerns small things. Who, except the erring, would deny that it is evil to approve of falsities as if they were true or to disapprove of truths as if they were false, or to hold uncertainties as if they were certain and certainties as if they were uncertain? However, it is one thing to think that a human being who is evil is good—that is an error; it is another to suffer nothing evil from that evil, as when an evil human being who is thought to be good does no harm. Again, it is one thing to think that a road is the right one when it is not; it is another when something good follows from the evil of the error, such as to be freed from the plots of evil men.

---

5. In an earlier chapter of the work, Augustine explains that he was once saved from harm at the hands of a band of plotting Donatists when he made a wrong turn at a crossroads and arrived at his destination by way of a long detour.

Select Bibliography

Biographies of St. Augustine:

Brown, Peter. *Augustine of Hippo: A Biography*. Berkeley, Cal.: University of California Press, 1967.

Van der Meer, Frederick. *Augustine the Bishop: The Life and Work of a Father of the Church*. Translated by Brian Battershaw and G. R. Lamb. London: Sheed and Ward, 1961.

Background Works:

Armstrong, Arthur Hilary, ed. *The Cambridge History of Later Greek and Early Medieval Philosophy*. Cambridge: Cambridge University Press, 1967.

Cochrane, Charles Norris. *Christianity and Classical Culture*. New York: Oxford University Press, 1944.

Jones, A.H.M. *The Later Roman Empire, 284–602*. 2 vols. Norman, Okla.: University of Oklahoma Press, 1964.

Works on Augustine and His Political Ideas:

Baynes, Norman H. "The Political Ideas of St. Augustine's *De Civitate Dei*" in *Byzantine Studies and Other Essays*. London: Athlone Press, 1955, 288–306.

Bourke, Vernon J. *Augustine's Love of Wisdom: An Introspective Philosophy*. West Lafayette, Ind.: Purdue University Press, 1992.

Brown, P.R.L. "St. Augustine's Attitude to Religious Coercion." *Journal of Roman Studies* 54 (1964), 107–16.

Chadwick, Henry. *Augustine*. New York: Oxford University Press, 1986.

Dean, Herbert A. *The Political and Social Ideas of St. Augustine*. New York: Columbia University Press, 1963.

Dyson, R. W. *The Pilgrim City: Social and Political Ideas in the Writings of St. Augustine of Hippo*. Suffolk: Boydell & Brewer, 2001.

Figgis, John Neville. *The Political Aspects of Saint Augustine's* City of God. London: Longmans, Green and Co., 1921.

Fortin, Ernest L. "Augustine and Roman Civil Religion: Some Critical Reflections." *Revue des Études Augustiniennes* 25 (1980), 238–56.

————. *Collected Essays*. Ed. J. Brian Benestad. 3 vols. Lanham, Maryland: Rowman & Littlefield, 1996.

————. *Political Idealism and Christianity in the Thought of St. Augustine*. Villanova, Penn.: Villanova University Press, 1972.

————. "St. Augustine," in Leo Strauss and Joseph Cropsey, eds. *History of Political Philosophy*. 3rd ed. Chicago: University of Chicago Press, 1987, 176–205.

Gilson, Etienne. "Foreword" to *The City of God: Books I–VII*. Fathers of the Church, Vol. 8. New York: Fathers of the Church, Inc., 1950, xi–xcviii.

Kries, Douglas. "Augustine's Response to the Political Critics of Christianity in the *De Civitate Dei*." *American Catholic Philosophical Quarterly* 74 (2000): 77–93.

Markus, Robert A. *Saeculum: History and Society in the Theology of Saint Augustine*. Cambridge: Cambridge University Press, 1970.

O'Meara, John J. *Charter of Christendom: The Significance of* The City of God. New York: Macmillan Press, 1961.

Schall, James V. "St. Augustine and Christian Political Theory," in *The Politics of Heaven and Hell: Christian Themes from Classical, Medieval and Modern Political Philosophy*. Lanham: University of America Press, 1984, 39–66.

Stevenson, William R., Jr. *Christian Love and Just War: Moral Paradox and Political Life in St. Augustine and His Modern Interpreters*. Macon, Ga.: Mercer University Press, 1987.

Swift, L. J. *The Early Fathers on War and Military Service*. Wilmington, Del.: Michael Glazier, 1983. 110–49.

TeSelle, Eugene. *Augustine the Theologian*. New York: Herder and Herder, 1970.

———. "Towards an Augustinian Politics," in *The Ethics of St. Augustine*. William S. Babcock, ed. Atlanta: Scholars Press, 1991, 147–68.

Bibliographical Tools:

Donnelly, Dorothy F., and Mark A. Sherman. *Augustine's De Civitate Dei: An Annotated Bibliography of Modern Criticism, 1960–1990*. New York: Peter Lang, 1991.

The *Revue des Études Augustiniennes* carries a critical bibliography of all the books and articles published each year on St. Augustine.

Reference Work:

Fitzgerald, Allan D., O.S.A., et al. *Augustine through the Ages: An Encyclopedia*. Grand Rapids, Mich.: Eerdmans, 1999.

Index